D0194867

THE
WESTERN
FRONT

THE
WESTERN
FRONT

Richard Holmes

TV Books

PICTURE CREDITS

BBC Books would like to thank the following for providing photographs and for permission to reproduce copyright material. While every effort has been made to trace and acknowledge all copyright holders, we would like to apologize should there have been any errors or omissions.

AKG London: page 86–87 (Musée d'Orsay, photo Eric Lessing); e.t. archive: pages 96, 104, 170–71 (courtesy Imperial War Museum), 174 (IWM), and 175 (IWM); Hulton Getty: pages 19, 20, 45, 53, 93 below, 98, 112 left,128, 143, and 158 left; Imperial War Museum: pages 26, 28–29, 37, 39, 43, 47, 58, 61, 64, 67, 72, 74, 80, 91, 93 above, 112 right, 118, 127, 129, 133, 136, 153, 158 right, 161, 172, 176, 179, 184, 185, 188, 192, 202, 211, and 212; Robert Hunt Library: page 110.

AUTHOR'S NOTE

Both Allied and German Armies were numbered, so to avoid unnecessary confusion I have referred to Allied Armies using 1st, 2d, 3d, etc., and First, Second, Third, etc. for German Armies.

Library of Congress Cataloging-in-Publication Data available upon request.

ISBN: 1-57500-147-0

The publisher has made every effort to secure permission to reproduce copyrighted material and would like to apologize should there have been any errors or omissions.

TV Books, L.L.C.
1619 Broadway, Ninth Floor
New York, NY 10019
www.tvbooks.com

Set in Times New Roman and Gill Sans by BBC Books
Manufactured in the United States of America

CONTENTS

INTRODUCTION

I am haunted by the Western Front: there is no other word for it. Yet the family connection is thin. My father was a boy during the First World War, which transformed jolly uncles into entries in lengthening casualty lists. He visited its battlefields in the late 1920s, and I still have some of his photographs, taken before the dignified memorials to the missing were complete, and when some graves were still marked by crosses, not chiseled headstones. I grew up in a part of Staffordshire that remembered the sacrifices of the local Territorial division, 46th North Midland, its bad day at Gommecourt on July 1, 1916, balanced by its triumphant breaking of the Hindenburg Line in September 1918.

If my family was touched by the war, it was bruised far less than many. A headstone near Cambrai commemorates a decorated infantry corporal in his thirties. His family proudly added the inscription telling us that he was one of five brothers that fell, every one a hero. Sergeant George Lee, Royal Field Artillery, killed on September 5, 1916, lies beside his son, Corporal Robert Frederick Lee, a member of the same battery, killed on the same day at the age of nineteen. And in Flatiron Copse Cemetery, in the shadow of Mametz Wood on the Somme, lie three pairs of brothers.

BACK TO THE FRONT

I first visited the Western Front in my early twenties. I remember standing under the Menin Gate at Ypres, with its almost fifty-five thousand names of soldiers missing in the Ypres salient—where Allied trenches bulged into German lines east of the town—before August 16, 1917; as I stood there, buglers of the local fire brigade sounded the Last Post. They had done so every night since November 11, 1929, with an interlude during the German occupation of 1940–44. Among the audience were many veterans of the war, mostly white-haired and spry, with First World War medals shining on their chests. Here was a Military Medal, there the purple and white of the Military Cross.

The war had ended just fifty-one years before: I was closer in time to it then than I am now to the Normandy landings of 1944. Veterans were neither hard to find, nor reticent when you found them. One stocky Welshman, with a South Wales Borderers badge on his blazer, pulled me up sharply when I started talking about something airily academic like the dissemination of information within the unit. He was a platoon sergeant. The officer read the map: he ensured that the boys followed in good order. "Dissemination of bloody information," the veteran mimicked in an English accent. Then his memories were back to the front, and his lilt was back to the valleys. "Lousy as rooks, we was," he said. "Lousy as bloody rooks."

Since then I have been back to the front perhaps three times a year for the intervening thirty, and in the process I must have spent as long on it as many of the combatants. When I began, there were hardly any graves of soldiers younger than I was. Now I am hard-pressed to find one older, and the growing weight of my own mortality seems to bend me closer to the men whose deaths I chronicle. I know Ypres in the autumn, slipping back almost guiltily for a hot bath and a good dinner—French quality and German portions—as early evening chills Polygon Wood, Nonne Bosschen, and Hill 60. Then there is the Somme in high summer, skylarks and poppies now as then, the iron harvest of unexploded shells at roadside collecting points still somehow as fecund as ever. Across into the French sector, there is the mournful ridge of the Chemin des Dames, speckled with memorials to an army that wasted so much French manhood by pitting raw courage against earth and concrete.

Through the forest of the Argonne lies Verdun, to my mind the most shocking of all the front's shocking battlefields. Business takes me to the Musée-Memorial at Fleury-devant-Douaumont (one of the many destroyed villages on the battlefield) every year, but I cannot take the museum's audio-visual show any more, with Brahms's *German Requiem* crashing out like a barrage and the faces of Lorraine peasants, sons and daughters of this butchered landscape, staring out from the sepia slides. Still the front snakes on, down to St-Mihiel, where souvenir hunters creep about the *tranchée du soif* ("thirst trench"), to emerge with shell nosecaps and steel helmets. Beyond it the hills rise and the blue line of the Vosges—almost a Holy Grail to prewar patriotic Frenchmen schooled to the need to recapture the provinces of Alsace and Lorraine, lost to the Germans after the Franco-Prussian War of 1870–71—fills the horizon. From the charnel hill of the *Hartmannswillerkopf,* known as *Le Vieil Armand* to the *poilus* ("hairy ones") who fought there, you can see the Alps.

Sometimes the front line cut through villages, like a border drawn by a malign boundary commission, leaving the inn in Allied hands and the school in German. West of Lille it ran through coalfields, trenches bisecting hard-

THE WESTERN FRONT 1914–18

faced rows of miners' cottages, barbed wire and barricades sealing tunnels below. It went through woods, curled across downland, slashed farms and great estates, sugar factories, backyards, and brickfields. At Mametz, on the Somme, it even desecrated the village cemetery: there was a German machine gun dug snugly (and indestructibly) under the concrete plinth supporting the crucifix.

The front ran from the Swiss border to the North Sea. Its length varied with the ebb and flow of battle, but was usually about 460 miles. Its defenses were as varied as the landscape it crossed. In some places—like Neuve Chapelle, below Aubers Ridge in Flanders—the water table was too high for trenches to be dug to full depth, so they were built up to form "high command" trenches. Veterans of the Northwest Frontier of India were reminded of the sangars—chest-high stone redoubts—built there as defenses. The easy digging of the Ypres salient meant that trenches there required careful revetting to shore up their sides and prevent them from caving in: Somme chalk was harder to dig but more robust. The dimension of no-man's-land, the debatable ground between the Allied and German barbed wire, also varied. It might be a few yards, so that whispered messages were in danger of being overheard by attentive enemies and rifle-grenades could be fired between trenches, or a few hundred yards, which left abundant scope for grim little patrol actions between the lines. There were places, such as marshy areas on the fringes of rivers, where there were no trenches at all, but wire curled down into the water to deter infiltration.

There was not even consistency as far as mutual hostility was concerned. The front had quiet sectors and dangerous ones. The latter were often areas where the loss of even a small piece of ground had tactical, and even political, significance: the Ypres salient is a good case in point. The Somme, in contrast, was quiet until the British began their prebattle bombardment in June 1916. We are told that when it began a German grenadier put on his best uniform and went to see his company commander, begging him to stop the foolishness before somebody was hurt. Some units fought without respite: others slipped comfortably into a routine of live and let live, punctuated by ritualized patrol excursions. Sentries sometimes conversed, and front lines might be close enough for songs, carols, jests or inquiries to roll across no-man's-land. One German shouted: "It is I, Fritz the bunmaker of London. What is the football news?" His adversaries were nonplussed to discover a fellow Chelsea supporter. "'E must be a damned good sort of sausage eater," muttered one of them.

'RIDICULOUS PROXIMITY'

As the war went on, the British army widened its hold on the front as it grew stronger. It moved southward down the front, from a small sector around Ypres in late 1914 to the Somme a year later and the Oise in early 1918. This territory was in what Paul Fussell has called "ridiculous proximity" to England. One officer "had breakfasted in the trenches and dined in his club in London"; another, going up the line by train, told two comrades: "Christ!...I was at *Chu Chin Chow* last night with my wife. Hard to believe, isn't it?" The rumble of the guns was easily audible in Kent, and the report of the mines exploded under Messines Ridge in 1917 could be heard in London. Newspapers arrived at the front only a day late: letters and parcels took two to four days. Officers' messes (and even well-found dugouts) sported copies of *Tatler* and *Punch*, although there was an understandable tendency for pictures of long-legged and flimsily clad beauties from *La Vie Parisienne* to find their way up onto walls. For the French, of course, the proximity was more striking and more poignant, as men went up the line through the ruins of a once-familiar town or even, in at least one documented case, died leading an attack into the family vineyard after savoring his last bottle of its produce.

CITIZENS OF THE FRONT

Contemporaries were aware that this counterfeit world, so close to the real one but somehow hideously malformed, swallowed a generation. Henri Barbusse, a French infantryman whose book *Le Feu* remains a classic, wrote of "the compact mass of men who, for several seasons, have emptied France to concentrate in the northeast." It was a great leveler, especially in the French and German armies, which had conscription from the outset. "Schoolteachers are rifle company NCOs or medical orderlies," wrote Barbusse. "In the regiment, a Marist friar is a sergeant in the medical corps; a tenor, the major's bicycle orderly; a lawyer, the colonel's secretary; a landlord, mess-corporal in headquarters company."

The British regular army tended to mirror the social structure of Edwardian England, its officers drawn largely from traditional elites and its rank-and-file soldiers disproportionately representing the urban unemployed. But the volunteer New Armies, raised in response to Lord Kitchener's call to arms, were a far less accurate reflection, and thousands of well-educated men served in the ranks. The historian R. H. Tawney was a sergeant in a New Army battalion of the Manchester Regiment, and the writer H. H. Munro ("Saki") died as a lance sergeant on the Somme. Conscription broke down even more traditional barriers, and in 1917–18 there were many middle-class, middle-aged men serving in the ranks. There is no easy correlation between rank and social class in the British army of the First World War. Regular sergeants in 1914 found themselves lieutenant colonels by 1918: Regimental Quartermaster Sergeant Fitzpatrick of the Royal Irish, who earned a Distinguished Conduct Medal by an act of remarkable bravery at Mons in 1914, may be the best-known example, but there are many others.

I know of at least two examples of the process in reverse. Harrow-educated Arthur Arnold Crow resigned his captaincy in the Loyal North Lancashire on account of ill-health in 1916. When he recovered he discovered that he could not regain his commission without giving up the chance of foreign service, so enlisted as a private in the Essex Regiment and was killed at Ypres in 1917. J. B. Osborne, invalided out as a lieutenant, joined the Argyll and Sutherland Highlanders and was killed as a private a month and a day before the war ended. He lies in Highland Cemetery at Le Cateau, and his headstone reminds us:

> He that humbleth himself
> shall be exalted.

PEN AND SWORD

In the years that I have known the Western Front, the reputations of the men who commanded there have also been prone to exaltation and humiliation. Books on the war are enough to keep one busy for a lifetime. Not least among the hazards of life as a military historian is the sheer difficulty of logging the shells fired in a literary bombardment which shows little sign of abating. Of course this mass of literature has changed the way I think about the war, and does so still. And it goes deeper than that. Some authors are personal friends and others are professional adversaries, and not a few manage to be both. The best of them share the same passion, and are nerved by the need to find some hypothesis that makes sense—if any can—of the First World War. In *The Swordbearers* (1963), a book that stands the test of time remarkably well, Correlli Barnett pointed to the continuing fascination of the war, which goes

> beyond the historical insights it gives. It is the fascination of events, of sentiments, as near as one's father's youth and yet as remote as the crusades; lances of the *Garde Ulanen* scratching the summer sky of 1914; the guns of Jellicoe's thirty-four capital ships firing the valedic-

tory salute to British sea-power into the mists of Jutland; horizon blue and field grey; the Motherland; the Fatherland; *La Patrie*.

To begin with, there was certainly more humiliation than exaltation. Critics tended to blame what have been termed "internal factors," primarily the incompetence of Haig, General Headquarters (GHQ), and senior British commanders, for the horror of the war. As a young man I was much influenced by A. J. P. Taylor's best-selling *The First World War* (1963), with its sharply honed laceration of commanders in general and those on the Western Front in particular. "Third Ypres," he tells us with characteristic directness, "was the blindest slaughter of a blind war." His mischievous captions drive the point home. Here is "Sir John French in training for the retreat from Mons," and there "Lord Kitchener with his keeper, Sir William Robertson."

No less hard-hitting were Leon Wolff's *In Flanders Fields* (1963) and Alan Clark's *The Donkeys* (1963). The former, a poignant evocation of Passchendaele, concludes that the campaign was simply "a caricature of war . . . unfairly and brutally conducted up to the highest level." The latter, a study of the abortive offensives of 1915, concluded that most senior and middle-ranking officers were grossly incompetent, and that "Haig, in particular, was an unhappy combination of ambition, obstinacy and megalomania." The fact that its title, derived from "Lions led by Donkeys," probably refers to a German judgment on French generals of the Franco-Prussian war of 1870–77, rather than to any comment on the First World War, seems not to have perturbed the author: the story is clearly too good to let that sort of detail get in its way. A 1962 *Spectator* article by Robert Kee sums up the genre, comparing the Western Front to a concentration camp in which "millions of brave men" suffered "in a hell comparable with nothing we know." The war was, he declared, "a gigantic swindle."

It did not end there. Douglas Haig's reputation has been repeatedly assailed, perhaps most cleverly by Gerard de Groot in *Douglas Haig 1861–1928* (1988) and certainly most excessively by Denis Winter in *Haig's Command: A Reassessment* (1991). John Laffin's *British Butchers and Bunglers of World War One* (1988) takes as one of its subtexts "Incompetence, Callousness and Vanity," significantly an *Australian* subaltern's comment on the *British* high command, and an indication of another eddy in the critical current. He goes on to conclude that Haig's great equestrian statue on Whitehall is in exactly the right place: it stands facing the Cenotaph, which commemorates the servicemen killed in the war.

The opposing school of thought stressed external factors, including what Keith Simpson has termed "pre-war British inexperience and lack of preparation, the problem of adapting to new technology, the fighting power of the German Army, restraints imposed by coalition warfare, and political interference." For some time the principal defender of Haig, and through him Allied strategy on the Western Front, was the redoubtable John Terraine. The appearance of his *Douglas Haig: The Educated Soldier* in 1963 gave even me, then at an age when I was instinctively more likely to sympathize with the Donkeys thesis, pause for thought. He depicted a general who had thought seriously about his profession, was capable of what he termed "grand scale imagination," and who recognized that the war on the Western Front was in essence a great continuous engagement which demanded the single-minded focusing of national resources, human and material. In successive works he has extended his argument, and has never flinched from assailing the "cheap advantage" which he detects to be sought by the Donkeys school.

Terraine's efforts have brought him as many brickbats as bouquets, not least a deftly aimed missile from John Keegan, who accused him of "trying to suggest that the generals who presided over the demolition of a whole British generation were somehow more respectable than idiots." Some academic historians bewailed his reliance on well-worn sources and jeered at his extraordinary personal commitment to his cause. But there is a consistency to his case, as unyielding—and perhaps this is no accident—as Haig's devotion to his own task. This is summed up in an article written a year before *Douglas Haig.* "Was the bloodbath on the Western Front inevitable?" he asks. "Was there no other way? My own view will have become apparent by now: there was not." The Germans were Britain's main enemy. They were in occupation of a huge swath of territory belonging to France, Britain's major ally. They would leave neither voluntarily nor by negotiation, and the status quo was clearly unacceptable to the Allies. The British bore an increasingly heavy share of the war's burden, and eventually "the task of engaging the main body of a main enemy in a continental war fell upon the British Army, for the only time in its history, and it carried out that task at very heavy cost with ultimately decisive effect."

It was not really until the 1980s that a middle path could be trodden with much confidence. A generation of military historians, writing with wide access to a rich variety of source material, began to draw the internal and external arguments together. In *Fire-Power: British Army Weapons and Theories of War 1904–1945* (1982), Shelford Bidwell and Dominick Graham put the development of British tactics into a wider context. In his book *The Killing Ground* (1987) Tim Travers developed the internal factors to look more deeply at the British view of the nature of war and the personalized structure of its prewar officer corps. Haig became the embodiment of the British army, warts and all. No less important was *Command on the Western Front* (1992), in which Robin Prior and Trevor Wilson examined the achievements of Sir Henry Rawlinson, divisional commander in 1914 and army commander 1916–18. The authors argued that historians who simply confined themselves to balancing internal versus external factors could not "see the essential story at all." At variance with some historians who have depicted the German army as such a wondrous organization that one might wonder why the shambolic British bothered to take the field at all, they go on to note "the suicidal manner in which the German authorities squandered their irreplaceable infantry" in 1918. Finally, they observe that even at that late stage in the war:

> it was required of Rawlinson (as of Haig) to prescribe objectives and devise ways of operating which were not manifestly silly, and to provide a command structure that would facilitate his technical experts and his rank and file in accomplishing these. That much Rawlinson achieved during the climactic stages of the First World War.

No reflection of the impact of other historians on this one would be complete without mention of Paddy Griffith, for many years a fellow member of the Department of War Studies at Sandhurst in the 1970s, original thinker and convivial host. His *Battle Tactics of the Western Front: The British Army's Art of Attack 1916–18* characteristically broke new ground. It contrasts the "amateurism, blundering and fumbling" of the first two years of the war with the battle-tested skills of "the numerous army and corps HQs who knew how to win so many victories during 1917 and in the [war's last] Hundred Days." This is a refreshing corrective to much of what had been written about the British army, although Dr. Griffith, like one of his infantrymen seizing a fleeting tactical opportunity, sometimes takes his argument further than the supporting evidence will justify.

And of course there was always much more to the war's literature than the work of professional historians. I had read Siegfried Sassoon's *Memoirs of a Foxhunting Man, Memoirs of an Infantry Officer,* and *Sherston's Progress* and Robert Graves's *Goodbye to All That* before any scholarly book on the war, and was powerfully influenced by the literature of the 1920s and 1930s that mirrored so much of the war's poetry. Generals and their staffs were usually stupid and unfeeling; soldiers were decent, simple souls, martyred by the incompetence of the men who led them; the war itself was a ghastly reflection of what Wilfred Owen so tellingly called:

> The old lie: *Dulce et decorum est*
> *Pro patria mori.*

Even now, drawn back to my books as I work on this, I experience the same overwhelming sense of what Owen called "the truth untold, the pity of war, the pity war distilled." Any military historian worth his salt must recognize the risk that he will be "beating his drum with the bones of the dead," and as far as the Western Front is concerned there are bones aplenty.

Yet there is another side to this. One did not need to be a psychopath to find some pleasure in the war. Sometimes it was the simple pleasure of celebrating survival. Ernst Junger, Germany's most decorated officer, thought that the war left most soldiers with two recurrent memories: one of its worst moments, the other "when the bottle went round as madly and merrily as ever it did in times of peace." There were moments when even battle had an insane rapture. At the beginning of the German offensive of March 1918 Junger and his comrades were "mad and beyond reckoning; we had gone over the edge of the world into superhuman perspectives. Death had lost its meaning." Malcolm Brown's *Imperial War Museum Book of the Somme*, based on first-hand accounts of the battle, includes Lieutenant Geoffrey Fildes's description of an attack, written shortly after the event. "Those were sublime moments," he wrote, "for we were England upon the field of battle; conquerors offering to her yet further renown, so, with our bodies throbbing the *pas de charge*, we burst through fences, ditches and ruins to our goal."

The front conferred its own sense of purpose, sometimes absent from civilian life. Graham Greenwell, who served in the infantry from first to last, admitted that "I look back on the years 1914–1918 as among the happiest I have ever spent." There were griefs and trials, but "to be perfectly fit, to live among pleasant companions, to have responsibility and a clearly defined job—these are great compensations when one is very young." Charles Carrington, another infantry officer, touched the very heart of the process that welded men together. "We were banded together by a unity of experience that had shaken off every kind of illusion, and which was utterly unpretentious," he wrote. "The battalion was my home and my job, the only career I knew." He resented what he saw as the postwar hijacking of all this. "It appeared that dirt about the war was in demand. . . . Every battle a defeat, every officer a nin-compoop, every soldier a coward."

The war has proved a fertile seam for filmmakers, who have tended to find the Donkeys thesis most compelling, whether tragicomically as in *Oh! What a Lovely War* or plain tragically as in *Regeneration*. On television Rowan Atkinson and Tony Robinson brought their own brand of humor to the front as Captain Blackadder and Private Baldrick. Such is the power of television that for tens of thousands of viewers Blackadder's aphorisms have become fact: the war's battles were indeed part of a long-running attempt to inch Field Marshal Haig's drinks cabinet closer to Berlin. A well-turned line of script can sometimes carry more weight than all the scholarly footnotes in the world.

THE FRONT IN PERSPECTIVE The Western Front presents a complex picture, whether analyzed through the recollections of veterans or the work of historians. It also shuns being neatly slipped into its own historical pigeonhole. For instance, trench warfare was not wholly surprising. Men had fought in trenches before, usually as part of siege warfare—which, in its way, the Western Front came to resemble. An English Civil War (1642–46) song includes the line "Engineers in the trench, earth, earth uprearing." Trenches figured in the American Civil War (1861–65) and, along with mines and barbed wire, were an even more common feature of the Russo-Japanese War (1904–5).

Nor was the front unique in terms of the suffering it caused. In the Second World War the eastern front imposed a far heavier cost in lives and, while it is impossible to compare human anguish in anything but the most superficial sense, the sheer misery of its battles equaled that of the Somme or Passchendaele. There were other theaters of the Second World War which, in their way, stand comparison with the Western Front in the First. John Ellis, whose work includes admirable studies of battle in the both wars, *Eye-Deep in Hell* for the First and *The Sharp End of War* for the Second, points to: "The Kokoda Trail in New Guinea, flooded Dutch polders, the Hurtgen Forest and the Reichswald, an Arakan monsoon, frozen foxholes in the Ardennes and the Apennines, the beaches of Tarawa and the putrid slime of Okinawa" as examples of Second World War combat that paralleled the Western Front but somehow failed to grasp the popular imagination in the same way.

Yet the Western Front retains its particular fascination for the British. In part this is because it was the British army's dominating experience of the war. Most British soldiers who came under fire did so in France and Belgium. The fact that a higher proportion of men served in the front line in the First World War than in the Second meant that there was a sense of common experience to the men of 1914–18 that was denied to soldiers of the next generation. As John Ellis put it: "For the public the First World War was the war in the trenches." In part, too, it is because of the burden of casualties—Britain and her Empire lost almost a million dead, and most of them perished on the Western Front. The "ridiculous proximity" of 1914–18 is a convenient proximity in the age of fast ferries, *Le Shuttle,* and *Eurostar*. I can visit the Somme and be home in one long day. I recently filmed after lunch in a flooded trench near Ypres—discovered while a car park was being built, and now buried under concrete—and supped at home. Lastly, there is the whole ineluctable poignancy of the Western Front. Every time I see it I am amazed afresh at what our grandfathers and great-grandfathers were asked to do—and at how well they did it.

THE FRONT IN CONTEXT Although, from the British, French, and German viewpoints, the Western Front was the principal theater of military operations during the First World War, it was not the only one. The war was a contest between two major alliances, with the Allies, chiefly Belgium, Britain, France, Italy, Serbia, and latterly the United States, facing the Central Powers—Germany, Austria-Hungary, and their ally, Turkey.

There was another major front in the east, where Germany and Austria-Hungary fought the Russians; and two theaters of war in the Middle East—in Egypt and in Mesopotamia (now Iraq). There was sporadic fighting too in Africa, where German colonies in Togoland and South-West Africa were swiftly overrun by Allied forces. Naturally, as military fortunes on both sides ebbed and flowed in these areas, operations in the Western Front were affected for good or bad—releasing more men and supplies or leeching them away. Similarly, the war at sea had its impact on the Western Front, the German submarine campaign trying to starve Britain out of the war; while the Allied blockade of Germany succeeded in restricting vital supplies.

In The War in Outline (page 216), I give a brief summary of the war as a whole, to clarify the strategic background against which the Western Front can best be understood.

OPPOSITE The misery of Passchendaele, 1917. The dreadful conditions, the result of the worst weather in memory and bombardments that destroyed the drainage system, made the battle a byword for the horror of the Western Front.

**THE WAY
AHEAD**

This book's six chapters examine the Western Front chronologically, from its waxing in the autumn of 1914 to its waning with the armistice of November 11, 1918. Each also focuses on a major theme. The first chapter looks at the ingredients, moral and material, of trench warfare, and describes how the front came into being. The second considers 1915, a year in which the British army in France expanded enormously and the government wrestled with the obdurate problem of feeding the hungry front with men and munitions. The French army and its defining battle, Verdun, are the subject of chapter 3. Chapter 4 considers the Somme, not from the perhaps familiar viewpoint of the men who fought there, but from the standpoint of the British chain of command. The fifth chapter asks how in 1917, the year of the French mutinies and Passchendaele, men coped with living and fighting on the Western Front. Finally, chapter 6 examines attempts to break the front, from the British tank attack at Cambrai in November 1917, through the German offensives of spring and early summer of 1918, to the great Allied offensive of the Last Hundred Days of the war.

MAKING
THE
FRONT

**THE ROAD
TO WAR**

Europe slid almost effortlessly into war in 1914. Although historians argue over whether the First World
War was inevitable, a combination of factors—economic
and colonial rivalry, lingering French resentment at the loss of her eastern
provinces to Germany following the Franco-Prussian War of 1870–71, and a
dangerously unstable system of alliances—certainly created a volatile mix, all too
easily ignited. There is a similarly inconclusive debate over the degree of individual and national responsibility for the outbreak of war. It is safest to say that
while there were warmongers on both sides, they were outnumbered by politicians and military leaders wrestling with problems quite beyond their resources:
the events of July–August 1914 smacked more of calamity than conspiracy.

The spark that blew the Old World apart came on June 28, when Gavrilo
Princip, a Bosnian Serb, shot the Archduke Franz Ferdinand, heir to the
throne of Austria-Hungary, in Sarajevo, capital of the then recently annexed
Austrian province of Bosnia-Herzegovina. Austria, confident of German
support, sought to punish the Serbs and, when Serbia rejected an ultimatum
designed to be unacceptable, duly declared war on her.

The Serbs had appealed to their Slavic brothers in Russia, who began a
partial mobilization in an effort to deter the Austrians. Germany warned that
she would answer a full Russian mobilization with one of her own. The Rus-

OPPOSITE The recruiting drive, August 6, 1914. Children
accompany recruits down Whitehall. They are marching,
ironically, toward the site where the Cenotaph now stands.

sians, undeterred but still hoping for a diplomatic solution, ordered full mobilization the following day. When Russia declined to cease her military preparations, Germany declared war on her on August 1. France, Russia's ally, was asked to provide a guarantee of neutrality in a Russo-German war, and declined to do so: Germany accordingly declared war on her on August 3.

Although Britain had no formal alliance with France, a series of informal staff talks had produced a plan to send an expeditionary force to France in the event of a German attack. Herbert Asquith's Liberal government hesitated briefly but, when German troops invaded Belgium, whose neutrality was guaranteed by a treaty to which Britain was among the signatories, Britain declared war on Germany on August 4. German violation of Belgian neutrality was the ostensible cause of Britain's entry into the war, but Sir Edward Grey, the foreign secretary, argued that the Europe that would follow a German victory would be wholly hostile to British interests.

THE IMPACT OF CONSCRIPTION

Between the outbreak of war in August 1914 and the end of the First Battle of Ypres the following November, the Western Front was created. Its ingredients were twofold: physical and psychological. The physical components of the front can be traced to the French and Industrial Revolutions. The former had inspired the great *levée en masse* of the 1790s, which produced armies that were not merely huge but also politically inspired, with "citizen-soldiers" and "intelligent bayonets," imbued with patriotic fervor, surging out against the stately, pipe-clayed armies of monarchical Europe. The latter not merely enabled these huge armies to be armed and equipped, but made possible the mass production of weapons of ever-increasing lethality.

The long peace that followed the Napoleonic wars saw armies shrink in size, but it was Prussia's perfection of her system of universal conscription that played a major role in her victories over Austria in 1866 and France in 1870–71. Thereafter continental powers recognized that the efficient mobilization of the nation's manhood was an essential component of military power. National policies varied, but in general the able-bodied young man could expect to be called up for two or three years' service after his eighteenth birthday. Thereafter he would be liable for recall: first as a regular reservist, fighting alongside his regular brother-in-arms, and later in a reserve formation with a less exacting task. One way or another, he would have a military service liability lasting for perhaps twenty years.

Many politicians argued that conscription did more than produce trained men: it also inculcated valuable social qualities, turning wild youngsters into steady, well-disciplined members of society. Middle-class sensibilities could be gratified by policies like the German "One-year Volunteer" system, which enabled a well-educated young man to serve for only a year, live out of barracks and, all being well, pass to the reserve as an officer when his full-time service ended. In Germany, victory in 1870–71 and the growing militarism that followed it had helped elevate the army's place in society: it was said that the young officer was a god, the reserve officer a demigod. An elderly professor, offered the appointment of honorary Privy Councillor (which brought with it the title of Excellency) wistfully replied that what he really wanted was promotion from lieutenant to captain on the reserve.

There was not, however, universal support for conscription. In France and Germany alike the left often complained of bullying NCOs, unjust discipline, needless hierarchical discrimination, and pointless drill. There was also, especially in France, a growing distrust of the army's role in support of the civil power: in 1906 the Confédération Général de Travail (CGT), the principal working-class organization, decreed that "antimilitarist and antipatriotic propaganda must become ever more intense and more audacious."

The left's suspicion of militarism cannot be wholly brushed aside. And, especially for France, the notion of the soldier as citizen too was to bring its own baggage to the Western Front. But the fact remains that in August 1914 conscription worked very much as its advocates had hoped. When call-up proclamations were read from town halls and mobilization notices appeared on the walls, men duly did what was expected of them and reported for duty.

THE CALL TO ARMS Some, especially the young, did it enthusiastically, and Berlin, Paris, Vienna, and St. Petersburg saw enormous popular enthusiasm for the war. The poet Charles Péguy wrote on August 3 that: "Whoever failed to see Paris this morning and yesterday has seen nothing." A German student was delighted to receive his orders: "This morning I met a young lady I knew, and I was almost ashamed to let her see me in civilian clothes." Another German, just turned sixteen, later wrote: "It is impossible to convey to anyone nowadays the genuine enthusiasm that animated us all." He did his best to volunteer, only to find that all the choice regiments were already full. He feared the war would be over by the time he was old enough. Eventually a kindly major let him into a dragoon regiment. Luckier than most, he was wounded and captured a year later. Louis Barthas, a barrel cooper (and militant socialist) from the wine-producing Minervois, heard a drumroll in his village square announcing that the mobilization notice had been put up. It was, he wrote, "the most terrible cataclysm which ever afflicted our humanity," but the announcement "to my great astonishment, raised more enthusiasm than gloom."

Most accounts of August 1914 emphasize this extraordinary excitement. They often fail to underline the darker side of mobilization. In a Breton village the order was greeted with "a petrified dumbness. Not a voice applauded. Someone sobbed, once, and the crowd stirred, and everyone went their various ways home." A French sergeant reported that the young peasants in his barrack-room were "sick at heart." Marc Bloch, history scholar and reserve infantry sergeant, traveled to a Parisian station in the back of a greengrocer's cart: the "slightly acrid odor of cabbage and carrots will always bring back the emotions of the early morning departure…" At the station, "an aged, white-haired father made unavailing attempts to hold back his tears as he embraced an artillery officer." Family men knew that they left hostages to fortune. Walter Bloem, a forty-six-year-old German novelist and drama critic called up as a captain with the 12th Brandenburg Grenadiers, enjoyed a last bottle of wine with his family and commented tellingly that "the tear season" had begun.

BRITAIN AND HER ARMY

There was no conscription in Britain. Her geographical position had meant that she never ran the same risk of invasion as continental powers, and her navy had long enjoyed primacy in national affection and defense funding. Her army, small by European standards, was largely a colonial police force and could be kept near its established strength by voluntary enlistment. However, Britain had made heavy weather of dealing with the Boers in the South African War of 1899–1902, and the army that went to France in 1914 was a child of the thoroughgoing reform that followed the war.

Much of it was the work of R. B. Haldane, the formidable Göttingen-educated Scots lawyer who became secretary of state for war when the Liberals took power in late 1905. A general staff was created, and almost immediately embarked on discussions with the French, at least in part in an effort to undermine the Admiralty's traditional primacy. The regular army was to produce an Expeditionary Force of six infantry divisions and a cavalry division. The nation's assorted nonregular forces—militia, volunteers, and yeomanry—were reorganized into a Territorial Force of fourteen brigades of yeomanry cavalry and fourteen infantry divisions.

The Territorial Force trained part-time, helped by a small full-time cadre, and it was not expected to take the field until it had received six months' training after mobilization: even then it was not legally liable for overseas service. There were many regular officers, with the revered figure of Field Marshal Lord Roberts prominent among them, who felt that the Territorials would never be much use, and who would have preferred conscription. However, despite the growth of anti-German sentiment and the suspicion that war was increasingly likely, old traditions died hard, and Haldane was right to recognize that, whatever the attractions of conscription to continental powers, most Britons found it repugnant.

THE FIREPOWER REVOLUTION Mass armies, swept into being by conscription, were, then, one ingredient of the Western Front. Two others were the weaponry they carried—and the railways that carried them. During the eighteenth century armies imposed ever-greater standardization on weapons, which were increasingly produced by government arsenals, like Potsdam in Prussia or Charleville in France, or by large-scale contractors, rather than by shoals of artisans filing musket-locks here or casting brass butt plates there. Although the huge armies raised during the Napoleonic Wars stretched national resources, making foreign purchase and capture useful sources of arms supply, soldiers were usually satisfactorily equipped with the muzzle-loading flintlock musket which was the characteristic weapon of the age.

From the mid-nineteenth century the pace of weapon development accelerated sharply. Breech-loading weapons became generally available, with the Prussian Dreyse "needle-gun" leading the way: the Franco-Prussian War of 1870–71 was the first conflict in which the infantry on both sides carried breechloaders. Moreover, these weapons were "rifled"—spiral grooves in their barrel spinning the bullet, helping to give it greater range and accuracy. Black powder, which burned slowly and gave off a dense, smelly smoke as it did so, was replaced from the 1880s by the more efficient smokeless powder. Soon infantry rifles used metallic cartridges, housed in a magazine below the breech or under the barrel, and loaded when the firer operated a turning bolt.

British regulars, products of an army that had taken the lessons of the Boer War to heart, were the most accomplished marksmen on the battlefields of 1914. With the .303 Short Magazine Lee-Enfield rifle in their hands, they were expected to hit a target three hundred yards away fifteen times a minute, and many could double this rate of fire with almost no loss of accuracy. In both precision and rapidity of fire there was simply no comparison between the magazine rifles carried by European armies on the eve of the First World War and the muskets shouldered by their grandfathers.

Artillery also improved. In 1870–71 the German rifled breech-loading field guns manufactured by Krupps of Essen dealt easily with muzzle-loading French weapons, and soon after the war the rifled breechloaders were adopted by most major armies. Not only did the new explosives impel shells with greater efficiency than black powder, but they also increased their bursting effect: high explosive shells, filled with chemical compounds like the British lyddite, were not only effective against troops in field defenses but also wreaked havoc on fortresses. In the Russo-Japanese War of 1904–5 Japanese heavy howitzers, their shells weighing seven hundred pounds, smashed the forts around the Russian fortress of Port Arthur. Engineers tried to keep pace with the new artillery by covering the stonework of old fortresses with earth and concrete, and taking their guns off unprotected ramparts and housing them instead in armored cupolas, but it was a duel in which the gunner usually had the edge.

The new explosives also made shrapnel more effective. This airburst shell had been invented by a British officer, Henry Shrapnel, during the Napoleonic Wars. By 1914 it had come of age. The shell, a hollow iron canister (still one of the most frequent finds on any First World War battlefield) contained round lead balls about the size of a fingernail, with an explosive charge below them. The gun's detachment, using information provided by the forward observation officer, set the brass fuse to burst the shell at a given time after leaving the muzzle. Ideally it would explode above, and slightly in front of, its target: the shell acted like a stubby shotgun barrel and the balls shot out in front of it. A British medical officer remembered its effects:

> A young gunner subaltern was on his way up to observe a machine-gun position. Just as he got outside my door a shrapnel shell burst full in front of him. The poor fellow was brought in to me absolutely riddled. He lay in my arms until he died, shrieking in his agony and said he hoped I would excuse him for making such a noise as he really could not help it . . . he was a fine looking boy, not more than nineteen.

For centuries cannon had bounded back on firing, compelling their detachments to manhandle them back into position after each shot. In 1897 the French introduced the famous 75 mm field gun, the *soixante-quinze*, the first genuine quick-firer. Its ammunition was "fixed," the shell fitting into a brass case, which made loading simple. When it was fired, most of the recoil was absorbed by hydraulic buffers: the layer, aiming the weapon, might need to make only a small adjustment before the next round was fired.

Gunners had long plied their trade using "direct fire," engaging targets they could see. As infantry weapons improved so this became more risky, for a field gun in the direct-fire role was vulnerable to the fire of magazine rifles, as British artillerymen had found to their cost in South Africa. A metal shield on the gun gave some protection to its detachment, but was no real answer. "Indirect fire," where guns were fired from behind cover at a target they could not see, their fire directed by an observer with a telephone, was the way ahead.

OPPOSITE A decorated train taking German troops to the front, August 1914. The events of the month owed much to this combination of popular enthusiasm and nineteenth-century technology.

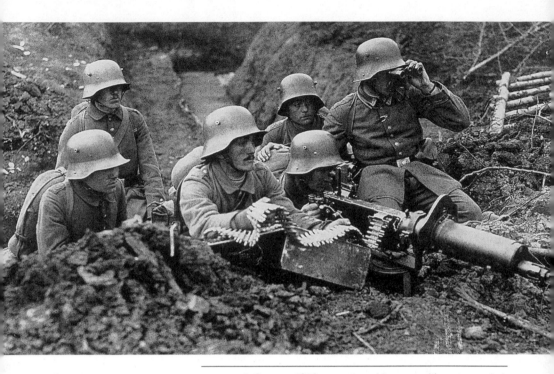

ABOVE A German 1908 pattern machine gun with water-cooled barrel clearly visible. The Germans adopted steel helmets in 1916.
BELOW The accurate and reliable .303 Short Magazine Lee-Enfield rifle, workhorse of British infantry throughout the war.

Field guns were deployed about twenty yards apart, and, using their dial sights, a form of military theodolite called a director, and basic trigonometry, they were laid so that their lines of fire were parallel, and a target hit by one gun could be hit by all. Targets could be "registered" by being hit, and their target information—the elevation and bearing required to hit them—was recorded, enabling gunners to bring down fire with the minimum of delay. Indirect fire was in its infancy in 1914, and in the first months of the war many gunner officers, by personal preference or tactical circumstance, found themselves using direct fire like their ancestors at Waterloo a century before.

The machine gun had first been regarded by some armies as an artillery, rather than an infantry, weapon. In 1870–71 the French had treated their machine gun, the Mitrailleuse, rather like a field gun, with the result that it was often knocked out by German artillery before it could do much damage to German infantry. The first machine guns were often cumbersome, complicated, and unreliable as their designers tried to solve the several problems connected with rapid fire. Most, like the Gatling and the Mitrailleuse, were multibarreled, but between 1883 and 1885 Hiram Maxim developed a weapon that used the force of the recoil to extract an empty case and push a new round into the weapon's chamber, making possible the single-barreled machine gun. A water-filled jacket fitted round the barrel to keep it cool, and ammunition was housed in fabric belts. The Maxim was adopted by Britain in 1888 and by Russia and Germany soon afterward.

These machine-guns fired between 450 and 600 rounds a minute, and were well described as "the concentrated essence of infantry." They were not available in huge numbers in 1914. A British battalion had two, and a three-battalion German regiment six, contained in its machine-gun company. As the war went on, however, not only were these heavy machine guns produced in ever-increasing numbers, but an assortment of lighter weapons, like the British Lewis and the German MG 08/15, were developed to increase infantry firepower.

WAR BY TIMETABLE

Technology did more than enable men to kill one another with greater facility. The military potential of the railway had been identified quickly. In 1840 the British moved a battalion by rail; six years later the Russians transported a corps of

14,500 men; and in 1859 the French sent an entire army, horse, foot, and guns, to northern Italy by train for their campaign against the Austrians. Prussia, with her central position in Europe and the ever-present risk of war on two fronts, was especially well placed to use the railway for military purposes, and not least among her reasons for success in the Austro-Prussian War of 1866 and the Franco-Prussian War of 1870–71 was the efficiency of the railway move to concentration areas.

After the Franco-Prussian War, staff officers across Europe studied the railway as if their lives depended on it—which, in a sense, they did. Moving troops to the frontier rapidly and efficiently was of fundamental importance: starting the process a day or two late might give the enemy an advantage that would prove decisive. The importance of railway timetables injected a note of desperate urgency into the events of July and August 1914. When, on August 1, the Kaiser summoned General von Moltke, Chief of the German General Staff, and told him that the political situation demanded war only with Russia and not with France, Moltke replied that the plan to send the bulk of the army westward by train was simply too complex to be altered. "I answered His Majesty," wrote Moltke, "that this was impossible." An appalled Kaiser, comparing Moltke with his uncle, architect of German victories in 1866 and 1870, snapped back: "Your uncle would have given me a different answer." And so he might, but in 1914 general staffs were rarely able to rise above the remorseless logic of the timetable.

THE CULT OF THE OFFENSIVE

The result of railway mobilization, universal conscription, and the revolution in military technology was a weapon density unparalleled in the history of warfare: the material origins of the Western Front. Yet its psychological origins are no less important: all the weapons in the world would not produce stalemate unless the soldiers using them proved resolute. And European armies and the societies they served had spent much time and trouble ensuring that the young men who rattled off to war in August 1914 would indeed be resolute.

Offensive war plans ruled. Russia planned to advance into East Prussia. France proposed to launch Plan 17, an all-out attack into the lost provinces of Alsace and Lorraine. And Germany sought to execute a plan named after a previous Chief of the General Staff, Alfred von Schlieffen. Schlieffen had concluded that the huge size of Russia and her population made it possible to win only "ordinary victories" in the east. Accordingly, if faced with the war on two fronts which the Franco-Russian entente made almost inevitable, he would leave a small force to check the Russians and throw the bulk of his armies against France. Because the French had fortified their common border with Germany—we shall see some of these fortifications loom large in chapter 3—he intended to send the strongest of his marching armies through Belgium, whence they would wheel down through France, the outer army passing west of Paris, to catch the French in a battle of encirclement somewhere in Champagne.

Moltke is often blamed for tinkering with Schlieffen's handiwork, but in truth the conditions that applied when the plan was new had changed by 1914. The Russians had embarked on serious military reform as a result of their defeat by Japan, and could no longer be relied on to wait, supinely, while their French allies were dismembered. And in any event there were some aspects of the Schlieffen plan, not least the logistic problem of sustaining over a million men on the march, let alone in the campaign's decisive battle, which had never been properly addressed.

The plan was a gamble, its risk magnified by the violation of Belgian neutrality, which would draw Britain into the war. If it did not produce a quick German victory, then Germany would find herself fighting the enormous human and material resources of Britain and her Empire. Indeed, one major reason for French interest in obtaining British support in August 1914 was not the tiny British Expeditionary Force (BEF) itself, but the fact that this was a promissory note for what might eventually be produced if, God forbid, the war was not over by Christmas.

These offensive plans were founded on the belief, held in slightly different forms by each of the combatant nations, that attack alone would produce decisive results. The British Field Service Regulations Part 1 of 1909 proclaimed: "Decisive success in battle can be gained only by a vigorous offensive. Every commander who offers battle, therefore, must be prepared to assume the offensive sooner or later." The French 1913 Regulations were even more extreme. "The French army, returning to its traditions," they decreed, "henceforth knows no law but the offensive."

But how were armies to relate their belief in the strategic imperative of the offensive to the ghastly reality, so vividly demonstrated in the Franco-Prussian and Boer Wars, that fire killed? It was certainly no simple task. Some theorists advocated the "defensive offensive," a thrust into enemy territory with all the war-winning characteristics of the offensive, but whose attacking units actually fought defensive battles when they met the enemy. Others, like the clear-sighted Emile Mayer, writing just after the Boer War, predicted that the next European war would witness the collision of two human walls: each side would try to outflank the other until stopped by the sea or a neutral border. This sort of outcome was not merely the prediction of leftist politicians or military commentators. In 1906 Schlieffen himself warned:

> All along the line the corps will try, as in siege warfare, to come to grips with the enemy from position to position, day and night, advancing, digging in, advancing again, digging in again, etc., using every means of modern science to dislodge the enemy behind his cover.

At a British general staff conference in 1909 the future General Sir Aylmer Haldane observed that it was "impossible to take a position which is well defended by machine-guns until these guns have been put out of action."

Regulations reflected the evidence of the Transvaal battlefields. The British, who had learned their lessons the hard way, redrafted their infantry regulations to emphasize that fire must pave the way for the successful assault. The 1904 cavalry drill book veered away from the charge altogether, and a preface by Lord Roberts decreed that "the sword must henceforth be an adjunct to the rifle; and that cavalry soldiers must become expert rifle shots and be constantly trained to act dismounted." In 1904 the French abandoned the shoulder-to-shoulder infantry tactics of the 1894 drill book and replaced them with the more flexible use of fire and maneuver. They even went as far as contemplating the abolition of the *cuirassiers*, heavy cavalry equipped with breastplate and helmet, whose charge had helped decide Napoleonic battles but had been of diminishing efficacy ever since.

In the decade before the war the pendulum swung back. It did so partly because many European theorists maintained that wars elsewhere were special cases: in South Africa, for example, ranges were unusually long and visibility good. The British, ran the argument, were scarcely a proper European army and their Boer opponents were not soldiers at all, just warlike farmers. For Frenchmen and Germans, who were in any case out of sympathy with British aims in South Africa, it was temptingly easy to claim that the British had often failed to take Boer positions because they had not been determined enough. A French officer, General Langlois, coined the phrase "acute transvaalitis," by which he meant "abnormal dread of losses on the battlefield." The British army was evidently infected by this, claimed its continental critics, and an army that was not would have pushed on through the dangerous zone of Boer rifle fire to win the battle.

The events of the Russo-Japanese War were used to support belief in the offensive. This time both combatants were recognizably first-rate armies: the Russians had a formidable reputation, and the Japanese had been trained by the Germans. Both sides had magazine rifles, breech-loading artillery, machine guns, and barbed wire. The Russians took up entrenched positions and lost: the Japanese attacked them and won. They did so by a mixture of careful preparation by their artillery and unstinted courage by their infantry. European observers were not slow to point up the "lessons." In Britain, Major General Edward Altham declared that the campaign in Manchuria, the region in northwest China contested by Russia and Japan

> showed over and over again that the bayonet was in no sense an obsolete weapon and that fire alone could not always suffice to move from position a determined and well-disciplined enemy....The assault is of even more importance than the attainment of fire mastery which antecedes it. It is the supreme moment of the fight. Upon it the final issue depends.

His fellow countryman General Sir Ian Hamilton declared:

> War is essentially the triumph, not of a chassepot [French breech-loading rifle] over a needle-gun, not of a line of men entrenched behind wire entanglements and fire-swept zones over men exposing themselves in the open, but of one will over a weaker will.

In France, General Joseph Joffre, appointed Chief of the General Staff in 1911, linked belief in defensive doctrine to the lethargic and politicized state of the French army generally, and welcomed the fact that "our young intellectual élite finally shook off the malady... which had upset the military world and returned to a more healthy conception of the general conditions prevailing in war." The influential Colonel de Grandmaison advocated "a conquering state of mind" and the need to "cultivate with passion everything that nears the stamp of the offensive spirit." In doing so he touched a popular nerve. The novelist Ernest Psichari wrote of "a proud and violent army," and at the Sorbonne the philosopher Henri Bergson spoke of *l'élan vital*: how better to demonstrate it than to impose your will on the enemy in battle?

Even artists rallied to the cause. Among the works in the Paris Salon of 1914 is one depicting a French dragoon looking east, where a German *uhlan* (lancer) holds prisoner two maidens, embodiment of the lost provinces of Alsace and Lorraine. Around the dragoon, uniformed specters from the Franco-Prussian War—here a *cuirassier*, there an Algerian *tirailleur*—rise to demand vengeance.

THE RIVAL WAR PLANS

The version of the Schlieffen Plan shown here avoided the Maastricht appendix of Dutch territory. This variant of Plan 17 was ordered on August 2, 1914, when it was plain that Germany was violating Belgian neutrality.

ENGLAND

Dover

Le Havre

Calais
Ostend
Ypres
Antwerp
Brussels
BELGIUM
Mons
Arras
Amiens
Charleroi
Maubeuge
Le Cateau
BEF
Forest of Mormal

Liège
Huy
Namur
Charleville-Mézières
Sedan
LUXEMBOURG
Longwy
Verdun
Metz
Nancy
Strasbourg

R. Rhine
R. Meuse
R. Somme
R. Oise
R. Aisne
R. Marne
R. Seine
R. Oise

GERMANY
Aachen
Trier

FRANCE
Paris

First
Second
Third
Fourth
Fifth
Sixth
Seventh
Alsace Group

5th
4th
3rd
2nd
1st
Alsace Group
1st Army

N
E
S
W

25 Miles
25 Kilometers
0

French armies
German armies
BEF
Frontiers

By 1914 the transformation was complete. The armies of Europe went to war expecting heavy losses and intending to impose their willpower on hostile firepower. The 1907 edition of British Cavalry Training set the tone. "It must be accepted as a principle," it announced, "that the rifle, effective as it is, cannot replace the effect produced by the speed of the horse, the magnetism of the charge, and the terror of cold steel." "Great victories," wrote the German Colonel Wilhelm Balck, "are nearly always accompanied by great losses." And so, as Sir Michael Howard has so tellingly written, "the casualty lists that a later generation was to find so horrifying were considered by contemporaries not an indication of military incompetence, but a measure of national resolve, of fitness to rank as a Great Power." Many, particularly young regulars, had steeled themselves for the test. Lieutenant Alan Hanbury-Sparrow of the Royal Berkshires expected a short war with very heavy casualties: he told his parents that they must not expect to see him again.

THE OPENING MOVES

Early on the morning of August 4 troopers of General von der Marwitz's cavalry corps rode across the Belgian frontier about seventy miles east of Brussels. Behind them, detraining on the wide platforms of the frontier stations, were the leading elements of the three armies of the German right wing: Kluck's First, Bulow's Second, and Hausen's Third. They were to move through the narrow gap between the hilly Ardennes to the south and the "Maastricht appendix" of Dutch territory jutting down from the north, marching on into Belgium and then curling down into France. On their left, the Fourth and Fifth Armies formed up around Metz and Trier, and further south the Sixth and Seventh Armies held the bulk of Alsace and Lorraine.

It was the essence of Schlieffen's concept that the right wing should be kept strong. If the French attacked into Alsace-Lorraine they would do him a kindly favor, for the further they got the more certain would be their own defeat as the northern armies swung in behind them. Moltke, as we have already seen, was no gambler, and over the weeks that followed he was to dilute Schlieffen's plan: first, by sending troops to the Eastern Front to shore up Germany's precarious position there; and second, by allowing the very capable Crown Prince Rupprecht of Bavaria, from August 8 in overall command of the Sixth and Seventh Armies, to counterattack, thus pushing the French out of a net that might have engulfed them.

Moltke's fatal hesitancy was, however, still a thing of the future when the Germans faced their first major challenge. The fortress of Liège, its twelve main forts encircling an old citadel, blocked the German avenue into Belgium. Initial attempts to take it failed, and although Major General Erich Ludendorff, fortuitously on the scene, managed to bluff his way into the citadel, the forts held out. But not for long: they were battered into submission by mighty Krupp 420 mm siege howitzers, assisted by some Austrian-made 305 mms. The Belgian commander, General Leman, was pulled unconscious from the wreckage of the last fort to fall.

The Belgian army retreated on Antwerp as German columns poured through Belgium. It was often a brutal passage. Footsore and frightened young soldiers reacted harshly to rumors of snipers, and their commanders sometimes used terror in an attempt to break the spirit of a nation whose resistance both surprised and irritated them. Allied propaganda was to make much of German atrocities in Belgium, and many of the stories were certainly overblown. Still, the episode helped harden the cement of the Western Front by persuading many Allied soldiers—and, no less to the point, their civilian friends or relatives—that theirs was indeed a hateful enemy.

The French commander in chief, Joseph Joffre, had established his headquarters (Grand Quartier Général—GQG) at Vitry-le-François on the stately River Marne, roughly equidistant between the headquarters of his five armies. He undoubtedly had some evidence of the scale of German preparations in the north. However, the French believed that if the Germans were able to extend well into Belgium, it could only be by using reserve divisions in the front line, something the French, with their mistrust of reservists, would not countenance. Joffre's deputy, General de Castelnau, had previously greeted a skeptical regional commander and a local politician, concerned that there would be no troops left to defend the northeast, with the words: "If they come as far as Lille, so much the better for us." Just as Schlieffen had hoped that a French offensive into Alsace-Lorraine would make his own task easier, so the French believed that by extending far into Belgium the Germans could only weaken their own center—where the French blow was to fall.

The French attack showed the early flare of a false dawn. The 1st and 2nd Armies advanced on Morhange and Sarrebourg, and Crown Prince Rupprecht's men obligingly gave ground before them: Sarrebourg fell on August 18. But it could not last. The French infantry, in their long blue overcoats and

---

OPPOSITE General Joseph Joffre, flanked by Castelnau, his deputy (left), and Pau (right), who lost a hand in 1870 and was recalled from retirement to command the Army of Alsace.

red trousers, pushing on into broken ground unsuited for this sort of offensive, were cut to pieces by German machine guns. German artillery, its fire directed by spotter aircraft, battered them mercilessly. Rupprecht, tired of defending against an enemy that was already losing momentum, begged Moltke to allow him to counter-attack, and Moltke weakly gave way.

What was called the Battle of the Frontiers raged from August 20 to 24, and there could be no doubt that the French were the losers as the doctrine of *l'offensive à l'outrance* (the all-out offensive) died on the wooded slopes and open fields of northern Lorraine. Captain Charles de Gaulle (leader of the Free French a generation later) admitted that:

> The first shock was an immense surprise.... Suddenly, the enemy's fire became precise and concentrated. Second by second the hail of bullets and the thunder of the shells grew stronger. Those who survived lay flat on the ground, amid the screaming wounded and the humble corpses. With affected calm, the officers let themselves be killed standing up, some obstinate platoons stuck their bayonets in their rifles, bugles sounded the charge, isolated heroes made fantastic leaps, but all to no purpose. In an instant it had become clear that not all the courage in the world could withstand this fire.

The first month of the war cost Joffre 212,000 men, about 20 percent of his mobilized strength and nearly 40 percent of his regular officers. And there was little sign that the Germans could be stopped. Ferdinand Foch, commanding one of Joffre's corps in front of Nancy, held his ground with a tenacity which marked him out for rapid advancement, but elsewhere the view from Vitry was one of unrelieved gloom.

Things were especially bleak in the north. Charles Lanrezac, commanding the 5th Army on the French left, was a brilliant but acerbic officer who had the unfortunate distinction of being wise before the event. He warned Joffre that there were Germans in strength to his north, and asked to be allowed to edge round to face them, rather than attacking northeast alongside the 4th Army on his right. Joffre reassured him, but on August 22 Lanrezac's men were badly mauled around Charleroi by the German First and Second Armies, and on the 23d he began to fall back.

OPPOSITE Field Marshal Sir John French, commander of the BEF till 1915. The mercurial French had made his reputation in the Boer War and was out of his depth on the Western Front.

<table>
<tr><td>**ENTER THE BEF**</td></tr>
</table>

Lanrezac's plight was of particular interest to the British Expeditionary Force (BEF), in position on his immediate left. Prewar planners had assigned this post to the BEF for perfectly good reasons. It was relatively simple for the British to get there, moving by rail from their main port of entry at Le Havre to a concentration area in the triangle Maubeuge–Hirson–Le Cateau. As there was no certainty that they would actually arrive, as Britain's commitment to France could not be guaranteed, it seemed to the French that the left flank, where nothing much was to happen, was just the place for the BEF to go. But Schlieffen, as we have seen, had other ideas.

The BEF went to war about one hundred thousand strong, with a large cavalry division and four infantry divisions, 1st, 2nd, 3rd, and 5th: 4th Division joined after the fighting had begun. In command was Field Marshal Sir John French, a sixty-two-year-old cavalryman who had made his reputation in the Boer War. His chief of staff, Sir Archibald Murray, was a charming but rather ineffectual officer who had made a bad recovery from a stomach wound received in South Africa. The real power on the staff was Henry Wilson, an ebullient francophile who had handled most of the prewar negotiations with the French. The BEF's quartermaster general, responsible for its supplies, was Sir William "Wully" Robertson, a man of great common sense who had been commissioned from the ranks and advertised the fact by deliberately dropping his aitches.

The BEF formed two corps, each of two divisions. Sir Douglas Haig commanded I Corps. A dour Lowland Scot, Haig had been French's brigade major (chief of staff) when French commanded the Aldershot cavalry brigade before the Boer War, and during it he served on French's staff. Their characters were very different. An officer who knew them both wrote that: "French was a man who loved life, laughter and women, whereas Haig was...the dullest dog I ever had the happiness to meet." French, who knew that he was not a natural staff officer, had a high regard for Haig, whose fluent prose gave form to some of French's airier conceptions. Haig was less impressed by French, writing: "In my own heart I know that French is quite unfit for this great command at a time of crisis in our nation's history." Although French had been on excellent terms with King Edward VII, whose amorous inclinations were similar to his own, he was less well regarded by George V, who disapproved of the field marshal's light-cavalry lifestyle. Haig, in contrast, was happily married to one of Queen Mary's ladies-in-waiting, and his relations with the King were good enough for him to be able to disclose his reservations about Sir John before the campaign had started.

Sir James Grierson commanded II Corps. A capable but overweight officer, he joked that the medal ribbons on his well-filled chest commemorated many a hard-fought battle with knife and fork. A heart attack killed him in his train on the way to the concentration area. French wired Lord Kitchener, who had just taken over as secretary of state for war, asking for Sir Herbert Plumer as a replacement, but to his horror received Sir Horace Smith-Dorrien instead. The poor relations between the two men were a matter of common knowledge in the army, and Kitchener believed that French cherished "great jealousy of and personal animosity towards" Smith-Dorrien. He seems to have made the appointment in the hope that Smith-Dorrien's sound professional judgment and robust moral courage would enable him to act as a sheet anchor on the mercurial commander in chief. However, Smith-Dorrien was subject to occasional fits of uncontrollable rage, which could make him difficult to work with, and it needed no deep knowledge of French's character to realize that he would be unlikely to forget that Smith-Dorrien had been foisted on him.

Before leaving England on August 14, Sir John French had been given written orders by Kitchener. These concentrate on the relationship between Sir John and the French, and in so doing go straight to the heart of the politics of the Western Front. "The special motive of the force under your control," wrote Kitchener,

> is to support and co-operate with the French army against our common enemies....
>
> It must be recognized from the outset that the numerical strength of the British force and its contingent reinforcement is strictly limited, and with this consideration kept steadily in view it will be obvious that the greatest care must be exercised towards a minimum of losses and wastage.
>
> Therefore, while every effort must be made to coincide most sympathetically with the plans and wishes of our Ally, the gravest consid-

eration will devolve upon you as to participation in forward move-
ments where large bodies of French troops are not engaged....

I wish you distinctly to understand that your force is an entirely
independent one and you will in no case come under the orders of any
Allied general.

John Terraine observed that in these orders "lay the germs of controversies
that would bedevil the British Command throughout the war." The relative
strengths and capabilities of the French and British armies would change, as
would the British government's attitude to "losses and wastage." From start
to finish the war on the Western Front was fought by a coalition whose major
partners had agendas, political and military, of their own: yet without that
coalition there could be no Western Front—and no Allied victory.

Sir John French's confidence in that Allied victory was unbounded as he
dined in Paris on August 14, noting in his diary that "the usual silly reports of
French reverses" were "all quite untrue." He visited Joffre the following day,
and on the 16th he went up to Rethel on the Aisne to meet Lanrezac. The latter was already preoccupied with reports of German forces moving round to
his north, and the meeting was not a success. Sir John spoke bad French, and
haltingly asked Lanrezac if he thought that the Germans proposed to cross
the Meuse at Huy. "Tell the marshal," snapped Lanrezac, "that in my opinion the Germans have merely gone to the Meuse to fish."

The BEF began to move forward on the 21st, and on the night of the 22nd
it halted with II Corps on its left, on the line of the Mons–Condé Canal, and
I Corps on its right, in front of Maubeuge. Reports from the Royal Flying
Corps and the cavalry confirmed that there were Germans to its front, and
late on the 22nd Lieutenant Edward Spears, liaison officer with the 5th Army,
told French that Lanrezac was in real trouble around Charleroi. If the BEF
continued to advance as planned, it would risk being exposed and cut off.

MONS   Early on the morning of Sunday August 23, French
spoke to his corps commanders, telling them some-
thing of his doubts and ordering them to be ready to move in either direction.
He then set off for Valenciennes, on his left, to inspect his lines-of-
communication troops, who had just been converted into an infantry
brigade. While he was away elements of Kluck's First Army collided with II
Corps on the canal in front of Mons, and the British army fought its first battle of the war. By nightfall Smith-Dorrien had pulled back to an intermediate

position south of Mons, and Haig had come up on his right. The action had cost the British just over sixteen hundred men, but the Germans, whose attacking columns had been cruelly punished by British rifle fire, lost at least five thousand men and perhaps many more. Walter Bloem spent much of the day trying to close with an invisible enemy: his regiment, 12th Brandenburg Grenadiers, lost twenty-five officers and five hundred men.

When he returned to his headquarters Sir John, buoyed up by the francophile optimism of Henry Wilson, at first hoped to hold his ground for another day, but around midnight he heard that Lanrezac had ordered a withdrawal, and deduced that 3rd and 4th Armies were also falling back. He ordered a retreat, and Murray left it to the corps commanders to sort out the details for themselves. On the 24th, I Corps, which had not been seriously engaged, broke away without difficulty. Smith-Dorrien moved 3rd Division, on his right, first: when it was clear he ordered 5th Division to pull back. The low ridge between the villages of Elouges and Audregnies was held by 5th Division's rearguard—a battalion each of Cheshires and Norfolks, with cavalry and gunner support. Orders to retire never reached the Cheshires, who were eventually overwhelmed: almost twenty-six hundred men were lost that day.

The 25th saw the two corps of the BEF separated by the Forest of Mormal, and that night they halted to its south, I Corps around Landrecies and II Corps west of Le Cateau. It was an eventful night. A party of Germans bumped into 4th Guards Brigade in Landrecies. Haig, whose headquarters was nearby, became uncharacteristically agitated, and told GHQ that he was under heavy attack. Smith-Dorrien, whose own rearguards were still on the road, was unable to help. Murray collapsed with the sheer strain of it all, and when Smith-Dorrien telephoned in the small hours to announce that he would not be able to withdraw as ordered because the Germans would be on top of him before he could move, French was not at his best. He sent a message which concluded: "Although you are given a free hand as to method this telegram is not intended to convey the impression that I am not anxious for you to carry out the retirement and you must make every effort to do so."

LE CATEAU   Smith-Dorrien hoped to hold his ground long enough to administer what he termed "a stopping blow," checking the Germans and giving his own men a chance to resume the retreat uninterrupted. The 4th Division, which had just arrived, albeit incomplete, fought under his orders, prolonging his line to the west. Le Cateau was a much bigger battle than Mons. It began soon after dawn and, although Smith-

Ancient and modern. The commanding officer of 1st Cameronians (center) confers with his mounted adjutant at Le Cateau.

Dorrien's men beat off frontal attacks with relative ease, the position of 14th Infantry Brigade, overlooking Le Cateau on the right of 5th Division, deteriorated rapidly, and 2nd Suffolks were eventually wiped out.

Early in the afternoon Smith-Dorrien felt that the moment had come to slip away, and ordered his divisional commanders to retire, starting with 5th Division on his right, followed by the 3rd Division, with 4th Division moving off last. There were inevitably some tragedies: a battalion of Gordon High-landers did not receive the order, and held on till it was too late. Many of Smith-Dorrien's guns were fought right forward with the infantry, and when the time came to get them away their teams were shot down. In all, 7,812 men and thirty-eight guns were lost. French's official dispatch paid tribute to Smith-Dorrien's "rare and unusual coolness, intrepidity and determination," and most historians now agree that the controversial decision to stand and fight was indeed correct. Privately, however, French continued to blame him for disobeying orders, and believed that II Corps had suffered far more se-verely than was in fact the case.

| **THE RETREAT GOES ON** | Colonel Huguet, French liaison officer with GHQ, cer-tainly took a gloomy view, and reported that the British had lost the battle of Le Cateau and with it all cohesion. |

Franco-British relations cooled markedly on August 26 when French and Jof-fre met at St-Quentin. Joffre discussed the creation of a new 6th Army on the Allied left, but French, whose staff had not yet told him of the scheme, was unimpressed. Relations thawed a little over lunch, when Joffre acknowledged that his plans had failed and expressed dissatisfaction with French's *bête noire,* Lanrezac.

The retreat went on, although the BEF was never in the same peril as be-fore. In the days that followed, Joffre showed his stature as a commander, dis-missing the incompetent or unlucky (Lanrezac was soon replaced by Franchet d'Esperey, known to the British as "Desperate Frankie"), sustain-ing the fainthearted, cobbling together the 6th Army to bolster up his left, and always striving to keep Sir John up to the mark. As his grip tightened, so Moltke's weakened. His headquarters (Oberste Heeresleitung—OHL) had moved up to Luxembourg on August 29, but Moltke was still far away from his marching armies. Joffre, in contrast, had himself whizzed between army headquarters by his chauffeur, one of France's leading racing drivers. He often listened in silence and said little, but somehow his calm, not often rec-ognized as a Gallic virtue, radiated through to his commanders. It was a time when this "imperturbable calm and rough good sense" really counted.

The crisis came in early September. On the 1st, Sir John French was con-sidering pulling the BEF out of the line altogether in order to refit, but was summoned to meet Kitchener in the British Embassy in Paris. There were no

The tide turns. A company of Cameronians crossing a pontoon bridge, manned by Royal Engineers, over the Marne at La Ferté sous Jouarre, September 10, 1914.

witnesses to what was doubtless a difficult interview, though by its close Sir John was left in no doubt that the BEF's fate was inextricably linked to that of the French army. The French government left Paris the following day, leaving the cadaverous but tough General Joseph Galliéni, its military governor, with instructions to defend it to the last. It was an aviator from the Paris garrison who brought the first piece of really good news of the campaign. The German First Army, drawn eastward by the nervousness of the neighboring Second Army and not sustained on its course by a strong directing will from OHL, began to turn in front of Paris, offering a flank that could be attacked.

THE MARNE

The Battle of the Marne took place in sweltering heat along the lovely valley of the Marne. It was not decided by a single brilliant masterstroke or decisive breakthrough: ultimately the will of the commanders was no less important than that of the exhausted young men who actually did the fighting. Manoury's 6th Army, reinforced by troops from Paris sent out in taxicabs, struck at Kluck's flank. Although Kluck blocked the stroke, in doing so he opened a gap between First and Second Armies. The British, despite Joffre's desperate entreaty, were slow to exploit this, but Franchet d'Esperey pushed 5th Army forward, and on his right the new 9th Army, under Foch, also attacked.

Moltke, already wrestling with his moral responsibility for all the killing—
his staff saw him weeping silently at dinner—was deeply worried, and sent out
a trusted staff officer, Lieutenant Colonel Hentsch, to visit the army commanders. It is not clear just how wide Hentsch's powers actually were, but a
long journey in an uncomfortable car through the rear areas of fighting
armies helped sap his resolve, and he was persuaded that retreat was the only
answer. Moltke might yet have won: either on the Marne, where the battle
still hung in the balance, or by switching resources to Rupprecht, who was
close to a breakthrough further east. But he was a sick and beaten man: in his
own defeat lay that of the armies he commanded. Not for nothing did the
French hail "The Miracle of the Marne."

THE AISNE   Between September 9 and 13 the Germans fell back to
the River Aisne, with the Allies close behind. The
weather, blazing hot during August, broke, and the Allies reached the swollen
river to discover the Germans securely dug in on the wooded spurs behind it.
It speaks volumes for the skill of French's engineers that they managed to
throw a number of bridges across the river, and for the valor of his infantry
that they pressed their attacks with such courage toward unattainable objectives. It was soon evident that the Germans, with their preponderant artillery,
were not to be shifted. Sir John noted in his diary that artillery was the dominant arm in this kind of battle, and told the King that: "the *spade* will be as
great a necessity as the rifle, and the heaviest types and calibres of artillery
will be brought up on either side."

**THE RACE
TO THE SEA**   Deadlock on the Aisne induced both sides to feel for
the open flank and to move troops northward in what
became known as "the race to the sea." Traditionally
this sort of outflanking movement had often proved decisive, with the larger
army able to lap round its opponent's flank and rear. In 1914, however,
armies were too big, and the coast too close, for this to happen, and between
September and October the trench lines groped steadily northward, across
the uplands astride the Somme, in front of Arras, down into alluvial Flanders, and on into the dunes of the North Sea.

OPPOSITE The genesis of trench warfare. Men of 2nd
Scots Guards in a shallow, hastily dug trench, near Ypres, in
October 1914.

The BEF moved north in early October. French felt that this would simplify his lines of communication and give him the best chance of acting against what he hoped to be the German flank, and on October 13 GHQ was established in the little town of St-Omer. His army had already grown larger, with one more division sent out from England and another, initially sent out to support the Belgians at Antwerp, falling back to join the BEF just before Antwerp fell.

Foch had been sent up to command French forces in the north, and he encouraged Sir John in his belief that there was indeed a flank to be found around the small Belgian town of Ypres, and on October 18–19 he cracked the whip, urging his commanders to push on for Menin and turn the German flank. In the process they encountered powerful German forces intent on turning the Allied flank, and the First Battle of Ypres blazed out as Allied and German troops collided in the lush, low Flanders countryside.

THE FIRST BATTLE OF YPRES

It was soon clear that it was the Germans who were doing the attacking. On October 31 they came perilously close to breaking the British line, taking the village of Gheluvelt just as their shells hit the nearby château at Hooge, which housed two British divisional commanders, killing one and wounding the other. A counterattack by a battalion of Worcesters sta-

THE FIRST
BATTLE OF YPRES
OCTOBER–NOVEMBER 1914

Houthulst Forest

Roulers

Langemarck

Pilckem

Passchendaele

St-Julien

Wieltje

Zonnebeke

Vlamertinghe

Nonne Bosschen

Becelaere

Ypres

Hooge

Sanctuary Wood

Zillebeke

Gheluvelt

Menin Road

Menin

Wytschaete

Kemmel

Messines

Warneton

N
W   E
S

Ploegsteert Wood

Ploegsteert

Armentières

0	5 Miles
0	5 Kilometers

Main Allied Line, 22 October 1914

Front Line, 22 November 1914

bilized the situation, but over the days that followed the fighting continued to be desperate. The cavalry corps, fighting dismounted with a skill that shamed many of those who had made jokes about "donkey-wallopers," held Messines Ridge, south of Ypres, and it was there that the London Scottish, the first of the many Territorial battalions to fight on the Western Front, went into a battle that cost it more than half its strength: thereafter there were fewer jests about "Saturday night soldiers." The battle reached its crisis on November 11, when the Prussian Guard, coming on at a jog trot through the mist, punched a hole repaired only by another stunning counterattack, this time by the Oxfordshire and Buckinghamshire Light Infantry. Ypres was held, but at what a cost: the BEF had lost over fifty-eight thousand officers and men. In each of the battalions that fought on the Marne and at Ypres there remained, on average, only one officer and thirty men who had landed in August.

The First Battle of Ypres had also hit the Germans hard. Many of the students who had responded with such enthusiasm to the call to arms had perished. On October 27 Captain Rudolf Binding, a cavalry officer serving with a German infantry division, wrote:

> These young fellows we have, only just trained, are too helpless, especially when their officers have been killed. Our light infantry battalion, almost all Marburg students...have suffered terribly from enemy shellfire. In the next division, just such young souls, the intellectual flower of Germany, went singing into an attack on Langemarck [north of Ypres], just as vain and just as costly.

The Germans called the battle the *Kindermord zu Ypren*—the Massacre of the Innocents at Ypres.

The Christmas overtones of this expression were not misplaced, for the battle died away with Christmas not far off. It was a miserable December, with rain giving way to freezing cold, as the soldiers on both sides settled down to the war's first winter. There had already been some instances of fraternization between the French and the Germans, and on December 2 Smith-Dorrien noted that there had been "weird stories from the trenches" about Anglo-German fraternization, and decreed that such things would not go on in his corps. But somehow the human spirit was stronger than regulations, and there were a number of local truces that Christmas. They were small comfort to men who stood in trenches down in the Vosges, the chalk of Champagne, the mud of Flanders, or the dunes of the coast, garrisoning a front that stretched from the Swiss border to the North Sea. The war had gone to earth.

FEEDING
THE
FRONT

WESTERNERS AND EASTERNERS

The New Year opened with a debate which was to become sharper as 1915 went on. While what were called "westerners" maintained that the Western Front should continue to dominate British strategy, "easterners" suggested that, as there was evident stalemate on the Western Front, the Allies should look elsewhere for a decision. The dispute was more complex than any simple outline suggests, and there were many whose views changed with tactical circumstances. But it was fundamentally important, for 1915 saw the character of Britain's commitment change. The old regular army, which had gone to the war in 1914, began to be replaced by the mass army that, ultimately, would win it in 1918. The chief task of British military and political leaders in 1915 was feeding the front with men and munitions. Yet the question remained: which front?

The year was only a day old when Sir John French received what he termed "another incomprehensible letter" from his political master, Lord Kitchener, secretary of state for war. Kitchener told him that:

> The feeling here is gaining ground that, although it is essential to defend the line we now hold, troops over and above what is necessary for that service could better be employed elsewhere. The question *where* anything effective could be accomplished opens a large field and requires a good deal of study. What are the views of your staff?

Sir John was not pleased, for he already had firm views of his own. On December 27, 1914, he had visited Joffre at Chantilly and come to what he termed "a complete understanding as to future plans." The French would mount a two-pronged attack into the great German salient that bulged out malignantly toward Noyon, one thrust going in around Arras, in Artois, and the other in Champagne. The British, meanwhile, would take over the line between La Bassée and the coast as reinforcements arrived. French was hoping for a little more, as he had been encouraged by Winston Churchill, First Lord of the Admiralty, to mount an offensive along the Flanders coast, with the support of naval gunfire, in order to get the Germans out of the ports of Ostend and Zeebrugge. A gradual extension to the coast would delay this offensive.

The arrival of Kitchener's letter sharpened his concern, and made him increasingly anxious to push ahead with the coastal offensive, because doing so would help establish the primacy of the Western Front over the "sideshows" that were being discussed in London. On January 3 he assured Kitchener that given sufficient men and munitions the German line could be broken. Attacking Turkey, Germany's ally, would simply "play the German game . . . [and] draw off troops from the decisive spot, which is Germany herself."

By January the issues that would dominate 1915, and echo far beyond it, had been clearly set out. There were those "easterners" who, in Kitchener's words, were inclined to regard the Western Front as "a fortress which cannot be taken by assault," and to look elsewhere for a decision. The "eastern" solution was especially attractive to politicians like Churchill and David Lloyd George. On the other side of the debate were those who argued that there was no alternative to the Western Front. The bulk of the German Army was there, and the war could not be won unless it was beaten. Moreover, any British lack of commitment to the Western Front might weaken French resolve, and so imperil the very existence of the entente. Sir John French set out the case for the Western Front very clearly, and his successor Haig was to do the same.

French's note of January 3 highlighted the importance of men and munitions. The supply of both these commodities stood at the very forefront of British military policy. The "westerners" argued that the war could be won only if they were sent to France and Belgium. However, doing so would result in Britain confronting her major adversary in the principal theater of war, in a marked deviation of the practice of more than a century. Wellington had fought the French in Spain, a secondary theater, with the navy at his back: most major battles of the Napoleonic wars had been left to Britain's continental allies. In the circumstances of 1915 the "western" solution may well have been the only proper one, but, once adopted, it would commit the British army to the most obdurate test of its history.

RAISING NEW ARMIES

The war had already begun to transform the army. At the outbreak of war the regular army numbered almost 247,500 men, about a third of them stationed in India. There were, in addition, regular reservists, Territorials, and colonial troops, most of them Indian, but the fact remained that this was not a force organized on a continental scale. Moreover, the regular army, the small special reserve intended to help bring it up to strength on mobilization, and the Territorial Force were all underrecruited, and comparatively few of the latter had accepted a voluntary liability to serve overseas. It was small wonder that Kitchener's August 1914 instructions to Sir John French had emphasized caution. Yet by November 1918 over 5,700,000 men had passed through the army, slightly over 22 percent of the adult male population of the United Kingdom. "The creation of the country's first mass citizen army," writes Peter Simkins, "was the product of a gigantic act of national improvisation which had considerable repercussions throughout British society."

Kitchener had made his reputation overseas, first as commander in chief of the Egyptian army, at whose head he defeated the Dervishes at Omdurman in 1898; then as chief of staff to Roberts, and latterly commander in chief, in South Africa; and finally as commander in chief in India. In 1914 he was British Agent (effectively proconsul) in Egypt, and, fortuitously home on leave when war broke out, was appointed secretary of state for war, an unusual post for a field marshal but one apparently justified by his towering status with the British public.

Kitchener's virtues and vices were, alike, on a grand scale. He believed that it would be a long war, and planned accordingly, with a breadth of vision few could equal. Despite his suggestion that there might be more fruitful theaters than the Western Front, he recognized the crucial importance of supporting the French. He was enormously hardworking and energetic. But he was not a team player, and needed only to see a settled organization in order to swing his boot through it. He had no knowledge of Whitehall, little regard for politicians, and increasingly became an isolated, rather forbidding figure.

On August 7, 1914, Kitchener published his appeal for his first 100,000 recruits, and his face, its unblinking gaze emphasizing that "Your Country Needs You," glared down from the billboards. Recruiting soon became a flood, reaching 33,204 on September 3, the highest ever attained on a single day. In the first eight weeks some 761,000 men joined the army. Kitchener had no time for the Territorials, calling them "a town clerk's army," and raised his New Armies through the adjutant general's branch at the War Office.

TOP Recruits, whose clothing emphasizes their wide social mix, at Southwark Town Hall, London, in December 1915.

LEFT Field Marshal Lord Kitchener, secretary of state for war, whose personal appeal for recruits helped raise the New Armies.

ABOVE New recruits' medicals. Thousands rejected for service early in the war were called up later as medical standards fell.

The great majority of them were infantry, and formed service battalions of country regiments. Kitchener was astute enough to harness local enthusiasm, and some of the most distinctive New Army units were the Pals' Battalions, raised by mayors and corporations or recruiting committees of local industrialists and magnates. Typical examples were 10th (Service) Battalion, the Royal Fusiliers (the Stockbrokers Battalion); 16th Northumberland Fusiliers (the Newcastle Commercials); and 12th York and Lancaster (the Sheffield City Battalion).

Raising the New Armies was one thing: training and equipping them was quite another. During the first five months of the war the Western Front had guzzled Britain's trained manpower, and there was little enough left to train and command the New Armies. Battalion Commanding Officers were very often retired regulars, assisted, perhaps, by a young regular wounded at Mons and a handful of pensioner NCOs. In some Pals' Battalions a man's prewar status was often reflected in his military rank, and mill owners commanded companies containing their workers; in others there was a fierce pride in not taking a commission. In the ranks of 3rd Royal Fusiliers (the Sportsmen's Battalion) there were two England cricketers, the country's lightweight boxing champion, and a former lord mayor of Exeter.

There was far too little space in barracks for the New Armies. A few units were housed in huts, but others lived in tented camps while their huts were built, and discipline and health suffered. In the winter of 1914 thousands of men were billeted on civilians, which caused problems of its own. There were too few khaki uniforms to go round, and 500,000 suits of blue serge were issued to the discontent of the recipients, who feared that they resembled postmen. Modern webbing equipment was in short supply, and rifles were scarcer still: the Sheffield City Battalion received its full quota a week before it went abroad.

Because all combatants had gone to war in the expectation of a short conflict, all found themselves running short of artillery ammunition in the autumn of 1914. During the two and a half years of the Boer War the British fired 273,000 shells; between August 15, 1914, and February 15, 1915, the BEF fired a million. On a smaller scale, L Battery Royal Horse Artillery fired more shells on a single day, August 24, 1914, than it had in the Boer War. Shells were only part of the problem, for all armies had to provide that plethora of "trench stores"—barbed wire, sandbags, duckboards, picks, and shovels—to build and maintain their defenses. They also needed to produce the new weapons demanded by trench warfare, like flare pistols, light machine guns, and trench mortars.

Britain's problem was compounded because her army was expanding at a rapid rate, and she had to equip new soldiers as well as old. Kitchener observed that: "The old-fashioned little British Army was such an infinitely small proportion of the world's demand that looking after its equipment was not much more difficult than buying a straw hat at Harrods. But now I am going to need greater quantities of many things than have ever been made before." The supply of artillery ammunition had reached crisis point by November 1914, and the British official history acknowledges that two of French's three corps had little more than enough ammunition for one day's battle, and the third had even less. Robertson told the master general of the ordnance, responsible for ammunition supply, that it was a pity that his department had provided guns capable of firing ten rounds a minute if it took factories a day to produce these shells. In January 1915 he complained that there was a shortfall in delivery of 8,000 4.5-inch howitzer rounds, and it was difficult to plan operations properly without knowing what ammunition would be available. For men in the trenches the effect was dispiriting: observation officers might call for fire, only to be told that already the day's allocation had been expended.

The provision of ammunition was an enormous problem. Existing factories, whether private or government-owned, were far too small to meet the demand, and there were too few tools and too few skilled workers. Contracts were placed with overseas suppliers, but their capacity, too, required time to surge. Sudden changes in requirements did not help: the BEF went to war with no high-explosive shells for its field guns, because shrapnel had performed better in the Boer War, but immediately demanded them, forcing new production lines to be set up. And, in a mood where, in England, dachshunds were kicked and windows of German-owned shops smashed, the fact that the master general of the ordnance was named Sir Stanley von Donop was an added difficulty.

NEUVE CHAPELLE

Joffre planned to launch his two-pronged offensive as soon as the weather improved, and Sir John intended to support it by putting in an attack of his own. The BEF had now been restructured into two armies: Haig's 1st Army in the south, opposite La Bassée, and Smith-Dorrien's 2nd in the Ypres salient. French considered attacking Messines Ridge, near Ypres, and Aubers Ridge, near La Bassée, and eventually decided on the latter, in Haig's view because "he could never be sure of getting satisfactory results from SD, and...because my troops were better."

Joffre emphasized that his offensive depended on the British relief of two of his corps north of Ypres, to which Sir John had agreed. Then, on February 9, Sir John heard that the 29th Division—the last to contain mainly regular battalions—was to be sent to Salonica, in northern Greece, instead of France. Although he was to receive a Territorial division in its place, one could not "carry out, with a Territorial Division, what I had proposed with a regular one." Joffre was furious, and declared that because the British could not now relieve his troops as planned, the offensive was off. Sir John, undaunted, went ahead anyhow.

The attack was entrusted to Sir Henry Rawlinson's IV Corps, assisted by Sir James Willcocks's Indian Corps. Haig had ordered Rawlinson to capture the salient jutting into British lines at Neuve Chapelle, to "surprise the Germans, carry them right off their legs, and push forward to the Aubers... ridge... and exploit the success thus gained by pushing forward mounted troops forthwith." Rawlinson's preparations were meticulous. He concentrated 340 guns—as many as the whole BEF had taken to France in August 1914—against the salient, representing one gun for every six yards of front attacked. He took great care that they registered targets only a few at a time so as not to alert the Germans.

When the bombardment began at 7:30 on the morning of March 10, its effect was stunning. "The earth shook and the air was filled with the thunderous roar of the exploding shells," wrote a British officer. "To the watching thousands the sight was a terrible one: amidst the cloud of smoke and dust they could see human bodies with earth and rock, portions of houses, and fragments of trench hurtling through the air." The Germans had a single trench line with a few machine guns behind it and, because of the high water table, trenches had high parapets and were easy to observe: the damage was severe.

The first wave of the attack was generally successful, and Neuve Chapelle was taken. However, the late arrival of two howitzer batteries meant that a small section of German trench to its north was not effectively engaged, and its garrison included two machine guns. These lacerated two of the attacking battalions, 1st Middlesex and 2nd Scottish Rifles. The latter's story is admirably told in John Baynes's book *Morale*. In it he notes that the Scots' Commanding Officer had left it to his company commanders to decide whether their officers would attack with swords that day: two decided that swords would indeed be carried. At least one officer wore a sword on the first day of the Somme, but this may be the last occasion when several British infantry officers brandished swords in battle.

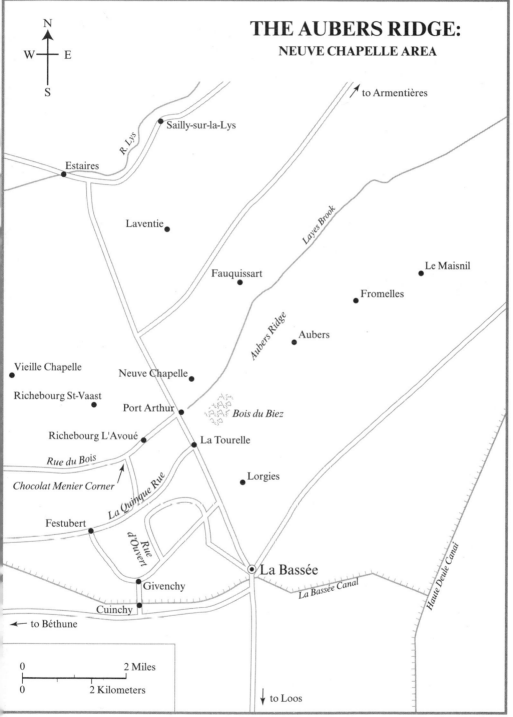

THE AUBERS RIDGE:
NEUVE CHAPELLE AREA

N
W — E
S

to Armentières

R. Lys

Sailly-sur-la-Lys

Estaires

Laventie

Layes Brook

Le Maisnil

Fauquissart

Fromelles

Aubers Ridge

Aubers

Vieille Chapelle

Neuve Chapelle

Richebourg St-Vaast

Port Arthur

Bois du Biez

Richebourg L'Avoué

La Tourelle

Rue du Bois

Lorgies

Chocolat Menier Corner

La Quinque Rue

Festubert

Rue d'Ouvert

La Bassée

Givenchy

La Bassée Canal

Haute Deule Canal

Cuinchy

to Béthune

0   2 Miles
0   2 Kilometers

to Loos

Neuve Chapelle, March 1916. Breastworks were built up because the wet ground made entrenchment difficult. German shells are bursting behind the British front line to prevent troops coming up.

If the sword was on its way out, the machine gun had certainly arrived. When the undamaged trench was bombarded late in the morning, its garrison promptly surrendered. Captain G. C. Wynne describes how "one officer and sixty-three men of the 11th *Jäger* Battalion, came out from it ... walking across the dead, estimated at about one thousand, lying literally in rows, whom they had slain that morning." The delay caused by this setback, coupled with the great difficulty Rawlinson experienced in assessing what had actually happened at the front so as to issue purposeful orders (the rapidly emerging problem in such attacks) meant that the second phase of the attack, the advance on Aubers Ridge, was delayed.

Rawlinson's critics have suggested that Neuve Chapelle was a tragedy of wasted opportunity, and had the advance gone on without pause the British would have made significant gains. Another of the great truths about trench warfare was emerging: it was generally easier for the defender, whose reserves were not moving across a shell-torn battlefield, to compensate for his failure, than for the attacker, whose communications became more fragile by the minute, to reinforce his success. There were German reserves in position behind the broken line by 9:30 A.M., and in truth the prospect of a break-through, after the first hour of the attack, was never great.

By nightfall the British and Indian attackers had overrun the defenses on a front of four thousand yards, penetrating to a maximum depth of one thousand yards. The battle went on until the night of the 12th, but neither fresh British assaults nor a German counterattack made much progress. French spoke warmly of "the defeat of the enemy and the capture of his position," but he had certainly expected more from the battle: it would show the French that they had an ally who knew his business, and demonstrate to Kitchener that feeding the Western Front was by no means pointless.

THE PROBLEM OF EXPLOITING SUCCESS

French had briefed his cavalry commanders personally. Rawlinson thought that their hopes that the cavalry would find an opportunity for effective action induced both French and Haig to prolong the battle longer than he himself thought wise. Mention of cavalry in the context of the Western Front still raises a guffaw, but the issue is more complex than it seems. Many commentators, including A. J. P. Taylor, who should have known better, have maintained that "most British generals were cavalry men." Both commanders in chief on the Western Front, French and Haig, were indeed cavalry officers. But by 1918, of seventeen corps commanders only one was a cavalryman, and of fifty-one divisional commanders, only five. As John Terraine has pointed out: "The overwhelming majority of generals actually handling troops in battle came, as one might expect, from the arm which produced the majority of those troops: the infantry."

The proportion of cavalry in the BEF dropped rapidly, from 9.28 percent in September 1914—a not unreasonable percentage for open warfare—to 3.88 a year later and 1.65 in March 1918. British cavalry were trained to fight dismounted as well as mounted—we have already seen them hold Messines Ridge with tenacity in the autumn of 1914—and there remained times when they provided a mobile reserve, although the small establishment of cavalry units and the need to detail horse holders meant that they generated less fire-power than comparable infantry formations.

For much of history the massed charge on the battlefield had been the most eye-catching of cavalry achievements. However, the pursuit after the battle, which converted a retreat into a rout, was often the finest achievement of the mounted arm. In 1914, exploitation remained a cavalry function, for there was, as yet, no other arm that could accomplish it. The proliferation of firepower, not to mention the cluttered nature of the battlefield, meant that exploitation and pursuit were difficult to achieve. They were not impossible—as the brilliant action of the Canadian Cavalry Brigade, which advanced eight miles, killed many Germans, and captured four hundred men and nearly one hundred machine guns at Cambrai in 1917, was to show. Yet there was, in essence, a technological gap that would be filled only by the development of the armored car and the tank.

THE LESSONS OF NEUVE CHAPELLE

Neuve Chapelle raised several issues, the difficulty of injecting cavalry into the battle only one of them. It highlighted the problem of achieving effective command and control on the battlefield. If Rawlinson deployed killing power that would have astonished the Duke of Wellington a century before, his communications had improved far less dramatically. The telephone was undeniably useful, but its wires were often cut by shellfire, and in an attack at this stage in the war the last links in the chain of command usually depended on runners toiling through the crater fields.

The unlearned lesson of Neuve Chapelle concerned the artillery. Rawlinson achieved a higher concentration of guns per yard of front attacked than he would on the Somme a year later, and because he had little ammunition he fired it swiftly. In doing so he achieved not only what the Germans called "the first real drum-fire [*Trommelfeur*] yet heard," but also surprise. Heavy fire, delivered rapidly and without warning, was to become a key ingredient of successful attacks toward the war's end: it made its unsung debut at Neuve Chapelle.

Haig planned to try again elsewhere, but it soon became clear that there was insufficient ammunition to permit him to do so. French told Kitchener: "Cessation of the forward movement is necessitated today by the fatigue of the troops, and, above all, by the want of ammunition." He went on to observe that unless sufficient shells arrived, "the offensive efforts of the army must be spasmodic and separated by a considerable interval of time. They cannot, therefore, lead to decisive results."

Over the next two months the issue of ammunition supply rose to become a crisis that would help bring down the government. Sir John's approach to it was never wholly objective. He knew that some of Rawlinson's difficulties had more to do with command and control than with ammunition, but was reluctant to say so. This was partly to excuse failure, partly to safeguard his own position as commander in chief (he remained worried that Kitchener

General Sir Douglas Haig, taciturn, reserved and single-minded, became Commander in Chief of the BEF in December 1915.

himself would bring the New Armies to France), and partly to maintain the primacy of the Western Front. Allied warships had already shelled Turkish positions on the Gallipoli peninsula, at the entrance to the Sea of Marmara on the sea route to Constantinople, and a landing would take place on April 25. For much of 1915 the Gallipoli expedition competed with the Western Front for scarce resources, and the knowledge did little to calm the mercurial Sir John French.

THE SECOND BATTLE OF YPRES

Joffre, meanwhile, had resurrected his plans for an offensive, and yet again Sir John agreed to relieve the French north of Ypres. Gallipoli cast its shadow over planning, however, and Sir John was unable to discover if or when extra troops would arrive. Nevertheless, in early April the British took over almost five miles of French front to the northeast of Ypres, finding the trenches "in a deplorable condition." It was here that the Germans struck on the afternoon of April 22, using gas for the first time. Their infantry went in behind a cloud of greenish-yellow chlorine, against which Allied troops in the sector had no effective protection. Within minutes men's eyes began to sting and their throats tightened. Soon they were fighting for breath, and the worst affected began to cough up blood.

It is not surprising that some French and British troops broke and ran: what is more astonishing is that some of the defenders held their ground. Private J. Lynn of the Lancashire Fusiliers fired his machine gun until the gas became too thick for him to see targets. Then he mounted it higher, on a stout fence post where the gas was thinner, and fired long bursts into German infantry until he collapsed, literally blue from the effects of gas; he died soon afterward. The stand made by the Canadian Division, its flank around St-Julien exposed by the attack, was a remarkable feat of arms and an early indication of the quality of Canadian troops.

The Germans were ill prepared to capitalize on their success, and the front was soon stabilized closer to Ypres after a series of bloody attacks and counterattacks that reflected little credit on the high command on either side. Sir John French was pressed to counterattack by Joffre and Foch, but was unconvinced that his men had much chance of success and became increasingly critical of the French. Being allied to them once in a lifetime, he complained, was more than enough. Smith-Dorrien, whose 2nd Army held the sector, sensibly recommended pulling back to shorten the line. French, ever more mistrustful of Smith-Dorrien since Le Cateau, first put Sir Herbert Plumer, one of 2nd Army's corps commanders, in charge of operations at Ypres, and then, on May 6, gave him command of 2nd Army. Wully Robertson had taken over as chief of staff from the exhausted Archie Murray in January, and he broke the news to Smith-Dorrien. "'Orace," he said, "you're for 'ome." When Plumer proposed retiring to a shorter line, French promptly agreed.

If the handling of the battle does not show Sir John at his best, it does shed light on his increasingly impossible position. He knew, from liaison officers at Joffre's headquarters, that Kitchener had made it plain that he would be replaced if Joffre thought it wise. Thus failure to support the French, even when their plans were unrealistic, could bring him down. Kitchener had already told Asquith, in words with which many historians would agree, that French "is not a really scientific soldier; a good capable leader in the field, but without adequate equipment and expert knowledge for the huge task of commanding 450,000 men." Then on March 31 Kitchener warned him that

> he considered Joffre and I were "on our trial"—that if we showed within the next month or five weeks that we could really make "substantial advances" then he would…always back us up with all the troops he could send. But if we failed it would be essential that the government should look for some other theater of operations.

Lastly, the strain of command weighed heavily on him. In March he had told Lord Esher, who visited him at St-Omer, that "It is a solemn thought that at my signal all these fine young fellows go to their death." He believed firmly in the immortality of the soul, and thought that his room was "*thick* with the spirits of my dead friends."

SPRING OFFENSIVE

On May 8, 1st Army attacked Aubers Ridge as an accompaniment to the French offensive further south in Artois. It was predestined to fail. As a result of Neuve Chapelle the Germans had been working like beavers on their defenses, doubling or tripling the depth of their barbed wire, strengthening the front-line trenches and beginning work on a second trench a short distance behind it, with dugouts for its garrison and communication trenches leading forward, to form a much stronger first position. Much further back, a line of concrete machine-gun posts formed rallying points in case the first position was broken. Over the months that followed, this would become a second position in its own right, almost as strong as the first.

In their painstaking study of Rawlinson's command, Robin Prior and Trevor Wilson observe that British gunners were able to bombard this improved line with only one-fifth of the intensity of shells delivered at Neuve Chapelle. The plan for the infantry assault was complex: some battalions had to make a 45-degree turn, under fire, in no-man's-land. It is small wonder that the attack failed disastrously. The British and Indians lost 11,500 men, and the German regiments facing them reported losses of less than a thousand. The diary of the German 57th Regiment expressed its admiration for the magnificent courage with which the British had attacked, as well as surprise at the repetition of attacks in broad daylight once the first had failed.

THE SHELLS SCANDAL

French was appalled. He had watched the battle from the tower of a ruined church, and when he returned to his headquarters he found an order to send 22,000 shells to Gallipoli. Charles Repington, a retired officer and *Times* correspondent, was staying with him, and Repington's article of May 14, with the headline "Need for Shells: British attacks checked: Limited supply the cause: A Lesson from France," was, it later transpired, the result of collaboration between the two men.

French also sent two of his staff to London with the same documents that had been shown to Repington. They were passed to David Lloyd George, a

Women munitions workers in the shell-filling factory at Chilwell near Nottingham. The wood-block floor was designed to prevent sparks, but there were several explosions, one of which gutted this building; it was rebuilt immediately.

member of Asquith's cabinet, and to the opposition leaders Balfour and Bonar Law. The Government would have survived the "shells scandal" had this been the only crisis facing it, but Lord Fisher had just resigned as First Sea Lord, and Asquith decided that the two events "would, if duly exploited...in the House of Commons at this moment have had the most disastrous effect upon the general political and strategic situation...." He decided to form a coalition government, in which Lloyd George became minister of munitions. Kitchener stayed on at the War Office, although his reputation was damaged by a press campaign against him in which French was heavily implicated.

Lloyd George's ministry unquestionably made a difference, though perhaps this was not as profound as its many publicists were to suggest. The first consignment of munitions it ordered did not arrive till October 1915, and the much-reviled War Office had actually supervised a nineteen-fold increase in output in the first six months of the war. Nonetheless, the ministry pressed ahead with energy, employing "men of push and go," experienced businessmen who, as Lloyd George put it, could "create and hustle along a gigantic new enterprise."

By the spring of 1918, 61 percent of the male industrial force was involved in war work. The number of women workers also grew: fewer than a hundred worked at Woolwich arsenal in November 1916, but there were twenty-two thousand six months later and thirty thousand a year on. The social and political effects of this expansion were considerable, but represented less of a uniform advance toward women's rights than is sometimes supposed. Many women lost their jobs after the war, and the 1921 census showed that the proportion of "gainfully employed females" was actually lower than it had been in 1911.

| FRESH OFFENSIVES | Although, as the official verdict put it, Aubers Ridge had been "a serious disappointment," the British continued attacking. On May 16, 1st Army tried again at |

Festubert, just south of Neuve Chapelle, this time after a deliberate three-day bombardment which embodied French's conviction, all too well justified in the light of Aubers Ridge, that "it's simple murder to send infantry against these powerfully fortified entrenchments until they've been heavily hammered." They were not hammered heavily enough: lack of shells saw to that. The bombardment seriously damaged the German trenches, but left many machine guns and dugouts intact.

Three divisions attacked at night and daybreak, overrunning much of the front line but being held up by machine guns that had survived the shelling and isolated parties of Germans hanging on in shell holes or sections of wrecked trench. The Germans eventually abandoned their first position and reinforced their second, but there was too little time and ammunition to engage this effectively, and although the British advanced a maximum of one thousand yards on a front of three thousand, it was for a cost of 16,500 men.

No sooner had Festubert ended than the British were again pressed to attack to divert German attention from an offensive of their own. Joffre initially suggested that Loos, at the southern end of the British sector, would be ideal, but the ground was unpromising and Haig gained permission to attack the Rue d'Ouvert at Givenchy, further north. Rawlinson was not convinced that Givenchy was much better, writing that: "it will cost us many thousands of lives before we are in possession of the place unless we get an unlimited amount of ammunition to smash the place to pieces before we go in." After a deliberate bombardment, with a slightly better ratio of guns to trench than at Aubers Ridge, IV Corps attacked, winning small lodgments which it could not hold when the supply of hand grenades—one of the key weapons in this kind of fighting—faltered. Rawlinson was not surprised that the attack on the Rue d'Ouvert failed, and admitted that: "A feeling exists that life is being thrown away on objectives which are not worth it.... Are we not asking too much of our infantry?"

Rawlinson made no efforts to explain his uneasiness to his superiors, and with good reason. In July a 3rd Army was formed, and although Rawlinson was the senior corps commander he was not given command, which went instead to Sir Charles Monro. He suggested in his diary that he could not "expect fair treatment with Sir John and old Robertson" against him. He was quite right. French had already come close to sacking him, and wrote the following year that: "No one trusts or believes in Rawlinson." This drew Rawlinson closer to Haig, the only real candidate for supreme command if French fell.

ALLIED PLANS

French and Joffre met at Chantilly on June 24 and gave a ringing vote of confidence in the Western Front. A passive defense in the west, they argued, would be "a bad strategy, unfair to Russia, Serbia and Italy, and therefore wholly inadmissible." They were united in their opposition to the Gallipoli venture, and urged that all available British troops should be sent to France. Another series of conferences in July, attended by the principal Allied leaders, established broad agreement that there should be a major offensive on the Western

German troops using two types of hand grenade, some carried by a messenger dog. The familiar 'potato-masher' is on the right.

Front. Joffre soon revealed that, unoriginally, he proposed to attack in Artois, with the French 10th Army around Vimy supported by the BEF to its north, while another major assault was delivered in Champagne. Cavalry, and infantry in motor buses, would exploit the breakthrough, whose final objective lay beyond the Belgian frontier.

Joffre was anxious for the BEF to attack on his immediate left, around Loos, into the area taken over by Haig's 1st Army in June. Haig was initially inclined to think that the sector offered good prospects for an attack, but soon changed his mind. On June 23 he reported to French that the ground was hopeless: the Germans were securely dug into an industrial landscape of mining suburbs, slag heaps, and pitheads. On July 12 French went up to Notre Dame de Lorette, a piece of commanding ground near Vimy Ridge (now crowned by a cemetery and ossuary housing many of the French soldiers who had died taking it), to see for himself. He too was not favorably impressed, for the terrain was "covered with all the features of a closely inhabited flourishing mining district. . . ." The only advantage was that artillery fire could be directed against it from high ground in Allied hands. Yet this was not enough. On 20 July he told a liaison officer with Joffre's headquarters that the most he could do would be to launch diversionary attacks and soon, prompted no doubt by Haig and Robertson, he decided against these too. He was quite firm, declaring that: "we should not be helping the French by throwing away thousands of lives knocking our heads against a brick wall."

Sir John could not hold his ground. Joffre leaned hard on him in August,

earnestly requesting his support, and, when Sir John replied that he would attack chiefly with artillery, Joffre demanded instead "a large and powerful attack . . . executed with the hope of success and carried through to the end."
French gloomily told Haig that "we must have big losses in order to achieve
any result," but privately suspected that success was impossible. Then Kitchener threw his weight into the balance. The Russians had just lost Warsaw and
were in full retreat. Sir John was bidden to attack "and do our utmost to help
the French, even though, by doing so, we suffered very heavy losses indeed."
In the face of this unequivocal order, GHQ and 1st Army set about planning
the battle. Perhaps because it was the only way out of his moral quandary, Sir
John's confidence improved, and a visitor to GHQ in late August found his
staff "quite optimistic."

A German officer had prophesied that his own side's use of gas at Second Ypres would earn Germany widespread criticism, but, having expressed
their moral outrage, her enemies would follow suit. He was perfectly correct,
for having condemned "that damnable gas," Sir John immediately demanded
a retaliatory capacity. By early September there was confidence that lavish
use of gas would make a real difference at Loos. Rawlinson was less sure, noting presciently that "we are not very good at these improvisations."

| LOOS

Haig's outline plan was simple enough. His I and IV
Corps would attack between the distinctive double slag
heap south of Loos and the La Bassée Canal, while his two other corps made
diversionary attacks. Once the German first position was broken, the General Reserve, Lieutenant General Haking's IX Corps and the cavalry, would
pass through the gap. Haking's corps was an unknown quantity. Its headquarters was newly formed and its staff largely inexperienced, and although
the Guards Division was built on a nucleus of well-trained men, its two New
Army divisions, 21st and 24th, had never fought before: some of their units,
indeed, arrived in France as the preparations reached their climax. Archie
Murray had written from London to tell French that the New Armies were
not really what they would term soldiers. Their artillery was "an unknown
quantity" (scarcely surprising, given its shortage of guns, ammunition, and
range space), and the infantry was not well enough trained to go straight into
the line. However, endless route marches meant that it was very fit, and would
do well if it could be thrown in once the battle was won.

French and Haig disagreed profoundly about the positioning of IX
Corps. French believed that it would not be needed until the battle's second

LOOS
SEPTEMBER 1915

La Bassée

Givenchy

to Hinges
(3m)

La Bassée Canal

Cuinchy

Cambrin

to Béthune
(4m)

Les
Briques
Farm

Auchy

Douvrin

Haisnes

Mad Point

Cité St-Elie

Hohenzollern
Redoubt

Quarries

Vermelles

Hulluch

Bois Carré

Lone Tree

to Béthune (5m)
and Lillers (15m)

Dud Corner

Chalk Pit
Wood

Loos Rd
Redoubt

Loos

Bois Hugo

Lens Rd
Redoubt

Chalet
Wood

Cité St-Auguste

Tower
Bridge

Hill 70
Redoubt

North
Maroc

Grenay

N

W — E

S

Double
Crassier

South
Maroc

Cité St-
Edouard

Lens

Cité St-
Laurent

Cité St-Pierre

0	1 Mile
0	1 Kilometer
Roads	
Railway	+++

British Front Line before attack on Sept 25 · · ·

British Front Line at end of battle, night of Oct. 13–14

German Front Line at start of battle - - -

German Second Line

day and could therefore be kept well behind the front, where he, as commander in chief, could commit it as required. French was an avid fan of Napoleon, and his handling of the reserve was very much in the Napoleonic tradition. Haig, however, argued that he would need the reserve much more quickly, stressing that he would have no spare troops and: "The whole plan of operations of the 1st Army is based on the assumption that the troops of the General Reserve will be close at hand."

French remained obdurate. His opponents were to suggest that this was because he wanted to initiate the decisive blow himself. It is, however, more likely that his initial fears about the battle had not fully subsided. If he put IX Corps at Haig's disposal from the outset, there was always the risk that Haig would commit it to battle come what may: French wanted to be sure that the gap really was there before Haking's green troops were shoved into it. Haig was not at all pleased that the General Reserve was being held back, and wrote that it was "impossible to discuss military problems with an unreasoning brain of this kind."

Rawlinson, for his part, had misgivings about even the first phase of the battle. The Germans had been working hard on their second position, some twenty-five hundred to three thousand yards behind the first, so that field guns used to bombard the first position would have to be moved forward in order to have the range to hit it, and situated on a reverse slope (behind the crest line of low ridges) so that it could not be seen from British trenches. Rawlinson noted that this second position was now fully protected by barbed wire, and was convinced that simply capturing the first position would be a real achievement. His dependence on Haig precluded him from raising his concerns, and at Loos in 1915, just as at the Somme a year later, there was no meeting of minds between Rawlinson and his immediate superior.

The attack was preceded by a bombardment, going on for four days, in which 533 guns fired more than a quarter of a million shells. But because the front was so wide—this was the biggest offensive in the British army's history to date—the ratio of guns to yards of front was far lower than at Neuve Chapelle. However, the attack was not wholly reliant on the shelling, for it was hoped that the 5,100 cylinders containing about 140 tons of chlorine would have a profound effect. Most German soldiers had primitive gas masks, but the gas release would persist far longer than these would retain even their marginal effectiveness: even the better gas masks issued to machine gunners would be unable to cope. Smoke was to be added to the gas cloud to confuse the Germans, and shrapnel would sweep their trenches when the gas was released and the defenders would be likely to man their parapets. Manhandling the heavy cylinders into front-line trenches was back breaking, and connecting them to release pipes, one vertical and one horizontal, was difficult work in poor light with cross-threaded nuts, jammed joints and spanners that sometimes broke or failed to fit. Nonetheless, by dawn on September 25 the 1,400 men of the gas companies had done a better job than either their own inexperience or the inherent difficulty of their task implied, and were ready to launch what the high command insisted on calling "the accessory."

There remained one problem. Successful use of gas relied on wind strong enough to carry it to the German lines but not so strong that it blew the gas cloud apart. Haig spoke to his meteorologist, Captain Gold, early that morning. Then, in the garden of his château at Hinges, he asked his senior aide-de-camp, Lieutenant Colonel Alan Fletcher, to light a cigarette. The smoke drifted gently toward the German lines and the leaves on the poplar trees rustled encouragingly. It was barely adequate but, aware that without gas only a much smaller-scale attack would be possible, Haig gave the order to launch the gas.

The gas behaved erratically. In the south it spread straight into Loos valley, where it lingered among the German trenches. Further north, it drifted obliquely between the trench lines, and some of it blew back into the British trenches, causing some of the confusion perhaps too vividly described by Robert Graves in *Goodbye to All That*. During the whole battle there were 2,632 British gas casualties, of whom only seven died, so stories about wholesale slaughter of friendly troops by gas are simply not true. Nevertheless, the British respirator, known as "the goggle-eyed booger with the tit," which consisted of cloth impregnated with chemicals with two eyepieces and a rubber mouthpiece, was no adjunct to effective fighting, and because the gas hung about in trenches, shell hole, and pockets in the ground men either had to wear them when no gas seemed evident or to do as most did and unmask in sheer frustration and take their chances.

The battle went well in the south where IV Corps attacked. The Territorials of 47th London Division took the southern part of Loos, and another Territorial division, 15th Scottish, poured through Loos itself, encouraged by the shriek of the pipes as several pipers risked the gas to play their comrades into battle. North of the Hulluch–Vermelles road, which bisects the battlefield, I Corps was less fortunate. As we have seen, the gas was less effective here, but 7th and 9th Divisions made some progress, entering the Quarries just north of the road and establishing a foothold on the Hohenzollern Redoubt, a strongpoint that dominated much of the northern sector.

TOP Loos battlefield, with the colliery winding-gear—Tower Bridge—from the British front line. Loos (out of sight) is to the right, and the German second position is over the horizon.
ABOVE Argyll and Sutherland Highlanders wearing the primitive gas protection issued in May 1915. Although gas masks were improved by the time of Loos, they were still uncomfortable and constricting.

The infantry attacked at 6:30 A.M., and half an hour later Haig sent an officer by car to French's forward command post at Lillers to announce that progress was good and to urge that IX Corps should be ready to move. At 9:30 he reported that his own reserves were committed and asked for IX Corps to be put under his command. French visited him just after 11:00 and agreed to put Haking's two New Army divisions at his disposal, driving off to give Haking the news in person. At 1:20 Haking phoned to announce that his two divisions were now under Haig's command and were on their way up. He added ominously that there were serious delays on the road.

The divisions had been on the march since early on the 24th, under rain coming down in stair rods and along cobbled roads congested with the traffic in 1st Army's rear. There was some less than meticulous staff work: one brigade commander was not allowed to take his men through Béthune because he lacked the correct pass, so had to march round it. Most of the advancing troops managed to eat once on the 25th: it was the last meal for all too many of them.

The Germans were also moving up reserves. Even on the first day their second position was held so strongly that an attack on it would have been difficult, but by dawn on the 26th it was more strongly held than the first line had been at the beginning of the battle and, to make matters worse, it had scarcely been touched by the British artillery.

It was not until the afternoon of the 26th that Haking's men advanced between Loos and the Hulluch–Vermelles road. They presented an impressive sight: German observers saw what seemed to be ten columns of extended lines of infantry, coming on as if on parade. Consternation turned to amazement, for there was no covering fire, and "A target was offered to us such as had never been seen before, nor even thought possible." The machine guns opened fire at fifteen hundred yards and, although men fell in the hundreds, the survivors pushed on. "Never had machine guns had such straightforward work to do, nor done it so effectively," recounted one German regimental history. "With barrels burning hot and swimming in oil, they traversed to and fro along the enemy's ranks unceasingly: one machine gun alone fired 12,500 rounds that afternoon." Some of the attackers actually got as far as the German wire but: "Confronted by this impenetrable obstacle, the survivors turned and began to retire." The two divisions lost over eight thousand killed and wounded.

The battle sputtered on for several more days. The Guards Division went into action to stabilize the situation, and in the fighting north of Loos, Rudyard Kipling's only son, John, a lieutenant in the Irish Guards, was reported

May 4th 1915

Royal Hospital
Huddersfield

My dearest mother. I hope you got my field P.C. all right and that you have not been working yourself up into a state about me being wounded. I sent it off from a field dressing station while waiting for removal to Hospital. Well, mother here is the whole thing from the start and that was on my birthday up to the time of writing. We went out on the 20th to take up Reserve Trenches, north of Ypres, we had practically nothing to do for the first two days, then it was on the afternoon of my birthday that we noticed volumes of dense yellow smoke rising up & coming towards the British Trenches, as I said my Coy. was not in the firing line and we did not get the full effect of it, but what we did was enough for me, it makes your eyes smart & run, I became violently sick, but it passed off fairly soon, by this time the din was something awful where we were, we were under a cross fire of rifles & Shells, we had to lie flat in the trenches, The next thing I noticed was a horde of those Turcos (French Colonial Soldiers, making for our trenches, some were armed, some unarmed, the poor devils were absolutely paralysed with fear, they were holding a French

A wounded soldier, J. D. Keddie, in hospital in Huddersfield, tells his mother about the first gas attack at Ypres on April 22, 1915.

missing, believed killed. The British lost over 43,000 men, including three major generals, and the Germans less than half as many. The French 10th Army's attack on the right fared no better.

HAIG TAKES COMMAND

After the battle came the recriminations. French's position, which was weak before Loos, was now untenable. Robertson, in London to assist the War Office, discussed his replacement with the King and Asquith. Haig had long been convinced that French should go, and now told Rawlinson that he should have been replaced after Mons. When the King came to France in October, Haig made it clear that "the C-in-C was a source of great weakness to the army," adding that he personally was prepared to serve in any capacity. There was a bitter dispute between GHQ and 1st Army over the mishandling of the reserves, and Haig ensured that the relevant papers were sent to the King. Asquith decided to replace French, and when attempts to persuade Sir John to resign failed, his old friend Walter Long, now a junior minister, phoned to say that he would have to go.

French suggested that Robertson should replace him, but everyone, Robertson included, recognized that his talents lay on the staff. He had, in any case, been earmarked for the post of Chief of the Imperial General Staff. French went the rounds making his farewells. Foch cried, and Joffre lamented: "If they do things like that, how can we hope to win the war?" On December 18, French met Haig, who was to succeed him. It was a painful interview. French had by now discovered what had been afoot. Both men were stiff and formal: one of French's staff saw that Haig never for a moment unbent, and another officer recalled that Sir John was "very bitter against Haig."

Haig had been in office for ten days when he received his own set of instructions from Lord Kitchener. These informed him that:

> The defeat of the enemy by the combined Allied Armies must always be regarded as the primary object for which British troops were sent to France, and to achieve that end, the closest cooperation of combined Allied Armies must always be regarded as the prime object for which British troops were sent to France.

He did his best to establish cordial relations with the French, inviting the head of their liaison team at GHQ to attend his daily staff conference. An inter-Allied conference at Chantilly in early December had concluded that decisive results would be achieved only if the Allies mounted coordinated attacks on the principal (Western, Eastern, and Italian) fronts.

Robertson, now indeed Chief of the Imperial General Staff (CIGS), passed on these conclusions to Haig, amplified with views of his own. Gallipoli would be evacuated, and every effort would now be concentrated on the Western Front, where the Allies were to mount a spring offensive. Despite the miseries of 1915—that sterile year—the British Army in France, increasingly well fed with men and munitions, was stronger and better equipped than ever before. It remained to be seen what use the new commander in chief would make of it.

HOLDING
THE
FRONT

FRANCE AND THE WAR Most of the Western Front cut through French soil. The great city of Lille and the mining belt around it lay behind the German lines, and the nose of the huge salient bulging out into France was as close to Paris as Canterbury is to London. Georges Clemenceau, the brilliant radical politician who became premier in 1917, reminded his parliamentary audience, speech after speech, that: "The Germans are still at Noyon." For part of the war Paris was within range of German superguns tucked into forests north of the Aisne: the Ecole des Mines, on the eastern edge of the Luxembourg Gardens in Paris, still bears the scars of shellfire from the siege of Paris in 1870–71 and shelling in 1918.

Tens of thousands of French soldiers came from towns and villages behind the German lines, and their miseries were sharpened by the knowledge that their homes were occupied. A broad swath of French territory was ravaged by the war, sometimes accidentally, but sometimes—especially before the German withdrawal to the Hindenburg Line in 1917—deliberately. In 1914 thousands of refugees from the advancing Germans found themselves on the wrong side of the lines when the front solidified.

Many Frenchmen were shot, imprisoned, or deported for resisting the Germans, but many, in this war as in the next, came to a working accommodation with the occupier. It was often difficult, especially in rural communities housing German soldiers who were themselves often countrymen, to preserve a necessary hostility. The war could not stand in the way of human nature. When French armies followed up the German retreat to the Hindenburg Line some soldiers, as Edward Spears, a British liaison officer, observed, went home to discover a flaxen-haired babe or pregnant wife. Many somehow managed to take this most poignant consequence of occupation in their stride, for they knew that nights were long and yearning deep.

Although the rumble of the guns could be heard in southern England, and prowling aircraft, airships, and warships sometimes brought death and destruction to Britain, the Channel provided a barrier between Britain and the war that was both physical and psychological. There was no such barrier in France: the line between the *Zone des Armées*, under military control, and the remainder of France was simply a line on the map. While French soldiers endured the sufferings of the front line and the dismal conditions in camps behind it, they knew that there was a world of theaters, cafés, and restaurants not far away. It was a world they seldom glimpsed and never sympathized with. The *embusqué*, the shirker, with a soft job, clean fingernails, and another man's wife, was the target of deep hatred reflected in the trench newspapers, which provide such a valuable understanding of the way the French soldier thought.

RED TROUSERS, WHITE GLOVES

Armies are, among other things, symbols of national culture, reflecting a nation's political and social structure and illuminated by its history. The French army of the First World War was colored by the Franco-Prussian War of 1870–71 and the political instabilities that followed it. In the summer and early autumn of 1870 the armies of the Emperor Napoleon III, nephew of a greater emperor, were destroyed by a German coalition under Prussian leadership in what was little less than a lightning war.

The Germans besieged and bombarded Paris and, in the provinces, fought a war of increasing bitterness against the Armies of National Defense, a hodgepodge of forces cobbled together by the government that had succeeded the fallen Empire. The war was concluded on humiliating terms, which included the loss of France's eastern provinces of Alsace and Lorraine. Government troops then took Paris from Communard insurgents in a brutal war which was to have a lasting impact on French politics. The Third Republic was established, with its president and bicameral legislature, and survived a sickly infancy menaced by royalist pretenders or flamboyant soldiers.

The French army entered a Golden Age after the war. Charles de Gaulle described the "exceptional prestige" enjoyed by the officer:

In the garrison, everyone treats him with respect. Tradespeople extend him credit. He is at the center of every activity. People admire his bearing. Women are favorably disposed. Families would be glad to have as a son-in-law this "man of honor" who, as they say, has a future, or at any rate a pension for later on.

It was a period characterized by the work of two of France's greatest military artists, Edouard Detaille and Alphonse de Neuville. Both specialized in historical paintings, with the wasted gallantry of the Franco-Prussian War as a recurring theme. And they looked ahead as well as back. In 1888 Detaille carried off the Salon's medal of honor with *Le Rêve* (the dream), a work that was both realistic and allegorical. The officers and men of a French regiment on autumn maneuvers sleep, rolled in their blankets: in the skies above, the warriors of old France lead the way to future glory.

French politicians had rarely agreed about the army. The Right traditionally preferred professional soldiers, or at least conscripts who served for so long as to be regulars in all but name, to short-service conscripts. The latter might prove unreliable in terms of political crisis, and go home having become all too familiar with the use of arms. The Left, in contrast, was suspicious of hired praetorians, and during the Franco-Prussian War reverted to the old Jacobin tradition which fused universal conscription and Republicanism.

The likelihood of a new war against Germany helped bring politicians together. In 1872 the National Assembly agreed on universal conscription, decreed that the army's peacetime organization would mirror that of war, and established officer and NCO cadres that would permit the army to double on mobilization. The army itself set about learning the lessons of 1870–71. A Staff College was created in 1875 and a proper general staff established in 1890. The swashbucklers of the Second Empire were replaced by a new generation of officers who read books and subscribed to professional journals. The sons of old noble families rediscovered the profession of arms. Weapons and equipment were comprehensively reformed. Forts arose on the bleak uplands overlooking the new frontier as engineers began to cast the framework of the future battlefield. Although political debate went on, there was widespread realization that the army must be kept out of political quarrels.

Clashes between troops and strikers started to tarnish the gilt. In 1894 the Dreyfus affair broke, driving a wedge between army and nation. Captain Alfred Dreyfus, a Jewish officer serving on the general staff, was accused of spying for Germany, convicted after a questionable trial, and imprisoned for life on Devil's Island in French Guyana. Doubts arose about his guilt, and in January 1898 Emile Zola published an article accusing the army of supporting the conviction of an innocent man. The nation was divided, some seeing the conviction as the embodiment of everything authoritarian and arbitrary, others claiming that the army's honor was being besmirched by Jews and radicals.

Dreyfus was retried, found guilty "with extenuating circumstances," and eventually cleared altogether, but the damage was enormous. The affair, coupled with other scandals, encouraged young men to turn away from military careers. The number of candidates for St-Cyr—broadly the French equivalent of Sandhurst or West Point—fell from 1,920 in 1897 to 871 in 1911, and over a similar period the number of NCOs who chose to reenlist fell from 72,000 to 41,000. With its prestige diminished, the army had few attractions: pay was poor and promotion slow. A colonel described how the most able officers became majors between the ages of forty-four and forty-nine, and thereafter it was a race between promotion and compulsory retirement.

THE TWO ARMIES

Some officers turned their backs on the burgeoning gloom of metropolitan France by soldiering in the colonies, where initiative might be richly rewarded and the bonds linking officers and men were closer. There were in effect two armies, a metropolitan army of yawning barrack rooms and jammed promotion lists, and a colonial army of dash and enterprise. The two were not on comfortable terms. Joseph Galliéni, governor of Paris in 1914, had turned down high command, fearing that the metropolitan army would not accept him. He tapped his button, with its marine infantry anchor, remarking: "It is a question of buttons." Joffre was a colonial sapper, and at least part of his messianic devotion to the offensive came from a desire to galvanize the metropolitan army into much-needed activity.

In 1905 military service was fixed at two years, loopholes through which the privileged had escaped were blocked up, and a total liability of twenty-five years was established. But in practice reservists were called for training less and less frequently, and the mistrust of regular officers for the reserves grew more marked. In 1913 the disparity between the French and German armies encouraged parliament to increase army pay and make it easier for warrant officers (confusingly called *adjutants* in French) to gain commissions, and after heated debate military service was extended to three years.

FRANCE GOES TO WAR

When France mobilized in 1914 her army bore the scars of the previous two decades. She had twenty-five hundred automatic weapons against the German army's forty-five hundred, and only thirty-eight hundred 75 mm field guns compared with the six thousand 77 mms in the German army. She was also pitifully short of heavier weapons. Emphasis on the offensive encouraged officers to regard the 75 mm as "God the Father, God the Son and God the Holy Ghost": it would have been nice, said one cynic, to have seen it surrounded by a few saints of heavier metal. True, there had been a marked revival of moral values in the years immediately before the war, and a student wrote that: "It is in the life of the camps and under fire that we will experience the supreme flowering of the French forces that dwell with us."

On July 31, 1914, the graduating class of St-Cyr swore to go into battle in parade uniform, with plume and white gloves. Many of them did so, and even in 1916 a French officer saw a comrade, some distance away, lying dead, his gloves flecks of white against his blue greatcoat. The officer who inspired the oath was luckier than many of his comrades: he lived till April 1915. The French army had suffered 955,000 casualties by December 1914, and in the next year it lost an appalling 1,430,000. The Champagne offensive of September 1915 cost 145,000 men. One general warned President Poincaré that the army could not go on like this: "the instrument of victory is being broken in our hands." In all, France's fatalities totaled almost a million and a half men, nearly half again as many as the 947,000 suffered by Britain and her Empire.

A French 75 mm field gun showing the barrel at full recoil after firing. France was pitifully short of modern heavy guns.

MILITARY POLITICS

There are strong political currents in almost any army, and in the French army they ran deep. There were complaints that the army was run by "generals from the Jesuit warrens," like Castelnau, Joffre's assistant in 1915–16: a lay member of a religious order, he was known as *"le capucin botté,"* the fighting friar. In contrast, there was General Sarrail, commanding the 3rd Army in 1914, with a reputation for confirmed republicanism. One broadsheet proclaimed that: "If General Joffre was unavailable for a period of two weeks and if supreme command were entrusted to General Sarrail, there can be no doubt that the Germans would be chased from the national territory." In late 1915 Sarrail was sent off to command the expedition to Salonica, and the need to keep him in a position suited to his political status became a powerful reason for not closing down a front that was widely regarded as a pointless sideshow.

Joffre himself had not had an easy time. He was characteristically modest about the Marne, declaring that he was not certain who had won it, but knew who would have been blamed for losing it. In September 1914 he replaced one-third of the French command. Generals were posted to the southern town of Limoges to await further orders, or *limogé*. In popular parlance they came unstuck *(dégommé),* a word the British plundered to produce "degummed." His offensives in 1915 failed largely because of lack of materials but, at the close of the year, as we have seen, he was anticipating a new offensive in 1916, which, it was subsequently agreed, would be mounted where the British and French armies joined, on the River Somme.

GERMAN PLANS

War is nothing if not two-sided, and it was never wise, in either world war, to assume that the Germans would behave as expected. General Erich von Falkenhayn had replaced the broken Moltke as Chief of the General Staff in September 1914 at the early age of fifty-three. He was, on the face of things, a surprising choice, originating in the thrifty junker squirearchy of East Prussia and enjoying a decidedly average career until attracting royal attention, and with it rapid promotion, just before the war. A biographer dubbed him "the lonely general," and his hard face and punishing lifestyle both testified to a single-minded strength of purpose.

It is still hard to fathom the man and the real logic behind the part he played in the events of 1916. The received wisdom is clear enough. In December 1916 Falkenhayn wrote a memorandum reviewing the progress of the war to date. France, he believed, was weakened almost to the limit of her endurance, and Russia had lost her offensive power. Britain remained the arch-enemy, but she was hard to reach. She could scarcely be invaded, and defeats in Egypt or Mesopotamia would not bring about her collapse. Attacking her armies in Flanders was impossible because of the state of the ground—a telling analysis. Launching unrestricted submarine warfare against her maritime lifelines might work, even at the risk of drawing America into the war, but it would take too long. He concluded that Germany's only chance of victory was to knock "England's best sword," the French army, from her hand. Then he went to the dark heart of the matter:

> Within our reach behind the French sector of the Western Front there are objectives for the retention of which the French General Staff would be compelled to throw in every man they have. If they do so the forces of France will bleed to death—as there can be no question of a voluntary withdrawal—whether we reach our goal or not. If they do not do so, and we reach our objectives, the moral effect on France will be enormous. For an operation limited to a narrow front, Germany will not be compelled to spend herself as completely.

He believed that there were two such objectives: Belfort, so bravely defended in 1870–71 that it had been retained by France at the peace, and Verdun. Preference, he argued, should be given to Verdun.

Although Alistair Horne's *The Price of Glory* was published as long ago as 1962, it remains one of the best works on the subject, and stands not least among its author's remarkable achievements. Its assessment that the Falkenhayn memorandum made military history because it was the first time any great commander had proposed to vanquish an enemy by bleeding him to death seems grimly fitting. We cannot, unfortunately, be absolutely sure that it is correct. There is no trace of the Falkenhayn memorandum in the archives: the only version we have is the general's own, contained in his autobiography. Falkenhayn is believed to have visited the Kaiser at Potsdam sometime between December 15 and 22, 1915, but the Kaiser's memoirs are silent on the point.

The possibilities continue to perplex historians. It may be that there was indeed a memorandum, all copies of which vanished so comprehensively that they were not available to the authors of the German Official History between the wars. It may be that there was never a memorandum as such, but that the views expressed in Falkenhayn's memoirs accurately summed up his mood at the time. Lastly, there is the possibility that Falkenhayn attacked at Verdun with the intention of taking the town, possibly hoping that by doing so he would unbalance the Allied armies on the Western Front and open the way for a successful offensive further west. By the time he wrote his memoirs it was all too evident that Verdun had not fallen, and the argument that he had never meant to take the town but simply planned to use it to sap the strength of the French army was a convenient justification after the event for a lost and bloody battle.

VERDUN Another factor complicates the question: the status of Verdun itself. Alistair Horne accurately describes it in 1916 as "a sleepy, duller-than-average French provincial town, unassumingly modest about its noble past and strangely insouciant about the future." Virodunum to the Romans, Verdun lies inside a ring of hills, the Meuse heights. It owed its military importance to its position, where the main road from Metz to Paris crossed the gentle River Meuse. To its east lies the boggy Woevre Plain, with the River Moselle and the great fortress city of Metz on its eastern edge. To its west stands the forest of the Argonne, with the open plains of Champagne beyond them. An invader advancing from the east needed to take Verdun before pushing through the defiles of the Argonne and debouching into Champagne, where he could maneuver more freely.

It is small wonder that Verdun's history was martial. It was sacked by Attila the Hun in 455, and in 843 Charlemagne's heirs signed the Treaty of Verdun, which divided his empire among them. One received "Lothar's kingdom," Lothari Regnum in Latin and hence Lothringen in German and Lorraine in French. Lorraine became, as Verdun's historian Alain Denizot puts it, "a stake in the game between France and the Germanic Holy Roman Empire." Between 925 and 1552 it was under German control. Its bishop, supported by the citizens, offered Verdun to France in 1552, and Henry II's occupation of the town was formally recognized in 1648 by the Treaty of Westphalia, which ended the Thirty Years War.

Fortifications surround the town like the rings of an onion. There are some medieval survivals, like the crenelated Porte Chaussée, grinning out across the Meuse, but most date from the seventeenth century. Jean Errard de Bar le Duc transformed the Abbey of St-Vanne into a citadel in 1624, and Sebastien de Vauban, the most distinguished military engineer of his age, built the ramparts, bastions, and ravelins that still mark the townscape. Verdun was taken by the Prussians in 1792—its governor committed suicide rather than surrender—but was soon recaptured. During the Napoleonic wars it housed British internees and prisoners of war: officers were allowed to live in relative comfort provided they did not attempt to escape. Correspondence in the charming Musée de la Princerie testifies to the fact that their presence was not wholly unwelcome. A citizen asked the Minister of Marine to allow a British midshipman to marry his daughter. She had become very fond of him and was expecting their second child, and so, suggested the bourgeois, it would be as well to regularize the relationship.

FORTIFYING THE FRONTIER
Verdun was taken by the Prussians on November 8, 1870, and was not returned to France until September 1873. With much of Lorraine lost, the new Franco-German border ran across the Woevre Plain, only a day's march from Verdun, and the town was incorporated into the frontier defenses laid out by General Séré de Rivières. A belt of fortifications ran from Verdun down the Meuse to Bourlemont. Another network of forts defended the confluence of Meuthe and Moselle around Toul. South of this lay the Charmes gap, into which it was hoped that an incautious enemy might venture for a mauling, and then more fortifications stood on the upper Moselle, from Epinal to Belfort and Montbéliard. North of Verdun, another ring of forts encircled Maubeuge.

From above, the forts looked like broad arrowheads, their points facing the enemy. Originally they mounted heavy guns on a flat fighting platform, the *terreplein*, with a stout rampart in front and masonry shelters between them. A deep, wide ditch, faced with stonework, surrounded each fort, with defenses in it to enable the garrison to deal with enemy infantry who got so far. Stout iron railings with sharp tips ringed the enemy side of the ditch, with a thick belt of barbed wire beyond them. Beneath the *terreplein* lurked barracks, kitchens, and hospitals.

By 1916 there were three layers of forts around Verdun. Forts Belleville, St-Michel, and Belrupt secured the high ground close to the town. An intermediate ring, including Souville, Tavannes, Moulainville, and Rozelier, protected the right bank of the Meuse, with Bois Bourrus, Marre and Vacherauville among the forts on the left bank. In front of this second line stood Douaumont, strongest of Verdun's forts, securing the long ridge that dominates a large part of the right bank, with the lesser Vaux to its east. Smaller *ouvrages* (defenseworks) and detached batteries helped fill gaps and strengthened likely approaches.

The forts were initially built of stonework about five feet thick, covered by up to sixteen feet of earth. The development of high explosive rendered them

FORT DOUAUMONT

Bourges Casemate

Entrance to Fort

A

Gorge bunker

Barracks (on two floors)

Magazine

B   ENEMY

Rue de Rempart

Ditch

Gorge bunker with flanking galleries

Railings

Barbed wire

Casemates

Rue de Rempart

Observation turret

75 mm turret

Glacis

Railings

Barbed wire

A   **Section through A-B**   B

Counterscarp galleries	75 mm turret
Ditch	155 mm turret
Observation turrets	Field of fire
Machine gun turrets	Tunnels

0 ___ 100 Meters
0 ___ 100 Yards

obsolete at a stroke. Guns on the surface were vulnerable, and the stone and earth layers were too thin to sustain direct hits. Unfortunately, the public mood had begun to swing away from military expenditure, and there were insufficient funds available to update all Séré de Rivières's work.

However, such was the importance of Verdun that most of its defenses were modernized. A shell of concrete up to eight feet thick encased the forts, with about thirteen feet of earth on top of it, and a layer of sand, to absorb the shock of explosions, between the concrete and the original stonework. Heavy guns were placed in armored turrets on top of the forts, with 75 mm pieces in concrete flanking defenses called Bourges casemates. Steel observation cupolas and machine-gun turrets speckled the forts. The number of guns they mounted dropped dramatically: the mighty Douaumont had only a single turreted 155 mm, two 75 mms in another turret, and another pair in a Bourges casemate.

Part of the reason for this apparent weakness was the belief that a single turreted piece, its gunners protected and ammunition supply assured, was worth a battery in open field. There was also a growing suspicion that despite all the expensive improvements, forts would remain vulnerable to high explosive, and might best be used as centers of resistance, providing observation posts and shelters for the defending infantry, rather than centers of resistance in their own right.

The events of August 1914 seemed to confirm this gloomy prognosis. The Liège forts, for all their armored cupolas and gallant defenders, were demolished by German heavy howitzers. In France, Fort Manonviller, built to command the Paris–Saverne railway line, was hit by seventeen thousand shells and surrendered: the fumes of the explosions made the place untenable. Joffre ordered that as many guns as possible should be withdrawn from forts and sent off to the field armies. Although the 75 mms in Bourges casemates could indeed be modified for field service, the stubby, turret-mounted 155 mm and 75 mm could not, and so they stayed on. He added that if the Germans attempted to surround Verdun, the town should not be held: the defenders should withdraw to the left bank and defend that. By 1916 the Verdun forts were held by skeleton garrisons, men whose advanced age and low rank testified to the sadly diminished status of these concrete monsters.

PREVIOUS PAGES Alphonse de Neuville's *Cemetery at St-Privat* shows Germans storming the village on August 18, 1870, after its gallant defense. This classic portrayal of French heroism helped nurture patriotism and the desire for revenge.

PROPHETS OF GLOOM

The town's military governor, General Herr, warned that his defenses were weak. His views were echoed, though much more forcefully, by one of the army's mavericks, Emile Driant. Born in 1855, Driant was an infantry officer who had married the daughter of General Georges Boulanger, minister of war in 1886–87. This might have proved a wise move in an army that quipped that there were three routes to promotion—seniority, selection, and son-in-law. Unfortunately for Driant, Boulanger, the classic political general, became the figurehead for a variety of anti-German political groups and was eventually exiled. Driant's career, already damaged by this association, was ruined when he protested at the keeping of dossiers on "clerical" officers.

He retired to write futuristic (and anti-British) works under the pen name of Captain Danrit, and was elected to the Chamber of Deputies. Recalled from the reserve in 1914, in 1915 he was a lieutenant colonel commanding two *chasseur* battalions on the Verdun front. *Chasseurs* had much in common with rifle regiments in the British army or *Jäger* in the German. They prided themselves on their marksmanship, and on tenacity which sprang in part from a greater degree of independence and initiative than was allowed to their comrades in line regiments.

Driant's men held the Bois des Caures, on the right bank of the Meuse and on the very chin of the French-held salient, formed by the defenses of Verdun, which jutted into German lines. Like his superior, General Herr, Driant had a low opinion of the state of defensive preparation at Verdun but, unlike Herr, he had powerful friends. On August 22, 1915, he wrote to Paul Deschanel, President of the Chamber of Deputies and an old personal friend, warning of "a sledge-hammer blow . . . on the line Verdun–Nancy. . . . If our first line is carried by a massive attack, our second line is inadequate and we are not succeeding in establishing it; lack of workers, and I add: lack of barbed wire." This warning was passed on to the minister of war, now General Galliéni, savior of Paris in 1914, who sent a delegation to Verdun. This reported that all was indeed not well on the Meuse front, and Galliéni duly forwarded a copy to Joffre, asking for his comments. They were barely printable.

"I cannot be a party," thundered Joffre, "to soldiers under my command bringing before the Government, by channels other than the hierarchic channel, complaints or protests concerning the execution of my orders." There were no grounds for Driant's concern. The Germans would not attack Verdun. And that was that.

The massive attack predicted by Driant was, as we have seen, exactly what the Germans had in mind. Yet, given the neglected state of the town's defenses and the French headquarters' orders that Verdun was on no account to be surrounded, how certain could Falkenhayn be that it would indeed be held to the last drop of French blood? The truth is that there was no certainty to it at all. Most of Verdun's significance to France stems from its role in 1916. Falkenhayn was painfully aware, when he wrote his memoirs, that he had indeed managed to touch something deep and primal in the French psyche. He cannot have been sure of this before the event, and this must strengthen the arguments of those who doubt the reliability of Falkenhayn's version of events. He may indeed have sought an attritional battle, and found the Verdun salient, where superior German artillery could be applied to a weak defense, an appropriate spot for it. Yet there is every chance that if the strength of French resistance astonished both France and her allies, it surprised Falkenhayn too.

THE ELEVENTH HOUR

The instrument of Falkenhayn's attack was the German Fifth Army, commanded by the Kaiser's son Wilhelm, Crown Prince of Prussia, which had come close to taking Verdun in 1914. The Crown Prince's Chief of Staff, General Schmidt von Knobelsdorf, enjoyed a close relationship with Falkenhayn and, in the months that followed, helped ensure that the Crown Prince did what Falkenhayn expected of him. In late December 1915 and early January 1916, however, Knobelsdorf found his loyalties strained as it became clear that Falkenhayn was not quite sure what he expected. Both the Crown Prince and his Chief of Staff wanted to attack on the left and right banks simultaneously. Falkenhayn maintained that there were insufficient troops for this, because a reserve must be kept to meet Allied attacks elsewhere. Indeed, these ripostes, he argued, might "bring movement into the war once again." Once they were repulsed, then more men could be used against Verdun. Crown Prince Rupprecht of Bavaria, an accomplished professional soldier commanding the German Sixth Army, suggested that Falkenhayn "was himself not clear as to what he really wanted, and was waiting for a stroke of luck that would lead to a favorable solution."

Little was left to luck in German preparations. New narrow-gauge railway lines were laid to enable the mountains of material needed for the attack to be brought to the front. Artillery ammunition had pride of place, for it was the essence of German plans that their gunners should make out a check

The Crown Prince of Prussia, commander of the German Fifth Army, talking to soldiers near Verdun. His men began the battle wearing the spiked helmet, but adopted the coal-scuttle helmet as it went on.

which the infantry would simply present for payment. Over twelve hundred guns were to be used on an attack frontage of twelve miles. They ranged from giant 420 mm howitzers, whose shells weighed over a ton apiece, long-barreled 380 mm naval guns, stocky Austrian 305 mms, and on down through the 210 mm, 150 mm, and 130 mm guns to numerous short-ranged trench mortars, heavy and light, to scores of 77 mms, workhorse of the field artillery. Targets were meticulously allocated: the heavy howitzers would take on the forts, naval guns would reach out into and beyond Verdun, and other guns, howitzers, and mortars would deal with French batteries, trench lines, and communications. They had two and a half million shells available for the first week of battle.

The experience of 1915 showed that attacking infantry were at their most vulnerable when the defender's artillery fire fell on crammed jumping-off trenches, whose crowded state in any case drew attention to what was to come. The Germans averted this problem by constructing numerous *Stollen*, large, deep dugouts in which the attacking infantry was to await zero hour.

The assault was initially scheduled for February 12, but the atrocious weather led to its postponement, much to the discomfort of waiting troops in the *Stollen*, many of them knee-deep in water.

Lastly, the Germans paid special attention to the air. All combatants had used aircraft for reconnaissance at the beginning of the war, and soon artillery spotting became a major task. It was a small step from harassing the enemy's observers to shooting at them, initially with a variety of weapons, private and official. In June 1915 the Fokker Eindekker single-seat fighter appeared at the front, pointing the way ahead: a mechanical interrupter gear enabled machine guns fitted to the fuselage to fire through the propeller's arc.

In early 1916 the Germans concentrated the bulk of their aircraft at Verdun. Fighter patrols denied French reconnaissance aircraft access to German territory, observation balloons and aircraft spotted for the artillery, and two-seaters attacked road and rail junctions with bombs, dropping forty-five hundred pounds in the first few days of the offensive. It was the first time in military history that air superiority had paved the way for an attack, but it was certainly not to be the last. Falkenhayn had christened the battle Operation Gericht—tribunal, judgment place, or even scaffold. As the short February days went by, the executioner prepared to drop the trap. Despite careful German precautions, the French were aware that an attack was coming. Prisoners admitted that something dreadful was in the wind. The occasional aircraft got through the German net and came back with news of dreadful preparation. And down in the chilly Bois des Caures, Emile Driant's *chasseurs* could hear the rumble of ammunition wagons.

THE ATTACK BEGINS

Early on the morning of February 21 a 380 mm naval gun opened the bombardment, its shell spinning high over chalk and woodland to burst in the bishop's palace at Verdun. It had been aimed at one of the Meuse bridges. Though a near miss at a range of nearly twenty miles was not bad shooting, the damage was seized upon by Allied propagandists as another example of Hunnish behavior. The main bombardment began three hours later, beating on the French positions like a metal flail wielded by some demented giant. In the Bois des Caures, Driant had wisely abandoned a defense based on continuous lines of trenches for a series of dugouts and bunkers, many of them made of concrete, consisting of small outposts, bigger *grandes gardes*, and even larger redoubts. Branches were lopped off, whole trees uprooted, and men were buried alive by direct hits on their bunkers. When the fire slack-

TOP Germans preparing a 305 mm howitzer in a forest near Verdun. Heavy guns like this required solid, level emplacements.
ABOVE An apparently unposed photograph shows French infantry attacking through barbed wire in the face of shell fire.

An evocative painting by Paul Thiriot shows French infantry counterattacking the village of Vaux.

ened toward midday and the survivors emerged to man the wreckage of their defenses, German artillery observers brought fresh fire to bear on centers of activity. Elsewhere, across the whole of the Verdun front, the story was the same. Forward positions were methodically plowed by shells, and a continuous barrage falling behind them boxed them off from support. Heavy guns and howitzers hit French batteries with a mixture of gas and high explosive: by midday the Germans estimated that only one gun per battery was still in action.

The infantry went forward at 4:00 P.M. The Germans were still wearing the prewar spiked helmet, its fabric cover bearing a stenciled regimental number: the "coal-scuttle" steel helmet would appear while the battle was in progress. Spikes had been unscrewed to prevent snagging trees or undergrowth, and the attackers wore white armbands so as to identify one another in the dangerous gloaming. Two of the three attacking corps heeded 5th Army's instructions that only strong fighting patrols were to advance that day, identifying breaches in the defenses through which the main assault would pour on the 22nd. General von Zwehl's VII Reserve Corps, attacking the Bois d'Haumont, northwest of the Bois des Caures, was less cautious, and its assault troops bounded forward, confident that there would be few Frenchmen in any condition to resist them.

The Bois d'Haumont fell quickly, but elsewhere German gains did not live up to their expectations. Although perhaps less than half of Driant's men had escaped death or injury, the survivors defended the remnants of the Bois des Caures with a grim tenacity, and XVIII Corps, attacking that sector, made little progress. The surprising thing about the bombardment was not the enormous physical damage it caused, but the extraordinary ability of men to live though it and somehow fight back.

On the 22nd the French, true to a doctrine that still insisted that ground lost should be retaken as soon as possible, put in local counterattacks that were usually shot to pieces but sometimes, against all the odds, bought an hour or two. However, assisted as always by their crushing artillery, and a fresh horror, the flamethrower, against strongpoints, the Germans took the village of Haumont, and, late in the afternoon, at last drove Driant's men out of the Bois des Caures. Driant himself was killed as he withdrew. Even in a battle as large and impersonal as Verdun the inspirational quality of valiant men made a difference, and Emile Driant, as physically brave in action as he was morally courageous out of it, had thrown the first substantial piece of grit into the German machine.

On the 23rd the defense was badly shaken by a sequence of order and disorder which led to the abandonment of Brabant, on the Meuse. The villages of Haumont and Herbebois, held with remarkable determination, were eventually taken, and Samogneux, too, fell after a ghastly misunderstanding in which newly arrived French 155 mm guns broke the back of a gallant French defense. On the 24th the Germans pushed right through the intermediate line sited by General de Castelnau, Joffre's deputy, when he visited Verdun the previous month. The battle had already crippled the 51st and 72nd Divisions of General Chrétien's XXX Corps, and when he flung in the North Africans of the 37th Division in an effort to patch the broken line it rapidly disintegrated. The leading elements of General Balfourier's fresh XX Corps were on their way, but combatants on both sides sensed that Verdun would fall before they reached it. The Crown Prince was to write that "the way was open to us," and lamented that, by not pressing on at all costs, the Germans missed the psychological moment. And a French general admitted: "Even were I Napoleon, I could not save the army from this disaster."

VERDUN 1916

Gremilly

Bois d'Haumont

Haumont

Bois des
Caures

Herbebois

Les Jumelles
d'Ornes

Beaumont

Maucourt

Louvemont

Bezonvaux

BEZONVAUX

Haudromont
Quarries

LORIENT

Bois d'Hardaumont

Vacherauville

Douaumont

HARDAUMONT

DOUAUMONT

Bras

Vaux

Charny

Thiaumont

Fleury

VAUX

Abaucourt

CHARNY

FROIDETERRE

Damloup

DAMLOUP BATTERY

R. Meuse

SOUVILLE

LAUFÉE

BELLEVILLE

Tunnel

TAVANNES

Eix

Woevre Plain

ST MICHEL

FIX

Station

MOULAINVILLE

Verdun

MANESEL

BELRUPT

REGRET

ROZELIER

HAUDAINVILLE

0	4 Miles
0	4 Kilometers

Main forts			French Line, 21 February 1916	——
Smaller forts (ouvrages)	◙	Roads	Furthest German advance, June 1916	– – –
		Railway	Front Line, 26 February 1916	- - -
			Front Line, 15 December 1916	••••

PÉTAIN TAKES COMMAND

A mixture of sound French decisions and serious German mistakes was to achieve more than Napoleon.

On the evening of the 23rd, General Langle de Cary, commanding Army Group Center and as such Herr's immediate superior, telephoned Joffre in his headquarters at Chantilly, seeking permission to give up the ground he held east of Verdun. Joffre was noncommittal, but before long Castelnau arrived, on the first of two visits, to warn him just how serious the situation was. We cannot be certain what happened in Joffre's quarters in the Villa Poiret that night—one version has the great man roused from bed in his nightshirt—but we do know that two key decisions were made. The first was that the 2nd Army, currently in reserve, would be sent to Verdun to hold the left bank. The second was that Castelnau would go to Verdun to see things for himself.

It was one of those moments in the war when much would depend on the line taken by a visiting staff officer. In 1914, Moltke's emissary Lieutenant Colonel Hentsch had allowed the pessimism of those at the front to infect

him. On February 25, 1916, however, Castelnau showed himself a man of sterner stuff. Sustained alike by heartfelt patriotism, deep religious belief, and the knowledge that three of his sons had already died for France, Castelnau left Chantilly not long after midnight. He was at Langle de Cary's headquarters at Avize before dawn, instilling calm there and telephoning ahead to warn poor Herr that if he gave up any more ground "the consequences would be very grave for him." Soon afterward he was with Herr in person, and at 3:30 that afternoon he telephoned GQG. Verdun could be held. Pétain should defend the right bank as well as the left, advised by the unlucky Herr until the latter could be gently sacked.

General Philippe Pétain's night was rather different. In 1914 he was an infantry colonel with unfashionable views on firepower and, at fifty-eight, close to retirement. The war transformed his fortunes. He commanded a brigade during the retreat, and was promoted *général de brigade* and given a division in late

Generals Pétain (left) and Joffre.

August. An elderly spinster kindly pried some stars for his cuffs from a dead relative's uniform. He added another star soon enough, and the autumn saw him *général de division* and a corps commander. In May 1915 his corps attacked Souchez, below Vimy Ridge, capturing three thousand prisoners and advancing two miles. It was lightning war by that year's dismal standards, and that summer, he was sent off to command 2nd Army.

Pétain was unmarried at the time, but was as adept in the courts of Venus as on the field of Mars. On the night of February 24–25 his trusted aide-de-camp Alain de Serrigny eventually tracked him down to the Hotel Terminus at the Gare du Nord. Outside the general's room, awaiting the attentions of the boot boy, were a pair of large field boots and a tiny pair of lady's shoes. Serrigny knocked, and Pétain eventually appeared, listened impassively to the news, and announced that they would set off for Chantilly in the morning. Meanwhile, the night imposed its own duties.

After pausing briefly at Chantilly, Pétain and Serrigny set off for Verdun. It was a difficult journey in appalling weather, and once they had left Bar-le-Duc to drive up the single road connecting Verdun with the outside world they could average only two miles an hour. The flotsam of defeat swept past in the other direction: civilian refugees with a few pathetic belongings on their carts, ambulances full of wounded, and the debris of broken regiments: one lieutenant, staggering back with a handful of survivors, saw tears glistening in the big general's eyes. Herr's headquarters at Dugny was so chaotic that Pétain could not stand it, and retraced his steps to the village of Souilly on the Bar-le-Duc road. There he met Castelnau, who gave him a written order to hold both banks of the Meuse, and to take command at midnight. Pétain had one piece of news for him, obtained at Herr's headquarters: Fort Douaumont had fallen.

THE FALL OF FORT DOUAUMONT

There could be no better evidence of the uneasy relationship between the Verdun forts and the commanders of the formations holding the ground on which they stood than General Chrétien's repulse from Douaumont. He had attempted to visit it in early February, only to be told by the fort's custodian, an elderly warrant officer called Chenot, that he opened the gates only to the governor of Verdun. This anomaly persisted, with the forts answering direct to General Herr rather than to the generals whose troops surrounded them.

It was not until early on the 25th that divisional commanders were told to maintain garrisons in the forts in their sectors. Chrétien, about to hand over the sector to Balfourier, assured him that the order had been passed on, and Balfourier, exhausted after his long approach march, took him at his word. In fact, nothing had been done and, at a crucial stage in the battle, with the German attack gaining momentum and French defensive responsibilities being reorganized, Douaumont had a tiny garrison.

Chenot commanded six regular and fifty-seven Territorial gunners; Private Meyer, responsible for the maintenance of the fort's oil lamps; and an engineer sergeant sent there to prepare demolitions in case the fort had to be abandoned. On the afternoon of the 25th the fort, despite having sustained some damage from shelling by 420 mms in February 1915 and during the bombardments accompanying the attack, was in good order, and its 155 mm turret was firing away steadily at a distant target, given to it some time before. Most of the garrison was in the bowels of the fort, listening to a lecture.

While Chenot's men went about their duties, the crack 24th Brandenburg Regiment advanced toward Douaumont Ridge, with its 2nd Battalion on its right, 3rd on the left, and 1st in reserve. The preparatory barrage had failed to materialize, but the regiment advanced anyhow, scattering some French and making excellent progress. The twenty-four-year-old Sergeant Kunze, with his section of pioneers, was on the left of the 2nd Battalion, and had been told to deal with obstacles in the path of the advance. After a brisk action against defenders in trenches, Kunze found himself under the lee of the fort. His men cut through the already damaged barbed wire around it, and got as far as the iron railings edging the ditch. Kunze was blown into the ditch by a shell that landed nearby, and his men followed him down. Ordering them to make a human pyramid, he scrambled up on their backs, pushed back the ditch-defense cannon protruding from an embrasure, and entered.

All but two of his men declined to follow Kunze into the fort but, wandering about the gloomy and unfamiliar corridors, he eventually found his way to the 155 mm turret and detained the gunners. Then, after managing to lock up the lecturer and his audience, he found a well-stocked mess-room and wolfed down a good meal. The gun came back to life when a relief crew arrived, much to Kunze's chagrin. However, by now two officers from the Brandenburgers, Captain Haupt and Lieutenant Radtke, had also managed to enter the fort. At the head of different parties, both had climbed from the moat onto the fort's superstructure. They eventually made contact with one another and with Kunze: Haupt took command, and by about 4:30 P.M., Douaumont was firmly in German hands.

Another Brandenburg officer, Lieutenant von Brandis, entered the fort after Haupt and Radtke, but, detailed to take the news back to regimental headquarters, appears to have been overgenerous with the truth and received one of the two Pour le Mérite, Germany's highest decoration, awarded for the action. He later wrote a best-selling book, *The Stormers of Douaumont,* in which his own role lost nothing in the telling. The other decoration went to Haupt. Kunze received nothing, and it was not until the 1930s, when he was serving as a police constable, that he read accounts of the capture and realized the part he had played. He wrote to his old commanding officer, who investigated the case. Kunze's claims were indeed justified and, although it was a little too late for the Pour le Mérite, he was given accelerated promotion to inspector.

Despite their propagandists' attempts to minimize its public and international impact, the loss of Douaumont was an appalling blow to the French. It was followed by something approaching panic in Verdun, and the shaken commander of 37th Division pulled right back off the Douaumont Ridge. Had the Germans not been overcautious there is little doubt that Verdun would have fallen.

THE FRENCH HOLD FAST

But if the German command faltered, the French did not. Pétain telephoned his senior officers to tell them that he was in command, but awoke on the 26th shaking with pneumonia. Using his trusted staff officers as intermediaries, Pétain managed to gather the reins of battle into his hands. The whole of XX Corps was now at the front and two more corps were on their way. Commanders were told to conserve their strength and hold their ground: no more wild counterattacks. And above all Pétain made it clear that this was a gunners' war. He began his telephone conversations by asking his commanders: "What have your batteries been doing?" The Germans felt the effect almost immediately. Fresh batteries were tucked in behind the ridges on the left bank and raked the gullies around Douaumont with their fire.

Men, guns, and ammunition could reach Verdun only via a little road from Bar-le-Duc and the narrow-gauge railway running alongside it. The task seemed impossible, for soon there were half a million men and 170,000 animals to be fed. However, Major Richard, responsible for transport, divided the road into six sectors, each with its repair crews and teams of engineers. Vehicles were commandeered all across France: the price of vegetables in Paris doubled in consequence. As the weather worsened, all available Territorials were set to road-mending, men working almost shoulder to shoulder. During the week beginning February 28, more than 25,000 tons of supplies and 190,000 men reached Verdun, and when the road was running at full capacity in June one vehicle passed a given point every fourteen seconds. In defiance of pre-war staff tables, the road maintained an army fighting at the highest intensity, and without it all that courage, determination, and suffering would have been in vain. This unremarkable provincial road richly deserved the title still proudly marked on the kilometer stones that measure its length: La Voie Sacrée, the Sacred Way.

THE LEFT BANK

Close as the Germans had come to taking Verdun, there could now be no escaping the fact that they had been checked. In early March they tried a major change of plan, sending the fresh VI Reserve Corps into action on the left bank—something that Falkenhayn's critics argued should have been done from the very start. The ground there was dominated by a long, irregular ridge, with Hill 304 at its western end, and the Mort Homme (dead man), its sinister name reflecting, perhaps, some grim tale from the Middle Ages, at its eastern end. Important though these crests were—for guns behind them could enfilade German lines on the left bank—they were but one rung of a ladder. Behind them, firmly held by its intact forts, lay Bois Bourrus Ridge. As it was, the German attack was too weak and too poorly prepared to succeed, and an attempt at a coordinated attack on the right bank fared no better. However, as March squelched into April the Germans maintained their pressure on the left bank, taking Malancourt, Haucourt, and Béthincourt.

On April 9 the Germans mounted a major offensive on both banks simultaneously, with General von Mudra commanding on the right bank and General von Gallwitz on the left. This time there was ample artillery support—the Germans fired seventeen trainloads of artillery ammunition—but the French, too, were well prepared and the battle seesawed to and fro below the crests of the Mort Homme and Hill 304. On May 3 the Germans concentrated five hundred guns against the ridge, and attacked after two days of concentrated fire which sent up a pillar of smoke twenty-five hundred feet high. They took Hill 304, and then, after another bombardment which, in the Crown Prince's words, left the Mort Homme flaming like a volcano, they took that too. By the end of May the whole ridge was in their hands. Yet Bois Bourrus was still intact, and the burden of losses, which had favored the Germans early in the battle, now seemed almost even.

THE PITY OF WAR

Many of the war's great battles had their own terrible distinctions. The fruitless heroism of the Battle of the Frontiers; the wasted hopes of the first day on the Somme; the mud of Passchendaele. But there was something peculiarly dreadful about Verdun. The front was so narrow (it is less than fifteen miles as the shell flies, from Hill 304 in the west to Damloup in the east) and the concentration of men and shells so great that many combatants remembered a battle that epitomized the impotence of the individual in the face of shellfire.

Men might be killed instantly, but without apparent damage, by concussion; blown to tatters by direct hits; cut up as if by some malicious butcher; crippled by flying fragments of their comrades' bodies, or shocked into babbling incoherence by a capricious hit which left them unscathed among the remnants of their friends. A French Jesuit, Sergeant Paul Dubrulle, summed up the great anguish of the combatants on both sides:

> To die from a bullet seems nothing; parts of our being remain intact; but to be dismembered, torn to pieces, reduced to pulp, this is a fear that the flesh cannot support and which is fundamentally the great suffering of the bombardment.

Evidence of death was all too abundant. Bodies hacked apart as men dug with pick and shovel; splintered trees turned to gibbets, heavy with dismembered limbs; glistening ropes of entrails. One French officer wrote feelingly of a "small compass where one cannot possibly distinguish if the mud were flesh or the flesh were mud."

A soldier recalled walking happily out into the sunshine, only to be confronted by a new shell hole.

> At the bottom, in the freshly turned earth, five bodies were spread, but in such a regular manner that you could see that the shell had burst in the middle of this little knot of men to send one in each direction, so that these poor bodies formed the five branches of some macabre review. The violence of the explosion had pushed them deep into the earth: three were almost completely driven into the lips of the crater, stuffed in like rags. The arm of one of these crushed bodies stuck straight up out of the clay: the hand was intact, and an aluminum ring encircled a finger.

After a storm of shellfire, another man found "nothing but a head in a red

puddle, a few bits of limb in a shell hole, and nameless scraps plastered to the parapet. That was all that remained here of our poor comrade."

Simply living in this blighted landscape wore men out. That common enemy, mud, was everywhere, as a soldier described in a trench newspaper.

It has rained since morning, one of those winter rains which nothing keeps out: cold, fine, eternal. The front-line trench is an earth-colored brook.... Water, mud. You stick in it, you slip down, dragged by some irresistible force. The molecules of the stuff open up at first, but then you feel them come back, sticking together with a tenacity that nothing prevails against.... Here the mud is obsessive. It is everywhere, under your feet, under your hands, under your body as you stretch out... it sticks to your clothes, penetrates right to your skin, and soils everything.

THE AIR BATTLE

High above the front the rival pilots fought it out, envied by many who raised their eyes from the squalor of the battlefield. Aircrew enjoyed flying pay, dry quarters, the prospect of rapid decoration, and a public adulation which not all found to their taste. And to earn it they climbed, muffled in fur and leather, into wood and fabric aircraft whose handling characteristics made them sometimes scarcely less lethal than enemy guns. When hit, they might be faced with the agonizing decision of staying in the doomed aircraft as burning petrol torched back into the cockpit, or jumping without a parachute to a different kind of death.

Some pilots hated the act of killing, but others, perhaps with comrades to avenge, felt a wild joy at the moment of victory. Albert Deullin put twenty-five rounds into a Fokker at a range of less than thirty feet, and recalled: "The fellow was so riddled that vaporized blood sprayed on my cowling, windscreen, cap, and goggles. Naturally, the descent from twenty-six hundred meters [eighty-five hundred feet] was delicious to contemplate."

The Germans had begun the air battle with numbers and technology on their side, but the French quickly concentrated their own air power at Verdun. That spring the Nieuport fighter arrived but, even before that, the pilots of the elite *Group des Cigognes* (Storks) had already made their appearance, with the legendary Jean Navarre shooting down two German aircraft over Fort Douaumont the day after its fall. Georges Guynemer, France's ace of

OPPOSITE A French soldier is buried on Hill 304.

aces, who was to amass fifty-four victories before disappearing above the Ypres salient in 1917, shot down twenty-one aircraft in 1916, including a triple kill in March. American volunteer pilots, forerunners of what was to become the Lafayette Squadron, were also on the scene, and Kiffin Rockwell opened their tally with a kill on his first combat sortie.

Like the fighting on the ground, the war in the air ebbed and flowed. The German ace Oswald Boelcke developed the *Jagdstaffel* (hunting squadron) whose coordinated tactics might have spelled disaster for the more gladiatorial French had Boelcke not been grounded in June on the news of the death of Max Immelmann: the Kaiser felt that Germany could not risk losing two aces so swiftly. Thereafter the skies above Verdun remained French, and as their lines were pounded by guns directed by spotter aircraft, it was German soldiers who paid the price.

COMMAND DECISIONS German commanders, less than unanimous about the battle even in February, bickered on. Mudra, thoroughly pessimistic about German prospects, was sacked in late April, but not before the Crown Prince had caught his mood and decided that the attack ought to be discontinued. "Although we had more than once changed our methods of attack, a decisive success at Verdun could only be assured at the price of heavy sacrifices, out of all proportion to the desired gains." Unfortunately the Crown Prince was not a free agent, and lack of experience left him at a marked disadvantage in the debate. The "oak hard" Knobelsdorf, his chief of staff, remained committed to the offensive, and replaced Mudra with the aggressive General von Lochow. Even Falkenhayn wavered, but after a series of meetings in May it was decided, against all the Crown Prince's instincts, to press on.

The French were scarcely more unanimous. For all Pétain's chilly exterior, the sacrifices made by his men moved him deeply, and the experience of standing on the steps of the town hall at Souilly on the Voie Sacrée, watching fresh troops going up the line and decimated survivors lurching back, never left him. At his insistence the French rotated divisions through Verdun, relieving them before they were exhausted: the Germans, in contrast, kept the same divisions and replaced casualties as necessary. Each system had its strengths and weaknesses. French troops were often fresher, but the dreadful experience of Verdun was spread across the whole army, and it became harder and harder for Joffre to harbor reserves for the great Allied offensive due that summer. The flood of fresh troops depressed German soldiers, but encouraged Knobelsdorf to believe that he was steadily wearing down the French army. His own system was depressing for front-line soldiers, who saw the effect of the battle on their own units and calculated that there were only two ways out of Verdun: the stretcher or the grave. Small wonder that they called it "The Mill on the Meuse": a mill that ground men, not corn.

Pétain's dogged caution, which Joffre had found so valuable in February and March, became increasingly unpopular at GQG. Yet Joffre could not sack the man of the hour without imperiling his own position. The solution was to kick him upstairs. On April 19 Pétain was told that he would replace Langle de Cary in command of Army Group Center. His place would be taken by General Robert Nivelle, a fifty-eight-year-old artillery officer whose rise had been scarcely less meteoric than Pétain's own. Cultured and eloquent—he was as fluent in the tongue of his English mother as he was in French—Nivelle charmed generals and politicians alike. He was powerfully influenced by two men: Colonel d'Alenson, head of his personal staff who was dying of tuberculosis and committed to winning the war before he perished, and by Charles Mangin, who commanded one of his divisions.

On May 22, Mangin attacked Fort Douaumont after a savage bombardment, which included some 370 mm howitzers. Despite an accurate barrage on their jumping-off trenches, the French infantry surged on across the fort's superstructure, and for a time it looked as if they had secured it. But their grip was never firm: the Germans leeched troops into the fort from the north, and they surged up from beneath the attackers. The French were dislodged on the 24th, and the failure bruised that morale which Pétain had done do much to foster.

THE FALL OF FORT VAUX

On June 1 the Germans began their biggest assault on the right bank since the beginning of the battle. Five divisions attacked with the aim of capturing Fort Vaux and then pushing on to the ridge crowned by Fort Souville, the French command post, from which Verdun itself was visible. Little Vaux had already been attacked without success, but in the process its single 75 mm turret, prepared for demolition, had been destroyed when a German shell exploded the charge. Its commander, the forty-nine-year-old Major Sylvain-Eugène Raynal, who arrived at the fort on May 24, had already been so badly wounded that he walked with the aid of a stick. Raynal estimated that shells hit the fort at the rate of fifteen hundred to two thousand an hour on June 1, and on the 2nd German infantry attacked. They lost men to the ditch-defense machine guns, but when one jammed the Germans were able to break into the northeast gallery. Captain Tabourot, Raynal's second-in-command, delayed them until he was mortally wounded. The other ditch-defense position fell later, leaving the Germans in possession of the fort's superstructure.

Raynal, however, had used the time to good effect, and sandbag barricades had been prepared along the tunnels connecting the galleries to the main body of the fort. Over the days that followed the French defended the galleries yard by yard. The Germans would blow up a barricade, killing its defenders, only to find another, as bravely held, behind it. Raynal recalled that "through the loopholes they poured flame and gas, which gave off an intolerable smell and gripped our throats." His men fought on in gas masks.

Contact with Fort Souville was maintained by signal lamp, runner, and pigeon. Raynal's last bird, carrying a message demanding relief, died delivering its message and was decorated for the feat. In the end it was lack of water that finished Vaux. The gauge on the fort's water tank was faulty, and men were reduced to drinking their own urine or licking moisture from the walls. Counterattacks petered out short of the fort, and on June 7 Raynal flashed his last message to Souville, and told his survivors that it was all over: they must surrender. "They understood," he wrote, "and together in one shout we repeated the last message which my instrument had just sent off: *'Vive la France!'*" He was taken before the Crown Prince, who noticed that he had lost his sword, and presented him with the weapon taken from another French officer. A chivalrous gesture on a barbarous field.

THE BATTLE'S CLIMAX

Elsewhere the Germans made steady progress despite dismal weather, and that second week in June saw Verdun in greater peril than at any time since February. Nevertheless it was saved, not simply by the courage of French soldiers, but by the fact that the members of both contending coalitions had obligations, and both of France's major allies, under tremendous pressure to distract the Germans from Verdun, honored theirs.

On June 4 the Russian General Brusilov attacked the Austrians in distant Galicia. Nearly half a million Austrians were captured, and for a moment it seemed as if the Eastern Front would collapse altogether: Falkenhayn sent three divisions eastward. And there were clear signs that the British were preparing to attack on the Somme. Falkenhayn hesitated, and in the time that it took him to order the Crown Prince to try again, Nivelle reestablished his line.

The last major German attack was launched on June 23 after a bombardment in which a new gas, specially designed to penetrate French respirators, played a lethal part. It came within inches of success, taking Fleury and lapping right up against Fort Souville. But on 1 July the British began their long-awaited offensive, and almost everyone—save the oak-hard Knobelsdorf—realized that Verdun could not remain the focus of German attention. It speaks volumes for his persuasive powers that he managed to persuade Falkenhayn to authorize one last attack. It failed, but not before a handful of Germans, briefly on top of Fort Souville, glimpsed the sunlight glinting off the Meuse in Verdun.

Knobelsdorf was one of the casualties of German failure, and was shunted off on August 23 to command a corps on the Eastern Front. Falkenhayn was not far behind him. He had predicted that Romania could not enter the war on the Allied side until the harvest was safely in, and when she joined the war on August 27, Falkenhayn's position was untenable. He resigned, and was replaced by the formidable combination of Field Marshal Paul von Hindenburg and General Erich von Ludendorff, who had made their reputation on the Eastern Front.

THE RECAPTURE OF FORT DOUAUMONT

There were dramas still to be played out at Verdun. On October 24, Nivelle and Mangin retook Fort Douaumont in a meticulously planned operation that left nothing to chance. The sector was boxed off by an impenetrable barrage while batteries methodically raked over the ground around the fort. So unnerving was the impact of French heavy guns that the fort's garrison withdrew to the comparative safety of shell holes outside, and when the French entered the fort they found it almost unoccupied.

The recapture of Douaumont set the seal on Nivelle's reputation, and when old Joffre was promoted marshal of France and appointed to a meaningless advisory post in December it was Nivelle who vaulted over the heads of the army group commanders to replace him. "We have the formula," announced Nivelle, "our experience is conclusive. Our method has proved itself. Victory is certain. I give you my assurance." What had been done at Douaumont could, he asserted, be done on a much larger scale. He was peddling victory, and it was a seller's market.

THE PRICE OF GLORY

Even now we cannot be sure what Verdun meant in human terms. Some French and German authorities suggest that Alistair Horne's estimate of casualties is too high, but it cannot be lightly dismissed. He suggests that the French lost

377,231 killed, wounded, and missing, and the Germans roughly 337,000. At least 700,000, and for 1916 alone: rather more than half the total casualties suffered by Britain and her Empire in the Second World War. Nine villages, which had stood on those uplands for a thousand years, were destroyed and never rebuilt. Woods and field were so polluted by metal, high explosive, and bodies that they were beyond cultivation. Declared *zones rouges*, red zones, they were cloaked in conifers and left to the recuperative powers of nature.

Some of the soldiers who died there were buried in military cemeteries, but the bodies of thousands could not be identified, or had lost all physical integrity. A temporary wooden ossuary was established to house their bones and, thanks to the efforts of Canon Noel and Monseigneur Ginisty, Bishop of Verdun, a permanent structure was begun on Douaumont crest in 1920 and inaugurated twelve years later. It contains the bones of around 130,000 unknown soldiers, French and German.

The psychological impact of the battle cut deeper than its physical wounds. "If the French succeeded in holding Verdun," wrote Philip Guedalla, "they had lost something far more irreplaceable upon the naked slopes above a town of no particular significance." French soldiers had fought a defensive battle summed up by Pétain's ringing order of the day: *"Ils ne passeront pas"*—They shall not pass. They had made extraordinary sacrifices. But there was less spring in their step, less glint in their eyes: theirs was an army running out of patience with its leaders.

The real price of glory: human remains at Verdun.

COMMANDING THE FRONT

RED TABS AND DUG-OUTS

Somehow it is hard to like First World War generals. In so many of their photographs they seem comfortable, secure, and well-breakfasted. Their uniform doesn't help. Breeched, booted, and spurred, they ride or stride their way about a world of châteaus and staff conferences. There is an age-old tension between the man on horseback and the man on foot: when mounted it is hard not to look, very literally, down on those below. On the Western Front polished leather and tailored whipcord conveyed a message that muddy folk in khaki serge did not always welcome, and at the end of the twentieth century it is hard to see behind the sepia image, foot flexed on château doorstep, chest quilted in medal ribbons. It is small wonder that one veteran was to write that all officers above the rank of lieutenant colonel should have been strangled at birth. Small wonder, too, that the general has been embodied in popular entertainment from *Oh! What a Lovely War* to *Blackadder* as the deadly buffoon, the cheery old card with the heart of flint.

The historical debate on British generals has, as I explained in the Introduction, now reached a remarkable maturity. While there are still historians who resolutely defend the thesis that British soldiers were indeed lions led by donkeys, the majority take a more balanced view, admitting that generals were called on to solve military problems of staggering complexity. Yet the scholarly debate has scarcely touched popular consciousness: to the ordinary man on the street, the generals of the First World War remain damned beyond hope of reprieve. This chapter is concerned with the British high command in 1916, the year of the Somme, but begins by looking at generals and

their staffs more widely, for it is only by understanding who they were and how they worked that we can begin to make sense of what they did.

The British army distinguished between units, lieutenant colonels' commands like infantry battalions or cavalry regiments, and formations, which were collections of units and which varied in size from the tiny brigade to the mighty army. A unit had its CO, Commanding Officer; a formation, its GOC, General Officer Commanding. During the First World War there were four grades of general officer. Armies were commanded by a general. He would have an indeterminate number of corps at his disposal, the precise number depending on the importance of his army's task. In July 1916 Rawlinson's 4th Army had five corps; 3rd Army, its northern neighbor, only three. A corps, with a lieutenant general at its head, normally comprised three infantry divisions, and had its own integral artillery and engineer support.

Divisions, commanded by major generals, contained three brigades, again with artillery and engineers. Their detailed establishment changed as the war went on, and numbers fluctuated as casualties were incurred and replacements arrived. In 1914 a division fielded a little over eighteen thousand officers and men, but by 1918 might, even without exceptionally bad luck, find itself half this size. While divisions were often shifted between corps, they tended to retain the same units within them, and to have a character that might survive repeated misfortune or the vagaries of a personnel system which, by design and accident, increasingly mingled regulars, Territorials, New Army men, and, from early 1916, conscripts. The brigade, with a brigadier general at its head, was the smallest of the formations, and the only one not to contain a mix of all arms. Until the winter of 1917 the infantry brigade contained four battalions, but thereafter manpower shortages reduced this to three.

Simply glancing at our GOC, as he genially asked us whether mail arrived promptly, or more curtly suggested that a haircut would not come amiss, might actually tell us little about him. He would be unlucky not to have medal ribbons from the South African War or a colonial campaign or two. Were he a general, lieutenant general, or rising star among the major generals, he would have a knighthood, or at least the companionate of an order of chivalry like the Bath or St-Michael and St-George.

His badges of rank would tell us only what he was at the moment. There were three sorts of rank in the army. Substantive (permanent) rank, of which

OPPOSITE Army commanders on the Somme: Generals Gough (right) and Rawlinson.

an officer could be deprived only by due process; temporary or local rank, given him for the duration of a particular appointment; and brevet rank, given as a reward for good service but not entitling its holder to employment in that particular grade. To take an extreme example: in 1908 W. H. Manning was inspector general of the King's African Rifles. He was a substantive captain, a brevet lieutenant colonel, and local brigadier general: at the time the latter grade was not a substantive rank in any event. The commanding officers of the units under his command were all substantive captains but local lieutenant colonels.

On the Western Front generals might well find themselves "acting up," in the case of brigadier generals by several ranks. Many brigadier generals were camouflaged majors, and even a few substantive captains commanded brigades. Substantive promotion took time to catch up with temporary rank, and its arrival—betokening pay, status, and pension that would not evaporate at the end of the war—was often very welcome. On December 29, 1916, Rawlinson heard that he had at last been promoted to the substantive rank of general, and wrote: "From Capt. to Full Genl in 17 years is not bad going after being in 3 Form at Eton too so there is hope for everyone." Hubert Gough was less fortunate: when he was sacked as commander of 5th Army in 1918 he was only a temporary general, and had to revert to his substantive rank of lieutenant general.

We have already seen how the British army expanded dramatically during the war. In the process it developed an enormous appetite for generals and staff officers. On the Western Front alone in 1914 it had one army headquarters, two corps, and seven divisions. By mid-1916 there were five armies, eighteen corps, and about fifty divisions. In addition, special staffs, such as artillery and engineer staffs, had proliferated. The *Army List*, which catalogs all the army's officers, is not always an accurate guide to temporary rank, and shows us only part of the iceberg, suggests that between 1914 and 1918 the number of major generals and above had doubled.

This fountain of promotion played most freely on prewar regulars. Australians, Canadians, and New Zealanders were different in this respect because their prewar regular establishment was so tiny and tradition of citizen-soldiering so strong as to make it easier for nonregulars to become generals. Indeed, one of the war's outstanding successes was Lieutenant General Sir John Monash, ANZAC corps commander in 1918, who was a civil engineer by profession. In the British army, however, the moderately competent regular could expect advancement. In 1918 nine substantive Royal Artillery lieutenant colonels were temporary major generals, another seventy-seven were brigadier generals, and among the fortunate majors was temporary Brigadier General Ironside, a future field marshal. Three of the five lieutenant colonels in the Grenadier Guards were brigadier generals.

Some generals were promoted on the basis of previous success. Among the divisional commanders in 1916 were Maxse, Davies, and Ingorville-Williams—the first an outstanding trainer of troops, the third killed on the Somme—given divisions after commanding brigades in 1914. Others were retired regulars "dug out" of retirement. The fact that Biddulph was sixty-one did not prevent his commanding a division very competently, and Bryan Mahon, brought back at the age of fifty-two, later went on to be GOC in Ireland. Broadwood, a retired lieutenant general, was brought back, unusually, in a temporary rank junior to his retired rank, and died of wounds as a major general commanding the 57th Division in June 1917. Most of the new brigadier generals needed in 1914–15 were dug-outs—retired lieutenant colonels were well placed—and the rest had made their reputations as COs in 1914.

A few nonregulars entered the charmed circle: in 1917 the Earl of Derby, then secretary of state for war, told the House of Lords that four Territorials had commanded divisions and fifty-two brigades. However, this included officers who had held these appointments on a temporary basis. The Territorial general was a rare beast, and the 1918 *Army List* shows only six Territorial brigadier generals. The regular army's control of key staff appointments was just as marked: only three Territorials held the post of GSO (General Staff Officer) Grade 1, a key figure at large formation headquarters.

None of this is particularly surprising, nor would it necessarily have been easy to have organized matters very differently. But it did mean that the field from which generals and their staffs were selected was very narrow. As there had been no prewar emphasis on training officers to step up in rank when war came, many generals, like the men they commanded, were learning on the job.

Promoted regulars and dug-outs alike brought with them much that was admirable. But they also often brought characteristics that chimed discordantly with the largest citizen army Britain had ever seen. We must beware of what can only be generalizations, but the British high command reflected the loyalties of the prewar army, where the bonds of experience shared (or personal antipathies aroused) in the same intake at Staff College or on the same campaign endured for years. Peacetime rings of influence rippled on into the war, and the private papers of almost any senior officer testify to cronyism that might make many real politicians blush. There were also many generals who were more brave than imaginative; found it hard to tolerate opposition, even when it was loyal and constructive; and equated the quality of advice with the rank of the adviser.

They were often prepared to hazard their lives, but sometimes less prepared to risk their jobs. Their motives here were by no means wholly dishonorable. Of course rank, pay, and the prospect of decoration cannot be ignored. Yet among letters and diaries there is frequent reference to their desire to be where it mattered, doing a job that counted. Losing the confidence of one's immediate superior, rightly or wrongly, was often fatal. French never forgave Smith-Dorrien—"wordy, windy and unintelligible"—for making his stand at Le Cateau. Rawlinson blamed Davies (8th Division) for errors at Neuve Chapelle. Davies, inches from dismissal, produced a dossier in his own defense. This persuaded French that Rawlinson should be sent home instead. Haig intervened, and although Rawlinson was saved it was made clear that further attempts to blame subordinates would see him relieved of his command. It was also clear that Rawlinson owed his survival to Haig, a point of no little importance in the story that follows. A debacle at St-Eloi, south of Ypres, cost Alderson command of the Canadian Corps in May 1916, and among the generals degummed on the Somme were Montagu-Stuart-Wortley (46th Division), Philipps (38th Division), Ryecroft (32nd Division), and Barter (47th Division).

Generals often fell between the hammer of a hard-driving superior and the anvil of the battlefield. Brigadier General F. M. Carleton, a dug-out who had left the army in 1908, was recalled in 1914 and commanded a battalion before being appointed temporary brigadier general in June 1916; he was relieved of command of 98th Infantry Brigade on the Somme. "I want no sympathy," he told his wife, "nor do I want to see anyone." His complaint was a common one: he had been sacked because his men had failed to achieve the impossible. "The men had been fighting for nearly six weeks, and had suffered enormous casualties," he wrote. "They were done to a turn. We were ordered to do something which was a physical impossibility.... I have been sacrificed to the ambitions of an unscrupulous general." The likes of Carleton were in an agonizing position. If they tried to do the impossible and failed, the butcher's bill would at least testify to the scale of their effort. If, recognizing the impossible, they objected or made a token attempt, they risked being branded as "sticky," the badge of professional suicide.

THE GILDED STAFF

Music-hall comics of the time joked that "if bread is the staff of life, the life of the staff is one long loaf."

Philip Gibbs, the best-known British war correspondent, was scarcely less scathing. "Within their close corporation," he wrote of the staff,

> there were rivalries, intrigues, perjuries and treacheries like those of a medieval court.... They worked late into the night. That is to say, they went back to their offices after dining at mess...and kept their lights burning, and smoked more cigarettes, and rang each other up on the telephone with futile questions.

Needless to say, things did not look the same from behind the staff officer's desk. Memoirs and diaries testify to cripplingly long days—it was not unknown for officers at GHQ to collapse at their paperwork. Brigadier General John Charteris wrote: "There are few, if any, officers who do not do a fourteen-hour day, and who are not to be found at work far into the night." And a staff job was often a mixed blessing. In 1916 Alan Hanbury-Sparrow told his mother that:

> I am feeling most frightfully homesick for my regiment and bitterly repent the day when my selfishness urged me to go onto the staff.... My conscience pricks me most horribly as I know I am far more useful with them than here.

Charteris spoke for many when he said that: "Perhaps the hardest thing of all is that we cannot share the dangers we send others to endure." Many staff officers repeatedly sought employment at the front, only to be told that they were too valuable to be released. Charteris lost his job in December 1917 and asked to go to the front. When told that Haig wanted to keep him on at GHQ as deputy inspector general of transport, he wrote: "It is a disappointment, but is softened by the verdict of the doctors that in any case they could not have passed me as fit for front-line work."

Nor were senior officers immune from personal risk. No fewer than fifty-eight generals were killed, or died of wounds received, on the Western Front. Of the first six divisions sent to France, three had their commanders killed and one wounded. Three divisional commanders, Capper (7th Division), Thesiger (9th Division), and Wing (12th Division), were killed at Loos in 1915. Haig's chief of staff at 1st Army, Johnny Gough (whose brother Hubert was to command 5th Army), was mortally wounded by a sniper while visiting his old battalion at the front. At least twice as many were wounded, many of them seriously. Big, brave Tom Bridges lost a leg commanding a division at Passchendaele: he had characteristically set off across the mud while it was "raining old iron."

There was bitter personal grief, too, for so many officers from military families. Walter Congreve, commanding XIII Corps on the Somme, was in the middle of a difficult attack when he was told that his son Billy had been killed. He paused, said, "He was a good soldier," and carried on with the battle. Edmund Allenby was commanding in Palestine when he heard that his boy Michael, a gunner officer, had died of wounds at the age of nineteen. Outwardly a hard man, he asked for no sympathy, but the level of his sorrow is marked by a letter whose strong, careful script is blotched by tears.

Corps and army headquarters would normally be found about eight to fifteen miles from the front line. Châteaus, a term that covers a broad band from manor houses to stately homes, were a logical choice for accommodation, for while the main house could often hold the general and most of his staff, servants' quarters and outbuildings could accommodate drivers, cooks, and grooms. There was also space within the grounds for temporary buildings, like those erected in the grounds of 1st Army's HQ at Hinges château in 1915 to house the intelligence staff.

The telephone exchange at GHQ, in casemates at Montreuil, operated here by the signals branch of the Royal Engineers.

Staff officers manned the main headquarters branches. At their head came the chief of staff, whose rank varied according to the level of his headquarters: a lieutenant general at GHQ, major general at army, brigadier general at corps, colonel at division, and major at brigade. The G (General Staff) Branch was responsible for all operational matters, developed plans and orders on the commander's behalf, was responsible for the acquisition and collation of intelligence, and coordinated staff work. The A (Adjutant General's) Branch oversaw appointments, promotions, and discipline, while the Q (Quartermaster General's) Staff dealt with supply and accommodation. Artillery and engineer staffs dealt with their own specialisms, and as the war went on the artillery staff grew in importance: by 1916 there was a Major General Royal Artillery at each army headquarters and an artillery adviser (from June, Major General Noel Birch) at GHQ.

All officers on the general staff, including aides de camp to generals, wore red tabs on their collars. In addition, colored armbands bearing a variety of symbols showed the branch to which an officer belonged. These signs, intended to be part honorific and part helpful, were often wholly irritating. There were jokes about "the red badge of funk," as well as unflattering doggerel:

> *He had red tabs upon his chest*
> *and even on his under-vest.*
> *He had the Military Cross*
> *and rode about upon a hoss.*

There is an age-old friction between those at the sharp end of war and those in safer jobs behind them, and relations between the staff and the men they commanded were often brittle. Again, there are no universal truths. Charles Carrington came close to finding one, suggesting that hostility was very much a matter of perception. Front-liners resented:

> the bloody munitions workers at home who were earning high wages and seducing your girl-friend; number four platoon in the next trench who made such a noise that they woke up the enemy gunners...and, of course, the staff who could conveniently be blamed for everything.

He acknowledged that "my colonel, brigadier and divisional commander were men I could respect," and added: "While every man in my company knew Brigadier Sladen and General Fanshawe by sight I doubt if one in ten knew the corps commander's name."

W. N. Nicholson, with wide experience of a divisional headquarters, thought the real breakpoint came between division and corps: "Lord Cavan [XIV Corps] was one of the rare corps commanders who was known by name to more than divisional commanders." He pointed out that senior officers were not universally unpopular. The men liked "Daddy" Plumer of 2nd Army because "he doesn't see red; and he looks after us." Nicholson felt that Haig's problem was partly presentational. In 1918 the commander in chief visited his division.

> It was the first time that any man present had seen the commander-in-chief. A man can issue orders till he's blue in the face; he can write— and the best of his orders and letters will be criticized. But if he'll come and let his soldiers see him, they'll do anything he asks them.

Such was this presentational problem that, soon after the war, the rank of brigadier general was abolished so that there would be fewer generals. It was briefly replaced by the untidy hybrid colonel commandant, and then by simple brigadier. Red tabs disappeared from all officers below full colonel. Second World War commanders remembered the damage done by the remoteness of their predecessors, and many cultivated a more personal style of command.

PLANS AND PRE-PARATIONS From December 1915 the British commander in chief was Douglas Haig, then a general but promoted to field marshal, the highest rank in the army, a year later. His headquarters moved to Montreuil-sur-Mer, a pleasant Picardy town from which the sea had long receded, in April 1916. He had attempted to translate his staff from 1st Army direct to GHQ, but his chief of staff, Major General Butler, was considered too junior, and instead Haig took Lieutenant General Sir Launcelot Kiggell. John Terraine, Haig's most acute defender, observed that "Kiggell never was, nor aspired to be, more than a mouthpiece for Haig." He adds that "a distinct weakness of Haig's period of command is a lack of forceful and energetic personality at his side until the last months of the War, when Sir Herbert Lawrence joined him [as Kiggell's replacement]."

Haig had been left in no doubt, by Kitchener's instructions of December 1915, that the defeat of the Germans by "the closest co-operation of French and British as a united army" was to be his objective. The Chantilly conference of early December had set out an Allied strategy, in which a combined offensive was to play a major role. Haig had his doubts about the level of French participation even before the Germans attacked Verdun, writing on January 14 that he thought the French unlikely to stand another winter's war, and so "the war must be won by the forces of the British Empire." This being so, he was reluctant to hazard his army in the "wearing-down fights" of which Joffre had spoken: he argued that there would be little merit in fighting such battles until the main offensive was imminent.

On February 14 he met Joffre at Chantilly. Although Haig could not agree to relieve the French 10th Army, currently sandwiched between the British 1st and 3rd Armies around Arras, the two commanders in chief were able to agree on a combined offensive astride the Somme, with a target date of July 1. Haig then told Rawlinson, designated to command the new 4th Army, to consider how this offensive might best be handled. But at the same time he ordered Plumer, commanding 2nd Army in Flanders, to plan for operations there, in an area where the German communications bottleneck presented an attractive target. At this early stage we can see the contradictions inherent in the choice of the Somme as a battlefield. There were no significant tactical objectives close behind it, and advance of even thirty miles would not strike a fatal blow. A much smaller advance from Ypres, however, would seize the railheads on which the northern wing of German armies depended. Sir James Edmonds, the official historian, complained that, this being the case, "the Somme offensive had no strategic object except attrition." That the Somme became a battle of attrition there is, as we will see, little doubt. But in early 1916 Haig saw it as something more: a potential breakthrough.

As soon as news of Verdun broke, Haig agreed to relieve the 10th Army, and on February 28 he saw Joffre "to shake him by the hand and place myself and my troops at his disposition." Over the coming months Haig had to balance conflicting priorities. The French urged him to attack as soon as possible to take the weight off them: given the importance of maintaining the alliance these demands could scarcely be ignored. But on the other hand Haig was all too well aware of the real state of his army, writing: "I have not got an Army in France really, but a collection of divisions untrained for the Field. The actual fighting army will be evolved from them."

There were sound reasons for delaying the offensive until the New Army divisions were better prepared, but sounder reasons for not imperiling the alliance. On May 26, Haig entertained Joffre in his modest château at Beaurepaire, near Montreuil. When he suggested that his army might not be ready

THE EVE OF THE SOMME, 1916

THE BATTLE FRONT OF THE BEF, JUNE 30, 1916

Canal du Nord

to Cambrai (10m)

to St Quentin (12m)

R. Sensée

R. Cojeul

R. Scarpe

Bullecourt
Queant
Croisilles
Wailly
VI Arras

Ginchy
Sailly Saillisel
Lesboeufs
Morval
Rancourt
Bouchavesnes
Péronne
Achiet-le-Grand
Bapaume
Gueudecourt
Longueval
Guillemont
Curlu
Clery
Maricourt
Chaulnes
Gommecourt
Puisieux
Serre
Pys
Le Sars
Martinpuich
Flers
Pozières
Ovillers
Montauban
Mametz
Bray
1 COLONIAL
XXXV
Fricourt
Albert
Thiepval
Courcelette
Beaucourt
Beaumont-Hamel
Corbie
Morlancourt
Villers-Bretonneux
Foncquevillers
Sailly
R. Ancre
R. Ancre
Daours (HQ)
Querrieu (HQ)
Boves (HQ)
R. Ayre
Doullens
RESERVE ARMY
Amiens
Dury (HQ)
R. Authie
R. Somme
Abbeville
Southern Boundary BEF
Blangy

3RD ARMY
VII
VIII
X
III
4TH ARMY
6TH ARMY

Legend:

Army HQ

GAN = French Northern Army Group

Belgian-held Front

British-held Front

French-held Front

Corps

VIII

25 Miles

0

25 Kilometers

0

N
E
W
S

to attack till August, Joffre declared that "the French army would cease to exist if we did nothing till then." Haig, an abstemious man, noted that:

> They are, indeed, difficult Allies to deal with! But there is no doubt that the nearest way to the hearts of many of them, including the "Generalissimo," is down their throats, and some 1840 brandy had a surprisingly soothing effect.

Rawlinson's newly formed 4th Army took over the right of the British line, about twenty miles of chalk downland from Foncquevillers in the north to Maricourt, just short of the meandering Somme, in the south. The Albert–Bapaume road slashed obliquely across its main feature, a long, irregular ridge running from Thiepval to Ginchy. Rawlinson himself took up residence in the delightful Château de Querrieu, about twelve miles behind the front. He thought it "capital country in which to undertake an offensive when we get a sufficiency of artillery."

It had previously been a quiet sector, and German defenses, prepared at leisure, were very strong. There were two completed systems, with a third in preparation. The first, composed of several lines of battle and communication trenches, incorporated fortified villages like Serre, Thiepval, La Boisselle, and Fricourt. The lie of the land made it immensely strong, for the villages enabled their defenders to bring flanking fire to bear on the sections of line between them. The second line was a mile or two behind the first, and both this distance and the intervening ridges meant that an attack on the second line would have to be distinct from the assault on the first. The firm chalk was ideally suited to the construction of deep dugouts. The Germans had built many, some of them thirty feet deep and impervious to direct hits by all but the heaviest guns. These were no surprise to the British, who had already captured one near Touvent Farm.

Rawlinson and his chief of staff, Major General A. A. Montgomery, developed their plan in March. It embodied what Rawlinson called "bite and hold," and was based on the mathematical calculation of the front that could be attacked by his troops and the two hundred heavy pieces available to support them. He concluded that he should be able to seize the German first line on a front of twenty thousand yards and then, in two distinct attacks, push on to take the German second line. Rawlinson knew that Haig was unlikely to welcome the plan, and wrote on April 4 that he had heard that the commander in chief favored wider objectives "with the chance of breaking the German line."

Here Rawlinson was perfectly correct. Haig declared that the methodical bombardment favored by Rawlinson would forfeit surprise, and complained that the whole scheme was far too cautious. He favored a more ambitious attack behind a short hurricane bombardment. The serious flaws in Haig's proposal, not least the difficulty of dealing with German barbed wire and strongpoints with a short bombardment, and bringing cavalry through to exploit the break-in, were apparent to Rawlinson. However, he declared himself "quite game to try although it does involve considerable risks." He told Haig as much, but added that he would do as he was told, and expected instructions in due course.

Haig eventually conceded that a deliberate bombardment would be necessary, but could not be deflected from his confidence in an ambitious attack that would break the German line and allow Lieutenant General Sir Hubert Gough's Reserve Army, then consisting largely of cavalry, to be pushed through the gap. Rawlinson never shared this enthusiasm. He warned his corps commanders that, despite the commander in chief's views on the subject, "I had better make it quite clear that it may not be possible to break the enemy's line and push cavalry through at the first rush." While on the whole he was "pretty confident of success," he expected that it would come only after heavy fighting, and expected ten thousand wounded a day, hardly an index of a clean breakthrough.

This was not the message conveyed to the soldiers of 4th Army. Brigadier General Gordon of 8th Brigade was expounding official orthodoxy when he told his men that they could "slope arms, light up your pipes and cigarettes, and march all the way to Pozières before meeting any live Germans." In the week before the attack British gunners fired a million and a half shells. The eighteen-pounders concentrated on the wire and trenches while heavier pieces hit German strongpoints and reached out to strike batteries. When the attack started, a creeping barrage which was a new concept developed by Major General C. E. D. Budworth, Rawlinson's Major General Royal Artillery—would move ahead of the infantry. Tunnels had been dug beneath German strongpoints, and chambers hollowed out and packed with explosives: these nineteen mines were to be exploded shortly before zero hour.

The expectation was that the shelling and mines between them would cut the wire, destroy or neutralize the first garrison of the first position, and cripple the German artillery's prepared response. The infantry was to advance at a walk, in extended lines, carrying full kit, in the belief that it was occupying ground already conquered by artillery. Rawlinson was well aware of the importance of the bombardment, and postponed the attack from June 29 to July 1 to give his gunners more time. Yet although the bombardment was dreadful for the Germans—the rats in some dugouts went mad and scrambled up the walls, where they were killed with spades—and conversely inspiring to the British, it failed to accomplish what was expected of it. The shelling of an exceptionally strong section of front was proportionately about half as heavy as that of the far flimsier defenses at Neuve Chapelle. The French, attacking on both sides of the Somme on the British right, had double the ratio of heavy guns per yard of front. About one-third of the shells fired failed to explode because of faulty fuses or shot-out gun barrels, which meant that shells tipped over and over in flight. Inexperienced artillery observers, and there were many in the New Armies, often moved sections of German wire but failed to cut it.

The interrogation of prisoners produced conflicting views of the state of German defenses. Some said that dugouts offered complete protection: others that they were being destroyed. Some patrols reported that the wire was cut; others found it intact. While Haig was convinced that the wire was indeed cut, Rawlinson was less confident, and was not "quite satisfied that all the wire has been thoroughly well cut." There was enough doubt in the efficacy of the bombardment for a private soldier, Rifleman Percy Jones, to write: "I do not see how the stiffest bombardment is going to kill them all. Nor do I see how the whole of the enemy's artillery is going to be silenced."

Rawlinson, as we have seen, had his own misgivings about the attack, some of which were shared by corps commanders. Yet 4th Army specifically warned that: "All criticism by subordinates...of orders received from superior authority will, in the end, recoil on the heads of the critics." The plan had become sacrosanct and even those who successfully deviated from it kept their intentions secret. Had Rawlinson been more morally robust, and the decision process less constrained by status, he might have argued his case more vigorously. As it was, he made what Robin Prior and Trevor Wilson call "an unhappy act of obeisance to Haig's authority," with the consequence that the result of July 1, 1916, was less "an unforeseeable misfortune...[and] more in the nature of a foregone conclusion."

THE FIRST DAY

The first day of the battle is marvelously chronicled by Martin Middlebrook's *The First Day on the Somme*, which remains one of the best books written on the war. In the south, Walter Congreve's XIII Corps had taken its objectives, thanks partly to the fact that French gunners, anxious to avoid

Men of 15th Battalion the West Yorkshire Regiment, known as the Leeds Pals. The battalion suffered heavily attacking Serre on July 1, 1916, its experience typifying blighted hopes of quick victory.

their own infantry being taken in the flank by intact positions on their left, had added their own fire to that of British guns. Henry Horne's XV Corps had made fair progress, taking Mametz and getting so close to Fricourt that the Germans gave it up next day. But further north the results were grievously disappointing. William Pulteney's III, Thomas Morland's X, and Aylmer Hunter-Weston's VII Corps had achieved few lasting gains. There had been some short-lived successes: the inimitable 36th Ulster Division, attacking north of Thiepval, had overrun the German first line but, with the defenses of Thiepval intact behind their right shoulders, the Ulstermen could not be supported.

The British army had lost 57,470 officers and men, 19,240 of them killed and 2,152 missing, on what remains its bloodiest day. Unusually in a war in which artillery was the major killer, about 60 percent of these casualties were caused by machine-gun fire. The Germans, sheltering in dugouts, emerged as the barrage lifted to fire into the massed ranks in front of them, and their batteries came to life to drop a curtain of shellfire across no-man's-land. Their official account observed that:

The training of the infantry was clearly behind that of the German; the superficially trained British were particularly clumsy in the movement of large masses.... The strong, usually young, and well armed British soldier followed his officers blindly, and the officers, active and personally brave, went ahead of their men in battle with great courage. But owing to insufficient training, they were not skilful in action.

The British official historian admitted that this appeared to be fair comment.

DEVELOPING THE BATTLE

Although the initial casualty reports that reached Rawlinson were optimistically inaccurate, even the real numbers could scarcely have deterred him, for the attack's operational imperative remained unaltered. On the night of July 1 he set out his vision for the next phase of the battle: 4th Army would hold on to what it had gained, and make fresh efforts to secure the many frontline

ABOVE Australians, wearing steel helmets rather than the familiar slouch hats, manning a Lewis gun in the antiaircraft role.
OPPOSITE The ravaged site of Guillemont, September 1916.

strongpoints where it had failed. This was a novel reversal of the principle of reinforcing success, and did not commend itself to Haig when he visited Querrieu on the 2nd. He gave Gough command of the two northern corps, VIII and X, and told Rawlinson to renew the attack in the south, where he had already made progress. Joffre demurred, perhaps fearing that operations in the south would leech away French resources too, but Haig, rightly this time, was adamant.

On July 3 attacks on Ovillers and Thiepval failed, and XV Corps could not exploit a promising attack at Contalmaison. That night XV Corps reached the southern edge of Mametz Wood, lying between the two German positions, and XIII Corps cleared Bernafay Wood, on the British right. Before he could attack the German second position Rawlinson had to secure Mametz Wood, and it was not until July 12 that he did so, after grim fighting which sadly mauled the New Army's 39th (Welsh) Division, whose composition owed much to the influence of David Lloyd George. In less that a fortnight 4th Army lost some twenty-five thousand men securing the start line for the assault on the second position. What is noteworthy is that these battles were fought without out overall direction from Querrieu. For example, when XV Corps attacked Mametz Wood on July 7, the artillery of XIII Corps remained silent. Attacks

46 Div

Hannescamps

Ayette

Ablainzevelle

Foncquevillers

Gommecourt
Wood
Gommecourt Park
Biez Wood
Gommecourt

Bucquoy

56 Div

Hébuterne

3rd Army
4th Army

Rossignol
Wood

Achiet-le-Petit

48 Div

Puisieux

Touvent
Farm

Serre

Miraumont

31 Div

4 Div

Sunken
Road

Beaumont-Hamel

Beaucourt

Grandcourt

Auchonvillers

St-Pierre
Divion

29 Div

Hamel

Schwaben
Redoubt

Courcelette

Thiepval

Mouquet
Farm

VIII Corps
X Corps

Mesnil-
Martinsart

Caterpillar
Wood

Leipzig Redoubt

Avenay Wood

Authuille

Pozières

36 Div

Ovillers

32 Div

Aveluy

Mash Valley

Contalmai

Usna
Hill La Boisselle

Sausage
Valley
Quadra
Woo

X Corps
III Corps

8 Div   Tara Hill

Bécourt

Fricourt

34 Div

Albert

Ma

III Corps
XV Corps

Bécordel-
Bécourt

Bois
Français

N
W — E
S

Méaulte

to Amiens

Dernancourt

R. Ancre

XV Corps
XIII Corps

18

0   2 Miles

0   2 Kilometers

Ville sur
Ancre

7 Div

British 4th A
French
A

Army boundary July 1   –xxxx–

Corps boundary July 1   –xxx–

Division boundary July 1   –xx–

British gains July 1   –·····–

Morlancourt

Bray-sur-Somme

THE BATTLEFIELD
OF THE SOMME
JULY–NOVEMBER 1916

Ervillers

Gomiécourt

ogeast
Wood

Achiet-le-Grand

Loupart
Wood

Grévillers

Bapaume

Butte de Warlencourt

's

Warlencourt-
Eaucourt

Beaulencourt

Le Sars

British Front Line Nov 17, 1916

Le Transloy

nan Road

Gueudecourt

Martinpuich

Flers

entin-le-
it Wood

High Wood

Lesboeufs

Bazentin-
le-Petit

Bazentin-le-
Grand Wood

Delville Wood

Sailly-Sailliser

Morval

Bazentin-
Mametz   le-Grand
Wood

Longueval

Ginchy

Bernefay
Wood

Guillemont

Combles

Trones
Wood

Montauban

Hardecourt-
aux-Bois

Maurepas

Bouchavesnes

rnoy

Maricourt
Wood

30 Div

Maricourt

to Péronne
(3m) →

Suzanne

R. Somme

Somme Canal

on one sector were disrupted by unsuppressed fire from another, and there was no attempt at cohesive action across the whole of 4th Army's front.

Yet Rawlinson was not idle. He and his staff were considering the problem of the German second line, leering down at them from the Longueval Ridge. Rawlinson proposed a night attack, and was only able to persuade Haig that the troops were well enough trained for this when Horne and Congreve, his remaining corps commanders, firmly assured GHQ that the plan was indeed feasible. Night attacks were no novelty, and often raised as many problems as they overcame. Forming up and negotiating the wire could be difficult, although the laying of miles of white tape helped men keep direction. Machine guns firing on fixed lines, and artillery engaging registered targets were as deadly by day as night. The Germans were amply provided with illuminating flares, and, like any defender in a night battle, knew their ground while the British did not.

Of course darkness did afford some shelter to the attacker, and contributed to the shock of a surprise assault. But what really made the July 14 night attack work was the fact that Rawlinson's gunners were engaging about six thousand yards of front as opposed to the twenty-two thousand yards of July 1, and that trench systems behind the front attacked on July 14 were no more than another twelve thousand yards. Although Haig's allocation of part of the old 4th Army to Gough had reduced the number of guns available to Rawlinson, in essence he had two-thirds as many guns with which to demolish one-eighteenth of the length of trench. There was steady bombardment on July 11–13, and at 3:20 on the morning of the 14th a five-minute blizzard of fire preceded the infantry attack. Its results were remarkable. The German second line, trenches and wire pulverized by a shelling proportionately five times heavier than that which fell before July 1, was overrun on a broad front from Bazentin-le-Petit to Longueval.

It proved impossible to exploit success. Getting the cavalry forward across slippery ground and deep trenches was a problem in itself and, despite Royal Flying Corps reports that High Wood was empty, it was in fact laced with trenches and German reserves were on hand. The battle was less a tragedy of missed opportunities than a successful instance of bite and hold, which, of course, is what Rawlinson had favored from the start. However, the fact that the Germans remained in possession of both Delville Wood and High Wood enabled them to slip reserves over the crest line behind them to turn the new line into a position it would take Rawlinson's men two bitter months to break.

Somme mud. Sledges used to drag wounded down the main road at Le Sars, October 1916.

On Rawlinson's left Gough's men made steady progress, taking La Bois-selle on July 7 and Ovillers on the 16th. Pozières, on the Albert– Bapaume road at the heart of the German second position, was attacked by the newly arrived Australians on July 23, and over the next two weeks the village was smashed to pieces as they fought their way through it. They were masters of it on August 7, but at what a cost. Three Australian divisions lost almost twenty-three thousand men, and with them their faith in British leadership. "If Australians wish to trace their modern suspicion and resentment of the British to a date and a place," writes the Australian historian Peter Charlton, "then July–August 1916 and the ruined village of Pozières are useful points of departure."

SUMMER STALEMATE

It was an atrocious summer, with rain turning the shat-tered woods and charnel villages into a stinking slough as the British and German armies slogged it out on the uplands. It is important to grasp the significance of these "forgotten battles" that defined the real character of so much of the Somme fighting. At this stage in the war German doctrine emphasized the importance of immediate recov-ery of lost ground. On July 2 Falkenhayn visited General von Below, whose Second Army held the Somme front, and emphasized that "the first principle in position warfare must be to yield not one foot of ground, and if it be lost to retake it by immediate counterattack, even to the use of the last man." Below immediately passed these instructions on to his troops, with the result that British and French attacks were almost always followed by German counter-attacks. Terraine castigated historians who portrayed the Somme as British troops rising from their trenches to be mown down: it ought, he pointed out, to be set beside an image of German troops doing precisely the same thing.

Nor is this all. One of the consequences of Falkenhayn's prior commit-ment to Verdun had been the concentration of German artillery in that sec-tor, and it was not easy to disengage guns for use elsewhere. As the Somme ground on, so Allied artillery preponderance became more marked, and the squat triangle of tortured earth with Bapaume at its apex was dominated by the gun. One of the less than fair consequences of the British army's regi-mental system, with its emphasis on county regiments—most now gone for-ever—was a tendency to undervalue the contribution made by the Royal Artillery. The remarkable improvement in artillery technique was an impor-tant legacy of the Somme. It is natural enough for a British audience to reflect on what German guns were doing to its grandfathers and great-grandfathers, and easy to forget what it was like on the other side of the hill. Between July 15 and September 14 British gunners fired 6.5 million shells, and the Royal Flying Corps' superiority over the battlefield meant that much of this fire was very well controlled.

Lieutenant Ernst Junger, who was to become Germany's most decorated officer, described the artillery landscape.

> The sunken road now appeared as nothing but a series of enormous
> shell-holes filled with pieces of uniform, weapons and dead bodies. The
> ground all round, as far as the eye could see, was plowed by shells....
> Among the living lay the dead. As we dug ourselves in we found them
> in layers stacked one on top of the other. One company after another
> had been shoved into the drum-fire and steadily annihilated.

The German army was extraordinarily resolute. Junger recalled being led for-ward to the front line through the village of Sailly-Saillisel one night in late August by a guide who was beyond hope and beyond fear. Nothing was left but supreme, superhuman indifference. "They attack every day," he said. "But they can't get through. Everyone knows it is life and death."

Yet by now there were cracks in this splendid edifice. A German regi-mental history described these days as "the worst in the War." On Septem-

ber 10 a reservist told his family: "You can form no idea what the poor soldiers have to go through here in this place and how cruelly and uselessly men
are sacrificed; it is awful." In August Sergeant Frederick Oehme, an ex-law
student, described Martinpuich, once "a pretty place," as "a region of horror
and despair. *'Lasciate ogni speranza'*—Abandon hope—are the words over the
portals of hell in Dante's *Divine Comedy*. I kept thinking of them as we tore
through the village." He was killed on October 25.

What is at issue is not the terrible damage that this fighting did to the contending armies, but whether the British could have inflicted this damage on
the Germans at less cost to themselves. There were too many small-scale operations, with the same objectives being attacked, time and time again, by too
few soldiers behind too light a barrage. Lack of progress coupled with heavy
casualties—4th Army lost about eighty-two thousand men during this period—led to growing disquiet in the British government, and on July 29
Robertson warned Haig that "the powers that be" were becoming more
restive. This induced Haig to give firmer direction to Rawlinson, and one of
the casualties of that dreadful summer was the commander in chief's confidence in 4th Army's commander.

ENTER THE TANKS The first tanks—so called because they were shipped to
France described as "water tanks"—were developed in
such secrecy that Haig did not know about them till
Christmas Day 1915. He took an early interest in them, writing in April 1916
that they might prove useful in the northern part of the Somme front, to take
the ridge around Serre, and discussing "the surprise and demoralizing effect"
likely to result from their first use. There would be too few available to use on
July 1, but during the summer stalemate GHQ remained anxious to accelerate
their arrival with a view to using them in a decisive battle. Haig was not a free
agent. Just as he had been pressed to initiate the Somme earlier than would
have been ideal, so Joffre demanded a decisive resumption of Allied attacks
on the Somme in order to keep the Germans at full stretch. The Russians were
in growing difficulties, and if the Somme faltered the Germans might be able
to shift some weight to the east. Haig realized that the attack would have to be
properly prepared, and refused to launch it before September 15, despite Joffre's pressure. But such was its importance that he felt it worth using as many
tanks as were available. If the summer's fighting had turned into an attritional
battle which had worn down the Germans, GHQ was clear that the next phase
of the fighting was to be "a decisive operation…"

all probability, dead). The want of preparation, the vague orders, the ignorance of the objective & geography, the absurd haste, and in general the horrid bungling were scandalous. After two years of war it seems that our higher commanders are still without common sense. In any well regulated organization a divisional commander would be shot for incompetence — here another regiment is ordered to attempt the same task in the same muddleing way. It was worse than Hooge, much worse — and it is still going on!

TOP Royal Artillery forward observation officers, one using a periscope, observe fire, while telephonists relay results to the guns.
ABOVE Quartermaster Sergeant R.A. Scott Macfie of the King's Liverpool Regiment tells his brother of the frustration caused by bungling commanders.

Rawlinson was skeptical about the tanks. On August 29, a fortnight before the battle, he told the King's assistant private secretary that:

> We are puzzling our heads as to how best to make use of them and have not yet come to a decision. They are not going to take the British Army straight to Berlin as some people imagine but if properly used and skillfully handled by the detachments who work them they may be very useful in taking trenches and strong points. Some people are rather too optimistic as to what these weapons will accomplish.

Rawlinson was preparing his ground in case the coming battle did not produce the decisive result hoped for by Haig: there was still no meeting of minds between Querrieu and Montreuil. Nor was Gough any more optimistic, and neither of the army commanders engaged in the first tank battle was inclined to use them save in small groups dotted along the front. Kiggell told Rawlinson that Haig wanted tanks "to be used boldly and success pressed in order to demoralize the enemy and, if possible, capture his guns." It is hard to resist the conclusion that Haig and Kiggell figured among the "some people" mentioned in Rawlinson's letter of August 29.

The first tanks, part of the Heavy Section, Machine-Gun Corps, arrived in France in early September and were moved up by rail to Bray-sur-Somme. In the meantime 4th Army had at last taken Guillemont and Ginchy, helping the French to push on and reach the Bapaume–Péronne road at Bouchavesnes. Although the French, recovering after this advance, were unable to attack on September 15, their heavy guns, reaching into the German flank and rear, made a valuable contribution.

Of forty-nine tanks available for the attack, thirty-two actually got into action. Tank D1 had the distinction of being first into battle on the morning of September 15 when it went forward, shortly before the main attack began at 6:20, to clear a strongpoint on the edge of Delville Wood. Gough allocated his tanks to 2nd Canadian Division, which planned to use them to spearhead its attack on the sugar factory near Courcelette. The attack was successful, though the tanks broke down or moved too slowly to keep up with the infantry. On their right, 15th (Scottish) Division of III Corps, Rawlinson's left-hand formation, took Martinpuich with the help of half the Corps' eight tanks.

Further east, High Wood—"ghastly by day, ghostly by night, the rottenest place on the Somme"—lived up to its evil reputation. Controversially, III Corps decreed that the four tanks allocated to 47th (London) Division would pass through the wood, despite the reasoned objection of the tank officers who argued that the ground was bad. Three ditched and the fourth reached the German support line, where it was destroyed by a shell. The first infantry attacks failed, and it was not until a trench-mortar battery had put 750 bombs into the wood that the morale of the Bavarian defenders cracked and the Londoners took the place at last. It did their commander, the well-respected Major General Barter, no good. He was sacked, and his supporters attributed this to the fact that he had been right about the tanks while the corps commander was wrong.

Further east, XV Corps made for Flers. The New Zealand Division, on its left, was initially held up by fire from High Wood, but on the right the attack developed with far greater promise. Twelve of the seventeen tanks allocated to the attack here went into action together. There was panic among some defenders, and 41st Division took Flers with close support from some of the surviving tanks. A pilot, echoed by war correspondents, reported: "A tank is walking up the High Street of Flers with the British Army cheering behind it." On Rawlinson's right, XIV Corps made disappointing progress, largely because most of its tanks, for which gaps had been left in the barrage, failed to materialize.

By the end of the day the British had taken a great bite out of the German third position, seizing strongpoints that had held them up for months and capturing ground from which to renew their attack. They had not broken through, and the attack had cost 4th Army alone nearly thirty thousand men. Success at Flers was, like success at High Wood two months before, to be overcelebrated: the truth of the matter was that the problem of exploiting success was still far from solution. The tanks could help break into the German position but, short-ranged, slow, prone to breakdown and ditching, bone-cracking and nauseating for their crews, they could not yet assist with the breakout.

THE END ON THE SOMME

If September 15 had brought no breakthrough, it had at least continued with the remorseless process of attrition. On September 25 Charteris observed that lads of the 1917 class, not due for conscription till the coming January, were appearing on the battlefield, "and if the weather holds we shall have worked through them pretty quickly." As usual he was optimistic. A bad summer blew into an awful autumn, and the conditions in which men lived and fought simply defy description. Even the Official History's prose rises to describe how, "in a wilderness of mud, holding water-logged trenches or shell-hole posts, accessible only by night, the infantry abode in conditions which might be likened to those of earth-worms, rather than of the human kind."

The British continued to make gains, taking Morval and Lesboeufs on September 25 and Thiepval—a July 1 objective—on the 26th, but their progress was painfully slow. The last blow in the battle was struck by Gough, whose men—renamed 5th Army on October 1—took Beaumont-Hamel, another July 1 target, on November 13. When Allied leaders met that month at Compiègne they agreed that it was time to halt for the winter. There would be another offensive in 1917, but it was evident to all that the burden of 1916 had, for British and French alike, been almost insupportable.

Even now it is impossible to say exactly what that burden was. Allied casualties on the Somme totaled about 600,000, two-thirds of them British. The Germans reported casualties on a different basis, and the British official historian, Sir James Edmonds, assessed them as 660,000 to 680,000. Even if, as some historians suggest, he was overgenerous, it is hard to place them lower than 600,000. One German officer described the Somme as "the muddy grave of the German field army, and of confidence in the infallibility of German leadership," while Ludendorff acknowledged that his army was "completely exhausted" at its end.

One of the many virtues of Malcolm Brown's *Imperial War Museum Book of the Somme* is its identification of the ambivalence at the heart of the Somme experience. While one officer called it "just slaughter," another, Charles Carrington, wrote:

> The Somme raised the morale of the British Army. Although we did not win a decisive victory, there was what matters most, a definite and growing sense of superiority over the enemy, man to man... We were quite sure that we had got the Germans beat: next spring we would deliver the knock-out blow.

Yet nobody reading Carrington's *A Subaltern's War* could doubt that he had indeed seen about the worst the battle had to offer.

This ambivalence extends to the generalship. Given the nature of Anglo-French relations and the emphasis that British politicians placed on maintaining the coalition, it is hard to see how Haig could have declined to attack on the Somme. Indeed, it took much of his moral strength not to be hustled into attacking sooner. Despite the advantages that the ground offered to the defender, and the lack of attainable objectives behind the front, the Somme was not inherently unsuitable for an offensive, and had the advantage of meeting French wishes to mount an Allied operation. Notwithstanding the losses of the first day, and the growing misery of the summer's fighting, the British could scarcely have stopped their attack: the need, first, to relieve Verdun and second, to prevent the Germans slipping troops to the east, saw to that.

In terms of tactics if not morale, the British army that emerged from the Somme was better than that which had entered it. As Paddy Griffith has written: "The five-month Somme battle taught the BEF many lessons and transformed it from a largely inexperienced mass army into a largely experienced one." However, the management of the battle does not redound to the credit of the British high command. The first day's plan was the bastard child of the differing expectations of Haig and Rawlinson. There was enough evidence to suggest that the scheme was unrealistically optimistic, and this was at best honestly discounted and at worst willfully suppressed. Rawlinson's handling of the battle thereafter was deficient: he behaved like the corps commander he had been, not the army commander he was.

His own insecurity did not help. One example shows precisely how his relationship with Haig affected the battle. Lord Cavan of XIV Corps formally protested at an order to attack Le Transloy on November 5:

> I assert my readiness to sacrifice the British right rather than jeopardize the French...but I feel that I am bound to ask if this is the intention, for a sacrifice it must be. It does not appear that a failure would much assist the French, and there is a danger of this attack shaking the confidence of the men and officers in their commanders. No one who has not visited the front trenches can really know the state of exhaustion to which the men are reduced.

Cavan pressed his point: Rawlinson went forward to see the ground, and agreed that the attack was impossible. After speaking to Foch, Haig reversed the decision, and XIV Corps attacked as ordered. Cavan lost two thousand men for no gains, and there is no evidence that his failure assisted the French.

The British won the battle on points and, as Sergeant R. H. Tawney— later a distinguished professor of economic history—wrote, were in danger of reducing "the unspeakable agonies of the Somme to an item in a commercial proposition." It seems certain that a knockout blow was still well beyond them: their opponent was simply too tough. The British were right to be on the Somme, but so many of them would not lie there today had some of their leaders shown a moral courage equal to the physical valor of the men they commanded.

ENDURING
THE
FRONT

In the year 1917 the Russian Empire collapsed; America entered the war; the French army mutinied; and Italy was badly beaten at Caporetto. All these events were to bear upon the Western Front, which was itself the scene of two major battles which cast long and terrible shadows: the Nivelle offensive of April, and the Third Battle of Ypres—usually known as Passchendaele, officially the name of one of its component actions—which groaned on through a wet summer and into a bitter autumn. A bleak year indeed: the year of Passchendaele.

Men were dying of exposure on the bare uplands in front of Bapaume, above the meandering Somme, when Allied military leaders met at Joffre's headquarters at Chantilly on November 15, 1916. Their conclusions were scarcely revolutionary: Germany remained the main enemy. Her rapid destruction of Romania in the late summer had showed all too clearly that she remained a formidable adversary, and the Allies were to mount "general offensive action" against her early in the New Year. Allied political leaders met in Paris shortly afterward and ratified this decision, and in early December it seemed as if the recipe for the coming year would be very much the mixture as before.

Then, in quick succession, key personalities changed. On December 7 Asquith was succeeded as prime minister by David Lloyd George. Appointed minister of munitions as a result of the "shells scandal" of 1915, Lloyd George had become secretary of state for war in July 1916. When he visited Haig that September it became evident that he and the commander in chief did not see eye to eye. Haig told his wife that "I have no great opinion of L. G. as a man or a leader," while Lloyd George was later to say that he found Haig "brilliant—to the top of his army boots." The antipathy was scarcely surprising. Haig was reserved, patrician, and reticent: Lloyd George flamboyant, populist, and voluble.

Lloyd George's reservations about Haig's conduct of operations had been deepened by the losses of the Somme, and in particular by the mauling of 38th Welsh Division at Mametz Wood. When he visited the front in September he asked Foch his opinion of British generals, and Foch reported the conversation to Haig, who was horrified by what he regarded as "ungentlemanly" conduct. In conversation with the journalist Charles Repington, Lloyd George described Haig as a "military Moloch," and he went on to tell Maurice Hankey that in his view the Somme had been "a bloody and disastrous failure." When he became prime minister, therefore, there was every reason to expect that he would question the primacy of the Western Front and the character of operations conducted there: he was "not prepared to accept the position of a butcher's boy driving cattle to slaughter."

The slaughter of the past two and a half years had weighed heavily on the French army, which felt its burden keenly: it had one man killed or captured for nearly every minute of the war. Much of the blame was leveled at old Joffre, whose oft-repeated assertion that he was nibbling away at the Germans rang increasingly hollow: the Germans seemed to be nibbling harder. Foch might have been considered as a replacement, but his star was not in the ascendant: he had commanded the French army group engaged in the Somme fighting, and it had (undeservedly) done little for his reputation. Nor did Pétain, the savior of Verdun, with his methodical approach and chilly manner, seem the right choice.

NIVELLE TAKES COMMAND

The hour had a new hero. In mid-December General Robert Nivelle, who had recaptured Fort Douaumont, at Verdun, became *de facto* commander in chief, with Joffre still hanging on to his office at Chantilly. The fraud was transparent, and on Boxing Day 1916 Joffre went off to a meaningless advisory post in Paris and was appointed Marshal of France, the first since 1870. Nivelle—charming, persuasive and fluent in English—

OPPOSITE General Robert Nivelle, the persuasive, half-English artillery officer who succeeded Joffre as French commander in chief.

soon set about moving his headquarters to the splendor of the Château de Compiègne, rebuilt in the eighteenth century and later the favorite residence of Napoleon III. It was bigger, grander, and closer to the front: new man, new style.

Nivelle had a plan. It was based on the combination of overwhelming artillery support and well-prepared infantry attacks that had served him so well at Verdun. And it would succeed in just forty-eight hours—or it could be called off. No more Sommes: no more Verduns. It now seems glaringly obvious that what had worked so well as a battle plan—on a narrow front against a strictly limited objective—would be less likely to succeed as a campaign plan, on a far larger scale, designed to bring the war to a sudden end. But we must not be too harsh on Nivelle's backers. He was peddling victory, and the French army and nation alike wanted to believe him, just as a sick patient desperately needs to believe in a miracle cure. "I have the secret," announced Nivelle, and men trusted him.

So, at first, did Haig. When the two men met on December 20, Haig found him "most straightforward and soldierly." His plan seemed sound, at least in outline: a surprise attack against an enemy worn down by the Somme. Its detail, which arrived a few days later, was more worrying. Nivelle intended to strike his sudden, violent blow with a mass maneuver of twenty-seven divisions which, of necessity, must belong to one nation—France. The British would launch subsidiary attacks to pin down the Germans and, in order to free French divisions for the offensive, would have to extend their line southward from the Somme to the Oise. Haig was welcome to plan for an offensive in Flanders, to be launched later should the need arise. For the moment Nivelle was anxious to gain agreement on the relief of French divisions between the Somme and the Oise: he wanted it completed by mid-January 1917.

| BRITISH VIEWS | Haig was not impressed. Sickness and shortage of drafts from home meant that he had only about fifty divisions available instead of fifty-six: he felt unable to |

take over the new line and put in the holding attacks demanded by Nivelle. He was also concerned that the scheme meant the abandonment of his own plans for an offensive in Flanders. We have already seen how this sector had been Haig's preferred choice for an attack a year before, and he had been diverted to the Somme by the inexorable logic of Anglo-French relations in the year of Verdun.

The attractions of Flanders were twofold. First, the rail junction at Roulers lay temptingly close to British lines, a little over twelve miles from Ypres as the crow flies. Its capture, or even domination by artillery, would imperil the German hold on the whole northern sector of the Western Front. Second, the Channel ports of Ostend and Zeebrugge had been recognized as important objectives since the autumn of 1914, and in November 1916 Asquith had informed Sir William Robertson, Chief of the Imperial General Staff, that "There is no operation of war to which the War Committee would attach greater importance than the successful occupation, or at least the deprivation to the enemy, of Ostend and especially Zeebrugge." German submarines based there not only sank warships and transports in the Channel, but forayed wider to add to the growing toll of merchant shipping based elsewhere sunk by U-boats. On February 1, 1917, at the considerable risk of alienating neutral opinion, Germany launched unrestricted submarine warfare, sinking suspect merchantmen on sight without applying the prize rules which had previously restricted their terms of engagement. On that day 23 of the 105 operational U-boats were based in Flanders.

Merchant shipping losses shot up, from around 300,000 to 350,000 tons a month in the winter of 1916–17 to 520,000 tons in March 1917 and an awful 860,000 in April. Losses on this scale raised the specter of Britain being starved to death. The First Sea Lord, Sir John Jellicoe, was gloomy. In April, shortly after America's entry into the war—an event that unrestricted submarine warfare had done much to provoke—he told an American admiral that "it is impossible for us to go on with the war if losses like this continue." In June he went further, telling the War Policy Committee that: "There is no good discussing plans for next spring—we cannot go on." Jellicoe's views were neither precise nor consistent, and they were, in any event, not universally held. However, the purely military attractions of Flanders were substantial, and Haig's reliance on cross-Channel supplies helped make the maritime argument a powerful one. All the more reason why Nivelle's plan worried Douglas Haig, and why, in a well-argued letter of January 6, he emphasized that he could not agree to Nivelle's proposals unless the clearing of the Belgian coast was provided for.

AN ALLIED ADJUSTMENT And there were other worries. In December Robertson warned Haig that Lloyd George was "off Salonika" but "on Egypt, and wants to get to Jerusalem." At the Rome conference in early January, Lloyd George spoke warmly in favor of sending troops to the Italian front to attack Austria, on the grounds that "if Austria were beaten Germany would be beaten too." He was vexed to discover that neither the French nor the Italians backed the scheme. Later that month, at a meeting in London, Lloyd George spoke warmly in favor of French achievements, and was clearly impressed by the Nivelle plan.

Then, in yet another conference, this time at Calais in late February, Lloyd George went even further. He not merely agreed to the Nivelle plan, but decreed that the British army would be placed under Nivelle's command for the duration of the offensive. Robertson, who, after all, was the prime minister's professional adviser on such matters, was stunned: an observer described how "his face went the colour of mahogany, his eyes became perfectly round, his eyebrows slanted outwards like a forest of bayonets held at the charge." Haig took the news with no outward display, but immediately wrote to the King offering to resign his appointment. The King's private secretary wrote back to dissuade him, relaying royal confidence that the two generals would soon be working on "the most amicable and open terms."

GERMAN RE-ADJUSTMENTS It was a vain hope. Although subsequent meetings repaired some of the damage done by Calais, it was hard to repair the mistrust that now existed between soldiers and politicians, British and French. And in the meantime the Germans were not idle. Ludendorff was later to admit that: "our position was uncommonly difficult, and a way out hard to find. We could not contemplate an offensive ourselves, having to keep all our reserves available for defense." The solution was twofold. Firstly, to shift troops from the Eastern Front, a process that was to become easier as 1917 wore on and Russia's commitment to the war weakened dramatically. Second, to give up the nose of the salient formed by the Western Front, falling back onto a well-prepared position and, by shortening the line, reducing the number of troops required to hold it.

German withdrawal to the Hindenburg Line was christened Operation Alberich, after the spiteful dwarf in the Nibelungen saga. It was well named. The retreating Germans left a desert behind them. Roads and railways were destroyed, bridges blown, orchards cut down, stately avenues felled across the roads they once shaded, wells poisoned, and booby traps left everywhere.

One German, horrified by what his own side had done, left a signboard in Péronne saying: "Don't be angry: Only wonder." Crown Prince Rupprecht of Bavaria, commanding the northernmost German Army Group, personally interceded for the splendid castle at Coucy, its keep the largest in Christendom. It was wasted effort: Ludendorff sent engineers who packed twenty-eight tons of explosive into the keep and blew it to bits.

THE NIVELLE OFFENSIVE

Although Allied propaganda made much of the German retreat, the well-handled withdrawal cast serious doubts over Nivelle's offensive. The Germans had pulled back from part of the attack sector. The newly liberated area was chaos, with roads to be rebuilt and the population fed. And Nivelle's political support slackened. The Briand government fell, and was replaced by an administration under Alexandre Ribot. Ribot's minister of war was the distinguished mathematician Paul Painlevé, and he discovered that even military support for the attack was less than firm. He then consulted the army group commanders, who were unenthusiastic. Painlevé made a last attempt to test Nivelle's resolve, and received a rhetorical tour de force in reply. Nivelle insisted that he knew what he was doing, and that his plan would work and win the war. Simply seizing the territory to be attacked would be only

> a poor little tactical victory. It is not for so meager a result that I have accumulated on the Aisne one million two hundred thousand soldiers, five thousand guns and five hundred thousand horses. The game would not be worth the candle.

The plan relied on surprise, a commodity in short supply. On April 4 the Germans captured a copy of Nivelle's plan which had unwisely been taken into a forward position. Soon they knew almost everything: date, times, and objectives. Information was circulated to their gunners to enable them to shell French trenches at their most vulnerable moment, just before the attack started. As we shall see later, the Germans had used the experience of the Somme fighting to formulate tactics based in defense in depth, with a lightly held front line absorbing the impact of the attack while counterattack formations moved up to deal with it. Their front along the Chemin des Dames and into the Soissonais region was already held in depth, well suited to roll with the sort of punch Nivelle planned to deliver. The attack's prospects would have been poor even if security had remained intact: with security compromised, its chances of success dwindled.

By now the course to tragedy was irrevocably set. At a last difficult meeting at Compiègne on April 6, Nivelle undermined his opponents by offering to resign. The plan had now been so heavily oversold that cancellation was unthinkable. And so, as Churchill was to put it:

> Nivelle and Painlevé found themselves in the most unhappy positions which mortals can occupy; the Commander having to dare the utmost risks with an entirely skeptical Chief behind him; the Minister having to become responsible for a frightful slaughter at the bidding of a General in whose capacity he did not believe, and upon a military policy the folly of which he was justly convinced.

As Edward Spears, a British liaison officer, observed, Nivelle had lost all touch with reality and was being swept along by his own rhetoric. And always at his elbow stood the chief of his personal staff, Colonel d'Alenson, mortally sick with tuberculosis and desperate to see the war won before he died.

The attack went in on the morning of April 16, in icy rain which turned to sleet, with French infantry going forward, as they had so often in the past, with a courage worthy of a better cause. The plan's sternest critics soon saw their fears confirmed. The bombardment had often left the German wire uncut, and the creeping barrage buzzed and roared its way hopelessly ahead of the attackers. Even where they penetrated the defenses they were taken on by flanking machine guns which had escaped the shelling or briskly counterattacked by Germans who had sat out the bombardment in the huge caverns that are a feature of the limestone landscape above the Aisne. By nightfall, far from being deep in the German rear, the attack had stalled. The medical services, counting on the light casualties envisaged by the plan, were overwhelmed. Spears saw French wounded depressed as never before. "It's all up," they said. "We can't do it, we shall never do it. *C'est impossible.*"

Nivelle refused to recognize failure. He ordered more attacks in the face of evident catastrophe and then tried to blame subordinates. By the time the battle formally ended on May 9 the French army had lost about one hundred thousand casualties. When he told Micheler, commanding one of his army groups, that he should be trying harder, Micheler rounded on him. "You wish to make me responsible for this mistake: me, who never ceased to warn you of it. Do you know what such an action is called? Well, it is called cowardice." Nivelle reeled like a drunken man as he walked to his car. And now his army, like a beast of burden flogged beyond endurance, began to mutiny.

THE FRENCH MUTINIES

On April 29 a battalion of the 18th Infantry Regiment refused to go back up the line. The ringleaders were arrested: four were shot and the remainder imprisoned. For a few days the episode was isolated. But soon similar outbreaks were reported elsewhere. The pattern was similar. Men, who had often drunk too much, refused to leave for the front or turned up at the transport without their rifles. Soldiers roamed the streets demanding more leave, better food, and above all no more attacks. This was quite unlike the sort of mutiny that the Russian army was undergoing. French officers might be jeered at or jostled—and even then usually not by men from their own units—but they were not murdered. True, somebody shot at a corps commander in Soissons, but that might have been simply to make the point.

The high command saw it as part of a deep-seated plot with links to extremist politicians, but this was never the case. The mutinies were spontaneous, and lacked organized leadership. They were more like strikes, carried out by citizen-soldiers who did not wish to see Germany win but would simply not throw away their lives in more hopeless attacks.

And it was not just the men who were disaffected. Private Louis Barthas, whose regiment had been kept at readiness to attack in appalling weather, saw a general order his colonel to attack. The tough, down-to-earth colonel took his pipe from his mouth, spat, and asked the general to look at his men. "They would have marched on the first day, but now they won't—and I won't either."

There was no doubt as to who should replace the broken Nivelle. On May 17 Pétain, soon heard to mutter, "they only call me in catastrophes," took over as commander in chief of an army that was beyond hope. His achievements over the months that followed are often, tragically, overshadowed by the role he played as head of the Vichy state in 1940–44. Yet there can be no doubt that Pétain deserved well of France that terrible spring. He immediately issued a directive forbidding major attacks: henceforth they were to be conducted "economically with infantry and with a maximum of artillery." Leave was increased: units out of the line might send 25 or even 50 percent of their men home. Steps were taken to ensure that men did not waste their leave waiting for trains that never came, at stations whose buffets charged prices they could never afford. Leave trains became more regular, and soldiers' canteens widespread.

Pétain visited his regiments, talking to officers and men, assuring them of his commitment to small attacks and determination to await the arrival of the Americans before launching a major, properly coordinated, offensive. He an-

NOUVELLE GÉNÉRATION

"Et toi, mon petit, qu'est-ce que tu feras quand tu auras vingt ans?"
"Je mourrai pour la patrie, m'sieur!"

This cartoon in the satirical journal *Le Canard Enchaîné* depicts an elderly man asking a boy what he will do when he is twenty. "I shall die for the country, sir!" he replies.

nounced a pay rise for veterans and the award of a decoration for distinguished units. He found out what men thought: monotonous food and decorations that seemed to get hijacked by the staff were common causes of complaint. He looked hard at the rear areas, ensuring that troops at rest were not worn out with fatigue duties and had proper facilities for getting themselves and their uniforms clean.

And he gripped discipline. For while Pétain was fair, he was unquestionably firm. On June 1 he delegated authority to convene summary courts-martial, and Painlevé managed to persuade the President of the Republic to waive his right to reviewing their sentences "in cases where discipline and national defense require an immediate penalty." Pétain went on to assure officers that those who acted with "vigor and energy" in suppressing mutiny were assured of his full support. Painlevé later claimed that only twenty-three men were shot. This is unquestionably an underestimate, but suggestions that whole batches of mutineers were led off to quiet sectors and wiped out by their own artillery err in the other direction.

There were two clear indications that the Pétain method was working. On Bastille Day, July 14, the government risked routing the traditional parade through the working-class district of Paris. There were no jeers and catcalls at the President, and growing applause from the spectators as the men in horizon blue swung past. Two weeks later the French launched an attack north of Ypres, taking three lines of German trenches for the loss of fewer than two hundred men killed. Other, meticulously prepared, attacks took the Fort de la Malmaison on the Chemin des Dames and the Mort Homme at Verdun. The French army was recovering its spirits.

It was to do so with weighty political support. On July 22 the seventy-five-year-old Georges Clemenceau rose in the Senate to denounce what he called the "anti-patriotism," and to attack ministers, who had failed to suppress the anti-military newspaper *Le Bonnet Rouge*. The government fell in September, and Painlevé headed a new administration which speedily ran into difficulties and folded in mid-November. President Poincaré summoned all the old names, but none would do; then, on the afternoon of November 14, he invited Clemenceau to form a government. The old man did so, going on to tell a packed chamber that his policy was simple enough: "to conduct the war with redoubled energy." He was harsh, autocratic, and remorseless. He stumped about the front in a battered hat and shabby coat, making it quite clear to all that his simple motto went to the heart of the matter: "I wage war."

ARRAS AND VIMY The British army, meanwhile, was waging war on its own account. On April 9 it launched the Battle of Arras, intended to pin German troops to Artois and prevent reserves moving south to face Robert Nivelle. The first day of battle was remarkably successful. The Canadian Corps, attacking with its four divisions side by side, took Vimy Ridge, a remarkable feat of arms which not merely secured this dominant ground against which the Allied wave had lapped for nearly three years, but struck a mighty blow for Canadian national consciousness. 3rd Army made good progress east of Arras, its gunners laying on heavy, well-orchestrated barrages in which the new 106 fuse, which burst when it grazed barbed wire, played a prominent part. Further south, 5th Army's attack on Bullecourt was mishandled, leading to acrimony between the attacking Australians and the tanks whose support had misfired.

Yet even at Arras, where the British had bitten deep into German defenses—Ludendorff acknowledged "a bad beginning for the decisive struggle of this year"—success could not be reinforced. It was not until the afternoon of the 10th that Allenby, the army commander, realized quite what damage had been done to the Germans. That night he told his troops that they were "pursuing a defeated enemy," and on the 11th sought to press the pursuit by sending in the cavalry.

By now the defensive crust had hardened, and the diary of the German 125th Regiment records: "We stood up as on a rifle range and, laughing, greeted this rare target with a hail of bullets." When a more formal attack went in on the 14th it was very roughly handled. The long ridges and shallow valleys enabled the Germans to employ elastic defense at its best, giving ground before the attack so that "the deeper [it] penetrates into the defender's position, the more it will find itself faced by surprise and unforeseen conditions." The collapse of the Nivelle offensive compelled Haig to continue the battle, and daily loss rates between April 9 and May 17 averaged 4,070 men, a figure matched only by the German March offensive the following year.

SINEWS OF WAR

By now the British were administratively prepared for battle to a remarkable degree. Logisticians are the Cinderellas of warfare, whose efforts are usually only recognized, by soldiers and historians alike, when they fail. By this stage in the war British logisticians had mastered their prodigious task. In part this was due to Haig's recognition that civilian experts, invested with temporary military rank, could solve problems on a scale that might baffle professional soldiers. In 1916 Sir Eric Geddes, a railway magnate, was appointed Director General of Transportation in France. His was an appropriate speciality, for by 1918 the BEF was using nine hundred locomotives, which traveled nine million track miles each month, carrying eight hundred thousand tons of equipment and two hundred sixty thousand of ammunition.

Increasingly efficient sea transport, docking, and warehousing helped the BEF import stores of all sorts. During the whole war 5,253,538 tons of ammunition were shipped to France, but even this was exceeded by the 5,438,603 tons of fodder for the army's horses and mules. The BEF's animal strength peaked at 449,800 in 1917. In the army's enormous reliance on horses and mules, we see another facet of the war's ancient and modern character, for by 1917 the BEF was also using six million gallons of petrol every month. By mid-1917 Haig's logistics, and the procurement system on which they in turn relied, were so robust as to give British planners the luxury of working with little constraint. For much of that summer British field gunners regularly fired a half million shells a day. Million-shell days were not uncommon and, during the Passchendaele battle, even this prodigious total was almost doubled on two occasions.

Haig, as we have seen, had long favored an offensive in Flanders, and he now found himself in a position to attack on ground of his choosing. We cannot be certain of the degree to which the French mutinies provided him with an added incentive for the Flanders battle, but it seems likely that the scale of the indiscipline was not fully known at GHQ. On May 15 Haig's intelligence officer, John Charteris, wrote that Lord Esher, with whom he had dined, told him that "the morale of the whole nation has been badly affected by the failure of their attack," and on the 19th he reported "very serious trouble" in the French army. Haig was visited by Pétain's chief of staff in early June, and confided to his diary that the French army was "in a bad state of discipline." At the very least this meant that there would be little French help for the Flanders offensive: Haig could certainly not rely on the sort of reciprocity extended to Nivelle that spring.

In Haig's mind the offensive had two linked aims. The first, well outlined in a sketch-map handed to Pétain on May 18, was for a two-phase advance from Ypres, the first extending as far as Passchendaele, and the second reaching out as far as Roulers and Thorout. A landing between Middelkerke and Ostend would be timed to coincide with the latter. The same month he told the War Cabinet that even if he failed in this aim, "we shall be attacking the enemy on a front where he cannot refuse to fight, and where, therefore, our purpose of wearing him down can be given effect to."

It was, in short, a repetition of the previous year's concept. There were objectives toward which the army would maneuver, and by doing so it would contribute to the steady attrition of German manpower. The notion of attrition continues to provoke shudders, but at the time its merits were, if not widely welcomed, then at least clearly articulated. When Lieutenant General Sir Ivor Maxse, whose biography is rightly called *Far from a Donkey*, addressed a platoon commander's course that May he told it: "*You have to defeat the German Army. You cannot measure your task by miles any more than you can measure a man's courage by his height.*" Early in May a conference in Paris concluded that the war-winning Allied offensive would have to wait until the Americans were present in strength in 1918. In the meantime, if they could not win the war, the Allies had to prevent the Germans from doing so, and could best accomplish this by mounting limited offensives. Haig briefed his army commanders on the 7th, confirming that the Arras operation would be scaled down as the army's weight was shifted to Flanders. There would be two distinct attacks: a curtain raiser designed to take Messines Ridge, south

British soldiers posted to France passed through Etaples for training. Instructors, called "canaries" because of their yellow arm bands, were notoriously unsympathetic, and troops mutinied here in 1917.

of Ypres, and then, some weeks later, the "Northern Operation" aimed at Passchendaele Ridge and beyond.

The whole of the Ypres salient was by now thoroughly battered after two and a half years of fighting, and Ypres itself, once crowned by its magnificent Cloth Hall, had been reduced to rubble. Yet the salient's topographical features endured. Although, like the planners of the period, we tend to speak of separate ridges, there is in fact one long, irregular ridge running down from Westroosebeke and Passchendaele northeast of Ypres, through Wytschaete to the town's south. Spurs, in effect smaller ridges in themselves, run off it. One goes almost north–south from Wytschaete to Messines, and another bulges eastward in the very center of the main ridge, to form the Gheluvelt plateau, with the Menin Road Ridge rising to its east. The ridge is low and undistinguished: the Gheluvelt plateau rises to only 213 feet and even Messines Ridge attains only 264 feet.

There were woods in the salient, especially around the Gheluvelt plateau, where Polygon Wood, Glencorse Wood, Nonne Bosschen, and Shrewsbury Forest still remained recognizable, though shelling was soon to change that. The many streams that drained the ridge's western slopes, like the Steenbeek and the Stroombeek, ran to join the little River Yser north of Ypres, their course often taking them across the British line of attack. As John Hussey has pointed out, the terrain is not dissimilar to, say, the area around York or Newark: low-lying, certainly, but not "some monsoon-like tropical swamp." However, the ground was not good for a war dominated by artillery: the drainage system was easily disrupted, and the soil—London clay, with layers of sand and silt—readily turned into mud.

None of this was a surprise to GHQ, which warned in May that a few hours of rain might swell the brooks and make operations impossible for twenty-four hours, while: "A few weeks' rain may make the whole country impracticable for prolonged operations for at least one week." This, coupled with John Charteris's assertion that in August the weather broke in Flanders "with the regularity of the Indian monsoon" has led Haig's critics to suggest that the battlefield would inevitably become flooded. John Hussey's careful analysis in the very valuable *Passchendaele in Perspective* disproves this. From a meteorologist's standpoint, "August might be expected to be reasonably dry, not abnormally wet." This expectation proved false. As Haig's chief meteorologist, Lieutenant Colonel Ernest Gold, later observed, the rainfall during the five months of the offensive was over five times heavier than for the same period in 1915 and 1916. The ground of the salient would certainly be rendered very difficult indeed by the combination of shelling and bad weather. The latter was not a foregone conclusion, however, and by attacking in the salient Haig took, as commanders sometimes must, a calculated risk. It did not pay off.

The German army's defense of the sector reflected the lessons of the Somme as embodied in its December 1916 pamphlet *The Principles of Command in the Defensive Battle in Position Warfare*. Anglo-American historians are sometimes given to overcelebrating German military excellence, but in terms of doctrinal development the Germans were clearly ahead of their opponents: they were good at analyzing the results of a battle, turning this analysis into doctrine, and then training troops in the latest methods.

The new principles, embodying the elastic defense we have already seen used against Nivelle, stressed that the defender should seek to disrupt the attacker, not to hold his ground at all costs. Ground should be covered by fire, not held by men. The defender should never surrender the initiative, and must consider depth—in the sense of depth from front to rear—whenever positions were sited. There would be a number of defensive positions, each consisting of three lines. First came a lightly held outpost zone, giving security and observation, probably on a forward slope. Next was the battle zone, ideally situated on a reverse slope, with trenches and pillboxes. Finally, the rearward zone or "artillery protection line" came about a mile behind the battle zone, with the bulk of the field batteries in and just behind it. The next belt of defenses, similarly organized, would be far enough behind for the attacker to have to shift his field guns after a successful attack on the first position. Although arrangements differed on Messines Ridge, where the narrowness of the ridge suggested slight changes, by the time the main battle opened the northern sector was held by a strong front position (the Albrecht and Wilhelm lines) with a third line and three successive belts of defenses—code-named Flandern I, II, and III—behind it. Flandern I was complete, Flandern II marked out by wire entanglements and pillboxes, and Flandern III simply sketched out.

In 1915 the Germans had dispensed with the brigade, and in 1917 their division consisted of three regiments of three battalions each, a three-battalion field artillery regiment, a heavy artillery battalion, and assorted supporting units. It would usually post its regiments side by side, with a battalion each in the three defense zones. Battalions in the battle and rearward zones were expected to counterattack when the opportunity offered. It was stressed that while immediate counterattacks often worked, if they were delayed by more than perhaps half an hour, the attacker would have brought up his own machine guns and adjusted his artillery fire; then they were likely to fail.

Formal counterstrokes were to be carried out by counterattack divisions, usually posted at the ratio of one for every two front-line divisions. They would try to choose the moment when the attacker was embedded in the battle zone, nearing the limit of his own artillery support and getting through key trench-fighting resources such as hand grenades. Then their barrage would wall him off from his supports and supplies while their infantry lunged forward. Counterattack divisions were specially trained in their tasks, and when actually used came under the command of the line-holding division whose commander, it was argued, would have his finger on the battle's pulse.

MESSINES RIDGE

The Messines attack was to be carried out by Plumer's 2nd Army. Generals' nicknames are indicative of their troops' regard for them, and not for nothing was Sir Herbert Plumer known as "Daddy." Although his red face, white mustache, and tubby build provided the model for the cartoonist Low's character Colonel Blimp, Plumer was an infantry officer with a deep understanding of trench warfare and a determination not to waste lives. His chief of staff, Sir Charles "Tim" Harington, was a careful planner and, as is often the case with successful "military marriages" between commanders and chiefs of staff, it was hard to see where one began and the other ended.

Plumer intended to take Messines Ridge by attacking on a ten-mile front with three corps in line and one in reserve. Each attacking corps would advance with three of its divisions up and one in reserve. Some preparations had been made for earlier planned attacks. Miners in particular had been at work since 1915, and there were now more than thirty-thousand men in Australian, British, and Canadian tunneling companies. The technical difficulties of digging around Messines were enormous, as miners had to penetrate a surface layer, then a layer of quicksand and finally enter blue clay, which expanded in contact with the air, to dig deep offensive tunnels beneath the German lines. A shallower defensive gallery, designed to detect and disrupt German mining, ran parallel with the front line. Mining was one area where the British enjoyed clear ascendancy, but German miners could not be disregarded, and hit back when they could, blowing in tunnels with small mines—camouflets—of their own, or breaking into them to fight at close quarters. The best modern research suggests that there were in fact twenty-four mines loaded with a million pounds of ammonal explosive, much of it sealed into metal containers to protect it from the wet.

Sapper Jack Lyon of 171 Tunneling Company Royal Engineers described how he worked as part of a twelve-man shift under a corporal. Three men worked at the tunnel face, one "clay-kicking," lying on his back on a plank inclined between floor and roof, using both feet to jab a short spade into the clay. One of his mates put the clay into a sandbag, and the third dragged the bag back to the start of the trolley rails. Three men worked the trolleys, another operated the air pump, and the remainder helped get the sandbags up to the surface. All were volunteers, either Royal Engineers or "permanently attached" infantry, usually miners who had joined the infantry at the start of the war. All worked three shifts in two days and then had a day's rest. After fifteen days, recalled Sapper Lyon, "We went down for a bath and delousing operation, the latter being only partially successful."

Other preparations were more recent. Water pipelines were laid to supply each corps with one hundred and fifty thousand gallons a day, and new light railways were built to carry ammunition and supplies forward. Plumer's own artillery was boosted by batteries from other armies to give him 2,266 guns, 756 of them heavy or medium, with an average of 1,000 rounds for each 18-pounder stacked on the gunline and a total of 144,000 tons of ammunition dumped. Pillboxes on the forward slopes of the ridge were engaged methodically by British heavy guns, and both trench lines and battery positions were repeatedly hammered: between May 26 and June 1 the Royal Artillery fired

MESSINES 1917

0 — 1 Mile	
0 — 1 Kilometer	
British Front Line	————
British divisions	**47**
British Mines	○ St-Eloi
German positions	{ --- --- / -·-·- / ·······
German divisions	35

to Ypres

X

Observatory Ridge

Caterpillar ○ Hill 60

Mount Sorrel

47

Ypres-Comines Canal

The Bluff

204

German Front Line

41
St-Eloi •

○ St-Eloi

35

19

British Front Line

Bois Quarante
Grand Bois

Second Line

Oosttaverne Line

Warneton Line

to Comines →

• Vierstraat

Hollandscheschuur Farm

2

Oosttaverne •

IX   16

○○ Petit Bois

Moedelstede Farm — ○

• Wytschaete

Peckham — ○

Spanbroekmolen
36

○○ Krùisstraat

3 Bav

Ontario Farm

Steenbeek

Messines ⊙

• Wulverghem

25

NZ

Petite Douve Farm

R. Douve

II ANZAC

Avenue Farm

4 Bav

• Warneton

N
W — E
S

Trench 127

Hill 63   **3 Aus**   St-Yves •   Trench 122

R. Lys

Ploegsteert Wood

LEFT Field-Marshal Viscount Plumer of Messines, who took his title from 2nd Army's victory, inspecting a guard of honor.
ABOVE An Australian tunneler demonstrates breathing apparatus used to filter gas or foul air. A caged canary gave warning of gas

three and a half million shells into the German lines. When the attack began there would be a creeping barrage moving ahead of the infantry, while standing barrages blocked off counterattack divisions and counterbattery groups took on German batteries that had escaped the preliminary bombardment. The fire was unusually effective. British artillery spotters enjoyed good observation from Kemmel Hill, and supplemented this with captive balloons and observation aircraft. Plumer had three hundred of the RFC's machines at his disposal, outnumbering the Germans by two to one. Seventy-two of the new Mark IV tanks were available, although in practice the terrain was too bad for them to prove very useful.

General von Laffert, of XIX Corps of the German Fourth Army, knew that an attack was on its way but was optimistic that he could deal with it. Because much British mining had been completed earlier, his own miners had been lulled into a false sense of security. At a meeting on April 30 the chief of staff of Rupprecht's army group suggested that Laffert might withdraw to the third (Oostaverne Line) or even the fourth (Warneton Line) of the defensive lines on and behind the ridge, but Laffert demurred: he would stay where he was.

At the end of May, XIX Corps had four of its divisions (from the north

204th, 24th, 2nd, and 40th) in line and two counterattack divisions (35th and 3rd Bavarian) behind it. Such was the toll inflicted on his line-holding divisions that Laffert used the counterattack divisions to replace the two hardest-hit, 24th and 40th. These were pulled out to refit, and two fresh divisions, 7th and 1st Guard Reserve, were given the counterattack role. This decision was to cost Laffert his job. The new troops did not know the ground, while their predecessors had rehearsed the counterattack task. The shelling also damaged Laffert's batteries: he had 630 guns, and had lost a quarter of his field pieces and nearly half his heavies before the battle started. Pillboxes, which resisted everything but direct hits by heavy guns, stood the bombardment well, but the trenches between them vanished, and their garrisons were worn out by the strain.

A German soldier described the anguish of enduring the bombardment. "All the trenches are completely smashed in," he wrote, "no more shelter is to hand, battery emplacements up to six feet thick are completely destroyed, and even twenty-foot-deep galleries are not safe from guns of heavy caliber— thus we are forced out into the open without any protection."

At 3:10 on the morning of June 7 nineteen mines exploded below Messines Ridge with a blast so savage that it was heard in London and an observatory on the Isle of Wight detected it on its seismograph. The professor of geology at Lille University, over twelve miles away, sprang from bed thinking that there had been an earthquake, and looked out of his window to see German soldiers running panic-stricken about the streets. Some defenders were simply vaporized by the blast; others were buried by tons of earth. The war correspondent Philip Gibbs described the sight as:

> The most diabolical splendor I have ever seen. Out of the dark ridges of Messines and Wytschaete and that ill famed Hill 60 there gushed out and up enormous volumes of scarlet flame from the exploding mines and of earth and smoke all lighted up by the flame spilling over into mountains of fierce colour, so that the countryside was illuminated by red light.

Survivors were pale and half crazy: one British soldier recalled them "running toward us shaking like jellies."

The outpost line fell quickly, and the attackers regrouped for the assault on the second line, covered by a protective barrage. The second phase of the attack began at 7:00 A.M., and although some German units fought back with determination, they managed to hold their ground only on the far left of the attack. Frank Dunham, a stretcher bearer with a London battalion, saw just how successful the artillery had been in paving the way for the infantry.

> All the small dug-outs were bashed in and even some of the larger concrete ones were badly damaged. . . . These prisoners were scared and fatigued, and we learned later that due to our heavy shelling they had received very few rations and had served longer in the front line as relieving troops could not reach them.

As his company was making for its objective, a ruined château, he saw his former company commander, Captain "Gussy" Collins. "He was strolling about the battlefield," recalled Dunham, "carrying his cane and wearing his renowned monocle as though doing some training exercise. As he came level with our company he shouted, 'Haven't you captured the bally place yet?'"

The attackers paused again for the assault on the third line, but, halting on the crest of the ridge, came under heavy fire as they did so. Plumer, fearing that it would take longer than planned to bring up the reserve division in each corps to launch the next phase of the attack, postponed it by two hours, and it was not until 3:10 in the afternoon that it was delivered. It was generally successful, and by nightfall most of the third line had been taken.

The two counterattack divisions had been alerted at 3:30 that morning, but concern about the direction of the British attack persuaded 4th Army to retain control of them till after 7:00 and, being new to the area, it took them some time to make their way forward. Both were shelled as they moved up. 7th Division reached the third line only to find the attackers already there, while 1st Guard Reserve reached the outskirts of Messines just as the attack on the third line went in: it was shoved back with heavy losses.

The day was a considerable success for Plumer. Although he had lost nearly twenty-five thousand men, most of them from II Anzac Corps, he had taken more than seven thousand prisoners, 48 guns, and 218 machine guns, and killed or wounded at least thirteen thousand Germans. The battle is a graphic illustration of the strengths and weaknesses of the British army at this stage in the war, and sends echoes on into the Second World War. It was a classic "teed-up" battle, and the future Field Marshal Montgomery, then a junior staff officer, learned useful lessons serving with IX Corps. Preparation and planning were first-rate, and briefing and rehearsal had been comprehensive. The artillery fire plan was well conceived and flawlessly executed, and in it we see one of the ingredients of Passchendaele: the growing dominance of British gunners. The infantry attacked with a resolution that again foreshadowed Passchendaele.

Messines Ridge, seen from across the valley of the Douve:
a bombardment is in progress.

The training of British infantry had improved considerably since the
Somme. Yet at Messines there were times—notably during the long and
costly pause on the ridge—when British infantry seemed, at least to their opponents, to be lumpy and lacking in initiative. One German regiment, fresh
from the Eastern Front, thought the tactical handling of British infantry to
be worse than that of the Russian. Many German guns were in danger of
capture on the reverse slope of the ridge, and the delay enabled most of them
to be got away.

For all this the battle was an impressive victory. Even the redoubtable
Rupprecht was shaken, and suspected that the next blow would fall without
delay on what he regarded as the vital ground in his defenses, the Gheluvelt
plateau, where so many of his batteries were tucked into the woods or hidden
behind the ridge. Why else, he argued, would the British have attacked
Messines Ridge if not to exploit its capture promptly?

**THE THIRD
BATTLE OF
YPRES**

Haig was in no position to follow the capture of
Messines Ridge with a swift second blow. The government had made it clear that the main Flanders offensive was conditional on French support, and Haig
knew that this would not be forthcoming on the scale for which he hoped.

Lloyd George had flirted with other theaters of war, and feared that an attack at Ypres could well turn into a ghastly rerun of the Somme. However, Haig remained anxious to attack in Flanders for the reasons we have already explored, and on June 12 he told Robertson:

> If our resources are concentrated in France to the fullest possible extent the British armies are capable and can be relied on to effect great results this summer—results which will make final victory more assured and may even bring it within reach this year.

Haig was authorized to "continue his preparations for the present" and it was not till July 25, six days before the attack began, that he was formally authorized to launch it.

Haig's instrument was Sir Hubert Gough of 5th Army, at forty-seven the youngest of the army commanders, a cavalryman with a reputation for dash which, it was felt, would prove useful if a German collapse was followed by mobile operations. Gough felt that it was a mistake to send him to "a bit of ground with which I had practically no acquaintance." However, he duly handed over the Croisilles–Havrincourt sector to 3rd Army at the end of May and moved his headquarters to Louvie Château, eight miles west-northwest of Ypres. GHQ gave him four corps, each of four divisions—II, XIX, XVIII, and XIV—with the single-division VIII Corps in reserve and V Corps, also with a single division, in GHQ reserve. His artillery comprised 752 heavy and 1,422 field guns. He had three tank brigades of 72 machines each, and 406 aircraft. Staff officers used to 2nd Army's methodical ways noted the change at once. Major Walter Guinness, a brigade major in 25th Division, noted that 5th Army seemed "very haphazard in its methods," and there is little doubt that the slapdash qualities of Gough's staff played their part in what followed.

In outline the British plan made good sense. First, there were the flanking thrusts. On Gough's right, the much-reduced 2nd Army would attack the outposts of Flandern I to fix German reserves. On his left, the French 1st Army would thrust towards Bixschoote. Rawlinson, commanding the rump of 4th Army, would attack in the coastal sector, and an amphibious landing, with specially built landing craft, had been prepared. 1st Army would send diversionary attacks toward Lens and Lille in an effort to attract Rupprecht's attention.

Gough's main attack, to be launched on July 31, would take Pilckem Ridge north of Ypres and the Gheluvelt plateau to the town's east before swinging northeastward to reach the Roulers–Thourout railway on August 7–8. At this period the tide would favor Rawlinson's coastal attack and the amphibious landing, and Gough and Rawlinson would then link up and push on through Bruges to the Dutch frontier. Gough was quite clear that Haig really intended him to break through:

> He quite clearly told me that the plan was to capture Passchendaele Ridge, and to advance as rapidly as possibly on Roulers. I was then to advance on Ostend. This was very definitely viewing the battle as an attempt to break through, and Haig never altered his opinion till the attack was launched, as far as I know.

Just as Haig and Rawlinson had disagreed over the plan for the Somme, so he and Gough differed over the detailed planning for Third Ypres. This time it was GHQ that was conservative and army headquarters radical. Gough decided to make the third line of the front position his first objective. After pausing there for a few hours, the attack would push on to the line Broodseinde–Gravestafel–Langemarck, and go even deeper if German resistance slackened. Haig's staff found this overambitious, and although Haig allowed it to stand he warned Gough that the Gheluvelt plateau was the vital ground and suggested to him that the Germans would pivot on it if they lost ground further north.

In the meantime, Colonel Fritz von Lossberg, the German army's leading expert on defensive tactics, arrived at Courtrai to take over as chief of staff of Fourth Army. Arnim, who knew him well, gave him a free hand, and he immediately rejected any idea of withdrawal to conform with the ground lost at Messines, and ordered work to be redoubled on the three Flandern lines. On June 30 Rupprecht's chief of staff suggested pulling back to Flandern I to disrupt British preparations, but Lossberg disagreed, arguing that the first line, where he would fight the battle as long as possible, would take much of the sting out of the attack long before it reached Flandern I.

His men would shelter from the inevitable bombardment in the large concrete bunkers which remain a feature of the Flanders landscape, and when the barrage lifted they would emerge to fight from the surrounding shell holes. Junior commanders were allowed as much initiative as possible, and could move about to avoid heavy shelling. The brunt of the attack would be borne by III Bavarian Corps, holding the six miles of front from Pilckem to the Menin Road, with three front-line divisions and two counterattack divisions.

THE GERMAN FLANDERS POSITIONS
JULY 1917

**THE FIRST AT-
TACKS:**

PILCKEM RIDGE,
GHELUVELT
PLATEAU AND
LANGEMARCK

The bombardment began on July 16, and in its course the gunners of 2nd and 5th Armies fired four and a half million rounds. The target was wider and deeper than at Messines, and air observation was hampered by the fact that the Germans fought hard for the sky: it was not until the end of July that the RFC had the edge. Although the shelling wrought severe damage to German positions, killed and wounded many of their defenders, and pushed many more to the edge of collapse, it also broke up the drainage system and smashed the woods, making much of field and woodland alike impassable to tanks.

The long-awaited attack began at 3:50 on the morning of July 31. On the right II Corps fought its way into Westhoek and Shrewsbury Forest, gaining a firm foothold on the Gheluvelt plateau, and XIX Corps, on its left, took Frezenberg and reached the line Zonnebeke–Langemarck. The two left-hand corps, XVIII and XIV, did well at first, overrunning Pilckem Ridge, but were heavily shelled and counterattacked in the afternoon. And then the weather broke, turning the Steenbeek, straddled by the northern corps, into a quagmire: a gunner officer reported that the infantry were up to their waists in water. The day's advance averaged some three thousand yards at a cost of thirty thousand casualties—roughly similar to those suffered by the Germans in bombardment and battle. But already half the tanks were out of action, knocked out or bogged, and the battlefield was breaking up.

In the days that followed, Gough, heeding Haig's insistence that the Gheluvelt plateau was indeed the vital ground, renewed his efforts. However, the rain continued ceaselessly, converting the shelled area into a huge marsh, and German guns on the plateau were unusually effective. Second Lieutenant Gerry Brooks, his memoirs preserved in the wonderful Liddle Archive at the University of Leeds, was commanding the tank *Fay* on 2 August, and describes just how difficult the ground was:

The fun began when the tape we were following led through some very swampy ground. It was so wet we found it hard to swing. The four of us [tanks] got rather bunched and the Foam received a couple of direct hits and Harris her commander and two more of the crew were wounded. Harris was in great pain having his left arm nearly blown off from the elbow and also armor plate and rivets in his leg.... We passed a good many dead who had fallen on July 31st. Soon we came up to our infantry who were hiding in shell holes with very heavy machine-gun fire. This pattered against our armor and some came through in a fine spray so that we were all soon bleeding from small cuts.

Fay bogged down shortly afterward and her crew abandoned her: one was shot dead as he did so. Although Brooks found himself surrounded by counterattacking German infantry, he managed to escape.

When II Corps attacked on 10 August its center division, 18th, reached Westhoek and Glencorse Wood. That afternoon it was viciously counterattacked from Nonne Bosschen and Polygon Wood and driven back with heavy loss. Although the corps commanders proposed to try again, the weather was so filthy that the attack was canceled.

The weather prevented Gough from trying again till August 16. He had already committed eight divisions held in reserve, and another two, sent across from 2nd Army, were soon caught up in the battle. II Corps tried to improve the results of the 10th by sending its battalions forward toward Polygon Wood on a front of only 250 yards, pushing reserves through them as they paused on an intermediate line, but progress was poor. Further north, XIX attacked with 16th Irish Division on its left and 36th Ulster Division on its right. These formations had already fought hard at Messines, and had been living in the misery of the Ypres battlefield for a fortnight. It is to the enduring credit of soldiers from both sides of Ireland's cultural divide that they pushed well up the ridge beyond the Hanebeek and into the German pillboxes. Then the inevitable counterattack swept them away, and the corps commander pulled the survivors back to the start line. In the north, XVIII and XIV Corps, attacking Langemarck on better ground and with artillery support well-observed from Pilckem Ridge, took the village. To their left the French 1st Army pressed forward on to the St-Jansbeek.

There were further major attacks on August 22 and 24, and a number of minor operations. 5th Army had now lost sixty thousand men, and fourteen of its twenty-two divisions had been withdrawn to refit. Its gains had not been derisory, but the Gheluvelt plateau was still firmly in German hands. The weather was simply atrocious. Corporal Robert Chambers of the Bedfords wrote that it was "raining like fury. Everywhere a quagmire. Fancy fighting Germans for a land like this. If it were mine I'd give them the whole damn rotten country."

These appalling conditions were no secret to commanders and their staff. On August 16 Gough visited Haig, and "informed the Commander in Chief that tactical success was not possible and would be too costly under these conditions, and advised that the attack should now be abandoned." The next day Charteris assured Haig that German morale was deteriorating steadily, and that German manpower could not stand the strain "for more than a limited number of months (a maximum of twelve months) provided that the fighting is maintained at its present intensity in France and Belgium." Haig was determined to continue the battle, but decided to place its conduct in the hands of Plumer.

2ND ARMY TAKES OVER:
MENIN ROAD RIDGE, POLYGON WOOD AND BROODSEINDE

Plumer was directed to take the Gheluvelt plateau, and proposed a four-phase operation, spearheaded by X and I Anzac Corps with II Anzac in reserve. The southern part of his front was entrusted to IX and VIII Corps, with only three divisions between them. He had 1,295 guns to support the assault, and bid for 3.5 million shells. Although he had been required to take over 5th Army's front as far as the Ypres–Roulers railway line, he was still attacking with twice the force over half the frontage assailed on July 31, with about double the artillery support.

Plumer's staff had thought hard about the problem of dealing with deep defense backed by counterattack divisions. Artillery would not merely destroy defenses, neutralize defenders, and suppress German guns: it would protect the attackers from counterattack with standing barrages and also reach out to disrupt counterattack divisions on their way forward. Loosely grouped skirmishers would lead the advance, followed by main assault parties, with mopping-up groups moving at the rear. Each attack would have three bounds, with pauses between them to permit consolidation and allow fresh units to move up through those which had led on the previous bound. Reserves were on hand at the rate of a platoon per company, and so on up: behind each attack division stood a reserve division. This was attack in depth, and with units extended back for almost eight miles it looked not dissimilar to the defensive system it proposed to break. Characteristically, Plumer's staff paid special attention to sorting out roads and light railways in the rear areas. They were also lucky: the rain stopped, and troops found themselves basking in the sun.

The bombardment began on August 31 and the infantry attacked at 5:40 on the morning of September 20. They moved quickly behind the creeping barrage, and by midday 2nd Army had reached most of its objectives on the ridge, overrunning much of the Wilhelm Line. 5th Army, attacking on its left, also made good progress. Then, when the counterattack was launched, British guns drew a curtain of fire in front of the newly captured positions and raked the three fresh divisions as they came up, rendering them ineffective. General von Kuhl, Rupprecht's chief of staff, admitted: "our counterattack divisions arrived too late. Their blow came up against a defensive position already organized in depth and protected by an artillery barrage." Most remaining objectives were seized in the next few days, and Plumer's first step had taken much of the vital ground.

The battle looked different to participants. Lieutenant Firstbrooke Clarke of the North Staffordshires wrote:

> I suppose to people at home it is a fine victory. Well, so it is but they don't see the dead and wounded lying out and they don't have 9.2s bursting 10 yards away, machine-gun bullets scraping a parapet. I lost 17 of my platoon (4 killed) besides the casualties in the rest of the Coy [Company]. I was so sick of it and upset that I cried when I got back.

The second step, taken on September 26, saw Plumer's Australians take Polygon Wood while 5th Army took Zonnebeke. These gains made it easier for British observers to see counterattack divisions moving up, and the Germans now changed their policy, pushing more troops forward and emphasizing the need for full artillery preparation before formal counterattacks went in. The new system was put to the test when Plumer took his third step on October 4. The sheer vigor of the two Anzac Corps took them deep into Flandern I east of Zonnebeke. The prominent Windmill Hill, northwest of Zonnebeke on the Langemarck road, was stormed by 3rd Australian Division on one of the few occasions when large-scale bayonet fighting took place. 5th Army kept pace, gaining a foothold in Flandern I and taking Poelcappelle.

It was a bad day for the Germans. Ludendorff acknowledged that "the idea of holding the front line more densely . . . was not the answer." The Germans were now losing more men than the British, and they redrafted their defensive tactics yet again, this time relying on a thin line of sentries with a few machine guns, backed by a main line of resistance spread deeply about the shell holes and pillboxes behind it. There would now be one counterattack for one line-holding division, the latter on a frontage of only just over a mile.

By now the experience of Ypres, fighting in stinking mud littered with the ruins of farms and villages, the shattered stumps of trees, and the corpses of men and horses, had etched itself deeply into the minds of the soldiers on both sides. The mud was so deep that a gun platform for an 18-pounder needed a foundation of fascines (bundles of brushwood) and road metal, with two layers of thick planks laid on top: even then it might last for only twenty-four hours. Men who lost their footing moving up in the dark risked drowning in the mire. One unnamed soldier told how he and his comrades tried to rescue a man sinking slowly in the mud. They could not, and eventually: "I shot this man at his most urgent request, thus releasing him from a far more agonizing end."

Lieutenant Edwin Campion Vaughan of the Royal Warwicks sheltered in a captured pillbox while:

> From the darkness on all sides came the groans and wails of wounded men; faint, long, sobbing moans of agony, and despairing shrieks. It was too horribly obvious to me that dozens of men with serious wounds must have crawled for safety into shell-holes, and now the water was rising above them and, powerless to move, they were slowly drowning.

An Australian officer, Lieutenant Russell Harris, recalled "the feeling of frustration at having been unable at times to go to the help of men trapped in those mudholes.... It was impossible to shut one's ears to their cries, and when silence came it was almost like a physical blow, engendering a feeling bordering on guilt."

Both sides used gas from time to time, and its insidious presence added a further ghastly complication. Alan Hanbury-Sparrow sat in a dugout as it rocked with the bombardment, feeling only half a man in his gas mask. "You can't think; the air you breathe has been filtered of all save a few chemical substances," he wrote. "A man doesn't live on what passes through the filter, he merely exists."

The Germans were driven to "grey desperation" by the conditions which most reckoned to be worse even than those at Verdun. "The hard times experienced here exceed everything which we have gone through before," wrote one soldier.

> It is horrible. You often wish you were dead, there is no shelter, we are lying in water, everything is misery, the fire does not cease for a moment night and day, our clothes do not dry. The worst, however, is the setting in of vomiting and diarrhea.

PREVIOUS PAGES C.R.W. Nevinson's *After the Push* shows the blighted landscape of Passchendaele.
ABOVE A German pillbox near Zonnebeke, captured by the Australians in September 1917.

Although the bunkers withstood direct hits, they sometimes slid into nearby shell craters, trapping those inside. "There was no way of rescuing them," recalled an officer, "and we suffered rather heavy casualties this way, not to speak of the painfully slow death of those trapped inside."

LAST GASP:
POELCAPPELLE
AND
PASSCHENDAELE

The weather broke again after October 4, and on the 5th both Gough and Plumer told Haig that it was time the campaign ended. It was evident that its tactical objectives could no longer be achieved. Rawlinson's coastal operation had been thwarted by well-timed German shelling in mid-July (a deserter had given vital information), and the amphibious assault had been shelved. It now seems clear that Haig ought to have stopped, and Charteris admitted that most of those at the October 5 conference "though willing to go on, would welcome a stop." But the Australian Official History is more generous, saying: "let the student, looking at the prospect as it appeared at noon on October 4, ask himself: 'In view of three step by step blows, what will be the result of three more in the next fortnight?'"

The Battle of Poelcappelle began on October 9 and went wrong from the start. Charteris watched it—so much for the gilded staff which never left the château. He thought it "the saddest day of the year. It was not the enemy but the mud that prevented us doing better.... Yesterday afternoon was utterly damnable. I got back very late and could not work, and could not rest." Gains were negligible and losses high. The New Zealand Division had suffered heavily, losing twenty-seven hundred men in four hours on "New Zealand's blackest day." Its commander complained that "the artillery preparation was insufficient, the barrage poor.... Our casualties are heavy, [Lt. Col] Geo. King among others—I am very sad." Private Leonard Hart of the Otago battalion recalled that on reaching the crest of the ridge they found:

> a long line of practically undamaged German concrete machine-gun emplacements with barbed wire entanglements in front of them fully fifty yards deep.... Dozens got hung up on the wire and shot down before their surviving comrades" eyes.

Three days later II Anzac Corps, attacking in driving rain behind a thin barrage, strengthened its grip on Passchendaele Ridge. An Australian infantry officer gave a graphic description of the battle:

> On the night of the 11th we marched off at 6:30 P.M. and walked till 5 A.M. on the morning of the 12th ... Before 5 A.M. we had lost men like rotten sheep, those who survived had most marvellous escapes. I nearly got blown to pieces scores of times. We went through a sheet of iron all night and in the morning it got worse. We attacked at 5:25 and fought all day at times we were bogged up to our arm pits and it took anything from an hour upwards to get out. Lots were drowned in the mud and water.

Conditions in the whole salient were now so unreservedly terrible that the battle had clearly reached its dying fall. Haig pressed for one last try—his 3rd Army was preparing an offensive at Cambrai, and the Germans had to be pinned down—but agreed to wait until the weather improved slightly and even more artillery was available. The newly arrived Canadian Corps began its drive on Passchendaele on October 26, and actually took the village on November 6. The battle shuddered to a halt on November 20. Conditions were too dreadful to permit its continuation and, as we shall see in the next chapter, Haig now had other concerns.

The casualty figures for 3rd Ypres are just as controversial as those for the

Somme. Sir James Edmonds declared that the British had lost 244,897 killed, wounded, and missing, and estimated German losses at 364,320. He reached the latter figure by taking the admitted German loss of 217,000, and adding "wounded whose recovery was to be expected within a reasonable time" who were not included in German statistics. Churchill, however, thought that the British had lost 400,000 men, while Lloyd George put the figure at 399,000. It is probably safest to say that losses were about equal, at about 260,000 each.

THE MAINSPRINGS OF MORALE

Anyone visiting the salient can hardly fail to be struck by the short distances involved—it is six and a half miles from the Menin Gate at Ypres to Passchendaele Church—and the crushing weight of cemeteries and memorials. Tyne Cot, just below the crest of Passchendaele Ridge, is the largest Commonwealth war cemetery in the world, with nearly twelve thousand graves, and the panels behind it list the names of over thirty-four thousand British missing. Almost fifty-five thousand more Australian, British, Canadian, Indian, and South African missing are commemorated on

OPPOSITE Eric Kennington's *Gassed and Wounded* depicts a crowded dressing station.
ABOVE Medals, awarded to an officer who transferred to the Royal Flying Corps, including (second and third from left) the War Medal and Victory Medal, nicknamed "Squeak" and "Wilfred".

the Menin Gate memorial. In the winter, with the beeks running deep and the wind whipping the rain past the dour, brick-built farms, the fundamental question insistently demands an answer: How did flesh and blood stand living and fighting in such a landscape?

Keith Simpson suggests that "Ultimately the British soldier obeyed his officers and military authority out of a combination of habit, social deference, the fear of the consequences of disobedience, and personal loyalty and respect." Discipline undoubtedly played its part, and recent work on the capital sentences inflicted on British soldiers during the war points to the fact that death sentences had a greater chance of being confirmed when a major battle was in progress and morale, in the high command's opinion, needed stiffening.

During the whole war more than 3,000 officers and men were sentenced to death. Most had their sentences commuted by the commander in chief, but 306 were executed for military offenses such as desertion or casting away arms. In 1998 the British government decided against pardoning these men, arguing that, as far as the extant documents show, most seemed to have been

Amateur theatricals helped relieve boredom. Here officers of the RFC's Kite and Balloon Section rehearse *Cinderella*.

justly convicted *by the law as it then stood*. It declared, however, that "those executed were as much victims of war as the soldiers and airmen who were killed in action, died of wounds or disease; as the civilians killed by aerial or naval bombardment; or those lost at sea."

This humane declaration has not gone far enough for those who continue to demand a blanket pardon, and it is not my purpose to debate the issue here. However, tragic though these individual cases remain, it is clear that an army that saw about 5.7 million men pass through its ranks was not dragooned into battle by fear of the firing squad. While formal discipline, backed by the brutal sanction of the death penalty, did indeed play its part in keeping men at their duty, it was part, as Keith Simpson suggests, of a much more complex package.

Soldiers brought part of this with them into the army. In his very important chapter in *Passchendaele in Perspective*, John Bourne maintains that by 1917 the Regular army had failed to impose its values on a huge citizen force. "The urban working class volunteers and conscripts of the First World War," he writes, "did not enter the alien authority system of the Regular army naked and without tried and tested survival strategies." Most of these had originated in the workplace. The British working man was used to tedium, regimentation, subordination, and physical hardship. He found solace in the military community, comrades, and distractions like sport, entertainment, and gambling, and often took pride in his trade. Working-class values, Bourne concludes, helped produce "an army with a remarkable degree of social cohesion, imbued with a resilient optimism, built to resist and to endure."

Good leadership also helped. Norman Gladden, a private in 7th Royal Northumberland Fusiliers, remembered his company commander, Captain West, as "a good, brave and truly gentle man." And he wrote approvingly of Lieutenant Hewitt, a Guardsman promoted from the ranks—as so many officers were by then. He was strict on parade, "yet off parade he was friendly without being condescending, an attitude which many of his amateur colleagues would have done well to emulate." Nor should we forget the impact of NCOs, and those "big men" among the private soldiers whose own quiet bravery meant so much to less courageous hearts. Siegfried Sassoon gives us a snapshot of Corporal Griffiths:

> doing his simple duty without demanding explanations from the stars above him.... Vigilant and serious he stared straight ahead of him, and a fine picture of fortitude he made. He was only a stolid young farmer from Montgomeryshire; only; but such men, I think, were England in those dreadful years of war.

This leadership was not confined to the regimental officers with whom men came into contact. Many senior commanders and their staff were well aware what the battlefield did to those who survived it, and recognized that units had to be rotated so that men spent some time in the line before coming back into reserve or, best still, to rest. In his chapter in *Passchendaele in Perspective*, Peter Scott stresses the importance of maintaining some kind of equilibrium between men's physical demands like food, tobacco, sanitation, shelter, medical attention, a reliable postal service, and regular leave, and the awful realities of life at the front. He notes that when the men of 113th Infantry Brigade of 38th Welsh Division came out of the line they were met by the division's senior logistic staff officer with a complete change of uniform, clean underwear, whale oil to rub into their feet, matches, cigarettes, and biscuits.

These creature comforts were extraordinarily important. The daily rum ration, in particular, looms large in British personal accounts. One soldier wrote of a smell of "rum and blood," and Robert Graves suggested that his men's rum tot, issued in his battalion as they stood to their arms at dawn, was "the brightest moment of their twenty-four hours." Sometimes it was used to prepare men for battle, but wiser units used it afterward. "For the boys who wanted rum there was plenty," remembered one Australian. "In the AIF [Australian Imperial Force] the rule was, no rum before a fight; the rum was given afterward when the boys were dead beat."

Buoyed up by the knowledge that if they survived the next two days they might live for another forty years, some men simply switched themselves off, and faced battle with sheer resignation. Advancing behind the barrage, Gladden experienced "a peculiar, almost dreamlike, illusion. Though my feet were moving with all the energy needed to carry me with my burden across the ground, I felt that they were, in fact, rooted to the earth, and that it was all my surroundings that were moving of their own accord." Charles Carrington felt much the same. He had a split personality just before the battle, and then withdrew himself altogether, "leaving a zombie in command of B Company, the 1/5th Royal Warwickshire Regiment." When the battle opened, "the Zombie took charge and I felt nothing at all. I think I should not have known if a bullet had struck me."

Regimental loyalty played a part in the equation. The future Field Marshal Slim remembered his men being rallied to a shout of "Heads up, the Warwicks, and show the blighters your cap-badges." They had no cap badges—they were wearing steel helmets—but this appeal to ancient pride worked. For conscripts, or wounded returning to the front through a replacement system that filled gaps in the roster without much thought for a man's regimental identity, the regiment often meant little. But even they formed part of a complex world of loyalties and responsibilities that started with the infantry section. C. E. Montague was right to say how small a man's world really was: "all that mattered to him was the one little boatload of castaways with whom he was marooned on a desert island making shift to keep off the weather and any sudden attack of wild beasts." At its best, this spirit could produce a spirit of corporate identity that went well beyond polished boots or bright badges. "We were bonded together by a unity of experience that had shaken off every kind of illusion, and which was utterly unpretentious," wrote Charles Carrington, who earned his Military Cross at Passchendaele. "The battalion was my home and my job, the only career I knew."

Few men were overtly patriotic: there was a generalized feeling that the Allies were right and Germany was wrong, and a belief that refusing to do one's bit was like failing a mate who was down on his luck. Real hatred of the enemy was comparatively rare. Both sides killed prisoners from time to time, usually in the heat of the moment, if they had maintained a stout defense too

The rum ration played its own part in maintaining morale.
Its issue was strictly controlled: these soldiers have either been
unaccountably lucky or, more probably, are posing for the camera.

long. "No soldier can claim a right to quarter if he fights to the extremity," argued Charles Carrington. Ernst Junger, on the other side of the hill, agreed:
"The defending force, after firing their bullets into the attacking one at five
paces' distance, must take the consequences."

The loss of a close friend—or the sheer difficulty of getting prisoners
back through the barrage—might cause lapses. Private Frank Richards of
the Royal Welch Fusiliers saw a comrade set off out down the Menin Road
with six prisoners. He came back soon afterward and admitted: "I done
them in... about two hundred yards back. Two bombs did the trick." The
man was killed seconds later. Richards, who served at the front throughout
the war, thought this behavior unusual, and believed that "the loss of his pal
had upset him very much."

These coping mechanisms helped bring the British army through the
nightmare of Passchendaele with its morale strained but unbroken. Yet those
who knew it well saw how tired it really was. "For the first time," wrote Philip
Gibbs, "the British army lost its spirit of optimism, and there was a sense of
deadly depression among many officers and men. They saw no ending of the
war, nothing except continuous slaughter."

BREAKING
THE
FRONT

TANK
ATTACK

1917—the year of the Nivelle offensive, the French mutinies, and the long, wearing slog toward Passchendaele—ended with a spectacular blaze that was to make the coming winter seem darker still. After 3rd Army's patchy performance at Arras in the spring of 1917 its commander, General Sir Edmund Allenby, was sent off to command the Egyptian Expeditionary Force. He was not pleased for, as his biographer Lawrence James explains, he saw himself "exiled to a peripheral and moribund front." In the event he was to distinguish himself there, and his energy and cavalryman's flair for maneuver were to be rewarded with a series of victories over the Turks. His successor, Sir Julian Byng, had commanded the Canadian Corps, whose capture of Vimy Ridge had been an unqualified success. While Passchendaele ground on, his staff developed plans for an offensive toward Cambrai.

That spring the British had followed up the German withdrawal to the Hindenburg Line to occupy a line running from St-Quentin, past Cambrai, and then turning to run north-northwestward in front of Arras. The front cut across the Cambrésis, whose sand and loam on chalk produces a landscape very like that of the Somme. The St-Quentin Canal, built by Napoleon, was incorporated into the Hindenburg Line, and west of Cambrai the Canal du Nord, so recently constructed that it was not yet filled with water, also formed part of German defenses. The whaleback mass of Bourlon Wood, between the two canals, still dominates the whole area.

Defenses were strong, with an outpost line running west of the Canal du Nord, crossing it at Havrincourt, and then swinging east in front of Ribécourt to pick up the line of the St Quentin Canal. The front system, Siegfried I, lay one to two thousand yards behind it, its trenches dug so wide as to make them uncrossable by tanks, with four rows of wire, ninety-five yards deep in all, slanted out in great wedges in front of them. The support system, also well dug and wired, was two to two and a half miles behind, with the Siegfried II system still further back.

Impressive though these defenses were, in the autumn of 1917 there seemed good reason for risking an attack on them. Breaking the Hindenburg Line at Cambrai would severely disrupt its northern run toward Monchy, and taking Cambrai itself would badly damage German communications. There were also more local agendas. 3rd Army, and its new commander, had been overshadowed by the fighting further north. General Sir Aylmer Haldane suggested: "The tail wags the dog, and army commanders who have their own advancement in mind submit schemes instead of GHQ." The Tank Corps, under the energetic Brigadier General Hugh Elles, with Lieutenant Colonel J. F. C. Fuller—later to emerge as one of Britain's outstanding military thinkers—as his chief of staff, sought an opportunity to show its mettle on firm ground, not the mud of the Ypres salient, and Cambrai seemed an ideal spot. Finally, Brigadier General Tudor, commanding the artillery of the 9th Division, had developed a method of marking artillery targets, and the gun positions from which they would be engaged, by accurate survey, so that they could be quickly and effectively engaged without the need for preliminary registration by fire. Tudor suggested that tanks, not guns, should cut the wire, and that an attack could be preceded by a short bombardment.

On September 16 Haig discussed the plans for an attack at Cambrai with Byng, but did not feel able to formally authorize the attack until the Passchendaele battle had ended. Losses in the fighting there, coupled with the need to send troops to Italy, where the Italian army had been routed at Caporetto, made him reluctant to hand Byng a blank check. One of the attractions of the Cambrai project was its limited liability. Fuller had envisaged a large-scale tank raid on to the German gun line. 3rd Army's plan was more ambitious. Two of its five corps, III and IV, would attack between Bonavis Ridge and the Canal du Nord. III would use 216 tanks to reach the St-Quentin Canal at Masnières and Marcoing. The Cavalry Corps would then push through this gap to take Cambrai and the crossings of the River Sensée. Further north, IV Corps, with 108 tanks, would take Flesquières Ridge and Bourlon Wood.

In all there were to be 378 fighting tanks, 54 supply tanks pulling sledges, 32 fitted with grapnels for dragging wire to make gaps for the cavalry, 2 carrying bridging equipment and 5 wireless tanks. Most would carry the large bundles of brushwood called fascines, which would be dropped into trenches to provide crossing points. Infantry and tanks practiced drills for working together so that mopping-up parties would be on hand to capitalize on the shock inflicted by the tanks. Over a thousand guns, using Tudor's new methods, would support the attack. Byng emphasized that if early results were not impressive, the operation could be halted after forty-eight hours, before it had become too costly.

Security was good. The tanks were moved up to their railheads by night, and crawled to assembly areas whence, after dark on November 19, they edged cautiously, in bottom gear with engines barely ticking over, to the forming-up line. At 6:20 on the morning of the 20th, with a glimmer of light

ABOVE Tanks and infantry advancing at Cambrai, November 1917.
OPPOSITE From 1916, dogfights routinely raged in the air above the battlefield, with hostile observation balloons an important target for fighters.

revealing the German outpost line, the barrage crashed down and the tanks went forward. The surprise and shock were too much for many defenders: some bolted and others gave up without a fight. By midday the outpost line and main battle line were overrun on much of the attack frontage.

There was a reverse at Flesquières, where 51st Highland Division became separated from its tanks. Most authorities have blamed the divisional commander, Major General "Uncle" Harper, for this, but it has recently been argued that bad luck and unhelpful ground were far more to blame. The defending division, 54th, was commanded by Lieutenant General von Watter, whose brother had encountered tanks on the Somme and warned him what to expect. He had trained his field gunners to pull their 77 mms out of their gun pits and take on tanks with direct fire: they had even practiced on moving targets. When the tanks crossed Flesquières Ridge, with the infantry now some distance behind them, they were taken on by determined gunners. Haig's official dispatch paid tribute to a German officer who had manned his gun single-handed until killed. The "gunner of Flesquières" story is largely myth. As the tanks lurched over the crest line they were at a temporary disadvantage: 51st Division lost twenty-eight of its tanks. If there was a particular German hero that day, it may have been Lieutenant Müller or Sergeant Major Kruger of the 108th Field Artillery Regiment.

If the break-in had gone well, the breakout (familiar story) was disappointing. III Corps got up onto the canal, and crossed it at Marcoing, but the tank "Flying Fox" had crashed through the bridge at Masnières. The handling of the cavalry was less than slick, and it was not until sunset that, hampered on its move forward by cluttered roads and uncertainty as to which villages were already occupied, it received orders "to push on with full strength through Marcoing and carry out the original plan of a breakthrough at that point." B Squadron of the Canadian Fort Garry Horse, given a special independent mission, had already crossed the canal near Masnières, ridden down a battery of 77 mm guns, and galloped through parties of German infantry. The squadron's survivors returned after dark, bringing eighteen prisoners with them. Its senior surviving officer, Lieutenant Harcus Strachan, wrote that "there would have been a remarkable opportunity for a great cavalry success had the operation in its original form been carried out." Nevertheless, the British had captured 7,500 prisoners and 120 guns, and had pushed some seven thousand yards into one of the strongest parts of the Western Front. It was such a palpable success that church bells were rung in England for the first time during the war.

The battle went flat over the days that followed. Tank losses had been heavy—179 of the 378 fighting tanks were out of action, 65 of them destroyed and the others ditched or broken down. On the 21st, III Corps began what was to become a long and debilitating battle for Bourlon Wood, for that evening Haig told Byng to persist with the offensive. His reasons were threefold. First, he was encouraged by Charteris to believe that the Germans showed "a disposition to retire" because they were "soft" as a result of the wearing-out battle of the past two years. Secondly, he was optimistic about the cavalry's chances, although the chance for bold action—such as it was—had now passed. And lastly, he hoped that the success would embarrass Lloyd George, who had been increasingly critical of the British command.

In the end it was Haig who was embarrassed. The battle for Bourlon Wood imposed a heavy drain on 3rd Army's manpower—the youngest British general of the war, Brigadier General R. B. Bradford VC MC, was killed there at the age of twenty-five—and the British soon found themselves holding a salient with tired troops. By sheer bad luck, orders were given for commanders to rest and hand over to their seconds-in-command, so when the German counter-

CAMBRAI 1917

Canal du Nord

Bourlon

Bourlon Wood

Fontaine Notre Dame

Cambrai

Moeuvres

Anneux

Flesquières

Marcoing

Masnières

Crèvecoeur

Havrincourt

Ribécourt

Lateau Wood

Villers Plouich

N
W—E
S

Gonnelieu

Banteux

Gouzeaucourt

Villers
Guislain

0   3 Miles
0   3 Kilometers

St-Quentin Canal

Front Line on November 19   ——————

Main direction of British
Tank advance   ———▶

Furthest British advance,
November 29   – – – –

German counter attacks   ───▶

Final Front Line, December 7   • • • • • • •

attack came on November 30 it caught the British flat-footed. The Germans tried the classic ploy of attacking both shoulders of the salient in an effort to pinch it out. They made poor progress on the Bourlon–Moeuvres front in the north, but on the southern flank they broke in between III and VII Corps around Villers Guislain. Things were very bad, and would have been worse had 1st Guards Brigade not been on hand to regain Gouzeaucourt. When the battle ended on the night of December 4–5, the British retained part of the old Hindenburg system around Flesquières, but had relinquished their other gains and lost fresh ground in the south. Both sides had lost about forty thousand men, with 158 British guns lost to 145 German.

PRINCES OF THE TRENCHES

Cambrai was not merely a disappointing battle for the British: it was an instructive one for the Germans. Just as the defensive fighting on the Somme in 1916 had helped them refine the defensive doctrine that was to cause the Allies such difficulties in 1917, so their experience of launching attacks of their own, most notably on the Eastern Front—where the city of Riga had been taken in a textbook assault by General Oscar von Hutier's Eighth Army in September 1917—had helped them develop offensive doctrine. It is now clear that the differences between German, British, and French doctrine were less clear than most historians once suggested, and we must steer clear of imagining that all British officers were hidebound martinets while their German opponents were clear-thinking innovators. Two of the most useful books on the subject, Paddy Griffith's *Battle Tactics of the Western Front* and Martin Samuels's *Doctrine and Dogma: German and British Infantry Tactics in the First World War*, come at the argument from opposite ends.

But in offensive as in defensive tactics, the Germans were better than their opponents at codification and doctrinal development. They were also clearer in the identification of tactical concepts, like the need to designate a *schwerpunkt* (focus of energy), the advantage of *aufrollen* (flank attack), and the importance of *schlagfertigkeit*, which was to tactics what quickness of repartee was to conversation. To promote the last the Germans reduced the number of levels of command until by 1917–18 there were in essence only two tactical levels, battalion and division: others were primarily administrative.

The practice of giving the commander on the spot authority over reinforcing units also helped. By 1918 the average age for promotion to captain in the German army was twenty-nine and a half, and an officer this age might find himself the *kampftruppenkommandeur* in a sector, controlling the three battalions of his regiment and any reserves sent there, effectively exercising the authority of a British brigadier general who might be ten years older and would have a more complex chain of command to tug. We have already seen the problems imposed on the British army by rapid prewar expansion, which inevitably diluted the trained manpower available and resulted in the promotion of the unfit as well as the fit. The Germans had not only a deeper pool of regular and reserve officers, but a formidable NCO corps. One British general reckoned that a prewar German NCO, on completing the two-year course at NCO school, was "as efficient as the average British subaltern of, say, five years' service." During the war NCOs commanded most platoons and, by 1917–18, were routinely commanding companies. They might be commissioned after further training, but in order to preserve the social exclusivity of commissioned rank the Germans developed the rank of *offizierstellvertreter* (deputy officer): these worthies had the responsibilities, though not the status, of subalterns.

When the Germans counterattacked at Cambrai they did so behind a creeping barrage that could be accelerated by signal lights fired by the infantry it supported. And in most divisions the attack was led by elite assault units. These had been developed from small beginnings after the Guard Rifle Battalion pioneered fluid assault in retaking a captured trench on New Year's Eve 1914. In March 1915 an assault detachment, of about half-battalion size, was created, and soon came under the command of Captain Willy Rohr, who had served with the Guard Rifles. Rohr developed tactics based on section-sized "storm troops," supported by machine guns, mortars, flamethrowers, and artillery, all coordinated at the lowest possible level to ensure the effective suppression of enemy defenses. Once storm troops had made a gap in these defenses, they rolled up enemy trenches by attacking along them with hand grenades.

The experience of Verdun encouraged the Germans to build assault detachments into larger assault battalions and to create more of them. Several *Jäger* (rifle) battalions were converted wholesale, and there were also regimental storm troop detachments. Establishments varied as the war went on, but a storm battalion might comprise up to five infantry companies, one or two twelve-gun machine-gun companies, a flamethrower section, an infantry gun battery with four to six guns, and a mortar company with eight mortars. The Germans had a functional approach to the various arms: troops and their weapons were considered for what they did, rather than what they were. Storm battalions needed to generate *Stosskraft* (assault power) as well as

German storm troops training for the spring offensive of 1918. They move quickly, rifles slung, seeking weak spots in the defense.

Feuerkraft (firepower), and it was logical to mix infantry and artillery within them, without letting traditional interarmy rivalries get in the way.

These units were more than just practitioners of the most up-to-date tactics: they were filled with the fittest, keenest officers and men, imbued with a spirit that made them "princes of the trenches." The soldier-poet Franz Schauwecker describes the ideal storm trooper:

> He moves from shellhole to shellhole in raging fire, by leap and bound, by creep and crawl like a seal, close to the earth like an animal, never discouraged, never irresolute, never forfeiting intent, always full of recourse, schemes and self-reliance, answering every blow with a counterblow...a new kind of man, a man in the highest exaltation of all manly qualities so harmonized and from a single caste that one sees a man in the word "fighter."

The Crown Prince of Prussia gave storm troopers his personal support, and when Ludendorff visited his headquarters at Stenay in September 1916 it was natural that a company of Rohr's assault battalion should form the guard of honor. Ludendorff was intrigued by their dress: the coal-scuttle helmet, fast replacing the spiked helmet in the infantry, puttees, mountain boots, and leather-patched tunics. This, thought Ludendorff, should become the model for the rest of the German infantry.

Storm troop tactics paid dividends at Cambrai. The short bombardment did not forfeit surprise, and behind it came the storm troops, supported by pioneer units dealing with obstacles and ordinary infantry to mop up bypassed positions. There was no sudden British collapse, and isolated groups of defenders fought back hard, forcing the Germans to take them on in detail. Well-prepared storm troopers were closely supported by "infantry accompanying batteries," one four-gun battery per attacking regiment, moving up with the infantry to provide direct fire, as well as by their own machine guns and mortars. They were followed by "assault blocks," up to battalion-sized teams of infantry, mortar men, and machine gunners, briefed to exploit success and maintain the momentum of the attack. The triumph of these methods at Cambrai suggested to Ludendorff that they were indeed the way ahead.

"BREAK-THROUGH MÜLLER" There was another useful lesson of Cambrai. The artillery fire support of storm troop attacks had been developed by Georg Bruchmüller. He had been a regular gunner officer with a modest background, and was on the retired list as a lieutenant colonel when the war began. Reemployed in 1914, he soon found himself commanding the artillery of an infantry division, and in 1916 masterminded a centralized artillery fire plan when a German corps counterattacked the numerically superior Russians at Lake Narotch. On May 1, 1917, he was awarded the Pour le Mérite, an unusual decoration for a staff officer, before being sent off to be artillery adviser to Hutier for his attack on Riga. In the German army appointment mattered less than formal rank, and the fact that Bruchmüller was still only a reemployed retired lieutenant colonel mattered not a jot. He soon had the nickname *Durchbruchmüller*—"Breakthrough Müller"—and, as General Max Hoffmann, chief of staff on the Eastern Front, was to write, troops "went forward with a fuller sense of confidence when Bruchmüller and his staff were in charge."

Artillery assets were divided into four groups. Close support for the infantry was provided by the *Infanteriebekampfungsartillerie* (IKA), with 75 percent of guns assigned to it. Some 20 percent of batteries formed counter-artillery groups (*artilleriebekamfungsartillerie*—AKA), whose task was counter-battery fire. The long-range guns of the *Fernkampfartillerie* (FEKA) reached out to hit command posts, ammunition dumps, and reserve concentrations. Finally, the *Schwereste Flachfeuerartillerie* (SCHWELFA) consisted of the heaviest guns, grouped to include their own air observation and survey units, which took on critical hard targets like railway bridges and reinforced command posts.

In addition, there were infantry assets: trench mortars; infantry-accompanying batteries of 77 mm guns; and infantry guns (captured Russian 76.2 mm guns with cut-down barrels), which were parceled out at the rate of one per attacking battalion and manhandled forward with the assault. Neither the infantry-accompanying batteries nor the infantry guns fired in the preparatory bombardment: their job was to take on targets like machine guns and snipers that had escaped other fires.

The essence of Bruchmüller's tactics was the centralization of control at the highest level consistent with the communications available, so that the artillery assigned to an operation played to the baton of a single conductor. His bombardments were short and violent, designed to neutralize rather than destroy the defender, and mixed gas, shrapnel, and high-explosive shells. Bombardments were divided into phases, each with a specific tactical objective, and could be mixed and matched as required. Bruchmüller understood the psychological effects of artillery fire, and often organized fire plans so that the same positions were hit time after time, making it hard for the defender to work out when it was safe to man his trenches to meet the real assault.

A creeping barrage—*feuerwalze*—would move ahead of the attackers, and although they were able to speed it up (by firing green flares), no method was devised for slowing it down. In the first half of 1918 Bruchmüller slowed the pace of the barrage, and by June it moved only 220 yards in ten minutes. He also authorized commanders to pull batteries out of the *feuerwalze* to deal with pockets of resistance, and made sure that they had enough assets to do this. By May 1918 Bruchmüller had developed the double creeping barrage, the nearer line of fire, consisting of high explosive, moving uniformly just ahead of the infantry, while the further line, consisting largely of gas, dwelled longer on likely lines of resistance.

Bruchmüller was increasingly suspicious of the need to register targets before an attack, as that inevitably compromised surprise. Captain Erich Pulkowski developed a method of adding daily meteorological influences to the special characteristics of individual guns and ammunition batches to make unregistered fire more accurate, and the British themselves had shown, with their barrage at Cambrai, just how effective unregistered fire could be. Bruchmüller backed the Pulkowski method against much high-level opposition, and managed to secure its partial adoption in February 1918.

LUDENDORFF'S DECISION   On November 11, 1917, Ludendorff met a select group of his advisers at Mons, the little Belgian town where British and Germans had first clashed in 1914 and now the seat of Rupprecht's army group headquarters. Among them were Major—soon to be Lieutenant Colonel—Georg Wetzell,

OHL's chief of operations on the Western Front, and Captain Hermann Geyr, a leading offensive ideologue and author of the pamphlet *The Attack in Position Warfare.* American entry into the war changed the entire strategic balance. Although Ludendorff and his officers were not to know it then, the tiny U.S. Army was to grow so swiftly that it would have a million men in France by July 1918 and over two million by the year's end. If the details of America's contribution were still unknown to the Germans, its general effect was not. Even if Germany succeeded in closing down the Eastern Front altogether, which she was already close to doing, she would inevitably be swamped by men and material pouring in from the United States. Her only chance, believed Ludendorff, was to attack before the Americans were present in strength.

One decision was simply made. Beating the French would still leave Britain in the war, and there was always the danger that an uncowed Britain, supported by the U.S.A., might continue the naval blockade which was doing Germany so much harm. Defeating the British, however, would turn the northern flank of the Western Front and provoke a French collapse. Ludendorff concluded that "we must beat the British."

Ludendorff's staff made several plans. Among them were schemes for attacks on both sides of Ypres—"George I" and "George II"—which would join at Hazebrouck and then swing northwestward to encircle a large part of the British army. Although there was much to be said for this scheme—for even a short advance would put important targets within German reach—the British had demonstrated with agonizing clarity that it was not easy to attack in Flanders. All might be well if Ludendorff could wait until the battlefield had dried out, but the need to strike before the Americans arrived in strength helped rule out "George" as a first option. Attacking in the Arras–Vimy sector— "Mars" and "Valkyrie"—would prove difficult because of the British hold on Vimy Ridge and the cluttered character of the ground.

Ludendorff's glance slid further south, to the land between the Rivers Sensée and Oise. Here the attackers could concentrate behind the Hindenburg Line, and for much of the attack front the defenders would have the wilderness of the old Somme battlefield to their backs. In the south, General von Hutier, back from the Eastern Front, would mount "Michael I" with Eighteenth Army securing the Crozat Canal as the attack's left shoulder and advancing astride St-Quentin. In the center, General von der Marwitz's Second Army would make for Albert ("Michael II") while General von Below's Seventeenth Army unleashed "Michael III" toward Bapaume. Once the front was broken, the attackers could swing northward, cutting deep into the British

The Germans captured some British tanks at Cambrai and brought them back into service with iron crosses painted on their sides.

rear. Below's right wing could then launch "Mars South" against Arras and, if the weather improved, "George" could be sprung last of all, exposing the British to a concentric attack which they would have little hope of resisting.

Ludendorff paid careful attention to morale. Many senior officers feared that the German army had degenerated into a mere militia, and part of the morale-building process included the reintroduction of the formal "goose-step" parade drill. Decorations were lavishly distributed, and military bands gave concerts featuring patriotic tunes. Ludendorff encouraged his men to believe that this mammoth offensive, the *Kaiserschlacht*, the Kaiser's battle, would win the war and end their miseries.

The balance of forces certainly looked encouraging. Some seventy-four German divisions, backed by 6,608 guns and 3,534 mortars, were to attack on a front of about fifty miles. They would be supported by over seven hundred aircraft, some, in the recently renamed battle squadrons, dedicated to ground attack, and others flying against British and French aircraft. Facing this panoply were the British 4th and 5th Armies, with thirty divisions between them. But Ludendorff was too experienced a commander not to recognize the flaw in his project. He was attacking where short-term tactical success was most likely, but in a sector where he could drive very deep into the British lines without necessarily doing fatal damage. Much would depend on how the British fought; how well his own men endured the pressure of the battle; and, above all, whether the alliance would hold together under its impact.

**AWAITING
THE BLOW**

The blow was to fall on a British army that was feeling the strain of a long war. If Passchendaele had worn down the Germans, it had also hit the British army hard. On March 1, 1918, Haig's infantry was just over half a million strong, only 36 percent of his total strength as opposed to 45 percent only six months before. Shortage of manpower compelled the reduction of battalions per brigade from four to three in British divisions (Dominion troops retained four), and 141 wartime-raised battalions, which could no longer be kept up to strength, were disbanded. Morale seemed to have recovered from its lowest ebb in the wake of Passchendaele, but the nation was scraping the bottom of its manpower barrel. In 1915 the German cavalry officer Rudolf Binding suggested that the quality of British troops compensated for their small numbers, but a year later he was complaining that prisoners were "rickety, alcoholic, degenerate, ill-bred and poor to the last degree." By 1918 many observers, British and German, testified to the growing numbers of schoolboys in the ranks, and a new military service act, which came into operation in April 1918, conscripted men aged forty-one to fifty.

Haig had reluctantly agreed to take over more ground from the French, and by January 1918 had extended the British front another forty-two miles, as far as the River Oise. This placed fresh demands on manpower, because French defenses were not organized on the scale required by the British. Moreover, British defensive tactics were themselves in the process of changing, and the new doctrine, heavily influenced by German experience, required existing trench lines to be remodeled. A GHQ memorandum of December 14, 1917, ordained that there would be three layers of defenses. A Forward Zone would be based on well-wired redoubts, whose machine guns covered the ground between them. A sprinkling of 17-pounders, sited individually, protected against tank attack. A mile or two further back came the Battle Zone, with more redoubts, the bulk of the artillery, and counterattack units to support the Forward Zone. Still further back was the Rear Zone, in theory organized much like the Battle Zone, protecting heavy batteries and supply dumps. Tanks, it was decided, would be grouped behind the front for counterattacks, not posted as individual strongpoints, or "savage rabbits."

There were two major weaknesses in this new structure. In the first place, it had not been properly taught, and there was a good deal of consumer resistance. "It don't suit us," grumbled one experienced NCO. "The British Army fights in line, and won't do any good in these bird cages." Many commanders, used to holding ground as far forward as possible, pushed too many men—and far too many machine guns—into the Forward Zone. They also failed to appreciate that the German system hinged on an unwritten contract between troops in the line and the high command. The former would hold on even if surrounded, and the latter would launch counterattacks as soon as possible. There are limits to men's tenacity, and a defense without hope of relief is something few citizen armies will sustain.

The second weakness turned on manpower shortages. Gough's 5th Army, holding the southern end of the British line, had only fourteen divisions to hold forty-two miles of front, and only 8,830 laborers in addition to fighting troops. When the German attack began there were no dugouts in his Battle Zone, and it was incomplete south of St-Quentin. The Rear Zone consisted only of its forward trench, the Green Line, simply marked out on the ground. Things were better further north, where 3rd Army had sixteen divisions for twenty-eight miles, but even here the Battle Zone was unfinished and the Rear Zone incomplete.

Gough pointed out the weakness of his line and, once he had discovered that Hutier was his opponent, predicted that his army would be in the path of the main assault. In February he was given permission to "fall back to the rearward defenses of Péronne and the Somme" if heavily attacked, but it was made clear that Péronne should be held at all costs. Haig visited the 5th Army front in early March, and recognized that things were far from ideal. "The French handed over to him a wide front with no defenses," he wrote, "and Gough has no labor for the work."

Haig was in growing difficulties. Cambrai had done very serious damage to GHQ's standing in the eyes of politicians: Haig himself, Kiggell, his chief of staff, and Charteris, his intelligence officer, were all under scrutiny. Kitchener had died in 1916, drowned on his way to Russia. On December 7 Lord Derby, now secretary of state for war, told Haig that "the War Cabinet are constantly saying that the statements and views you have put forward at different times regarding the moral and numerical weakening of the enemy are not borne out by the opposition your troops encounter, and so it seems to me and the General Staff here." Haig did his best for Charteris, but in December replaced him with Major General Herbert Lawrence, who had left the army after the Boer War when Haig had been promoted over his head to command the 17th Lancers. The two worked well together, but the fact that Lawrence was his own man, with a career to resume when the war finished, made him more robust in his dealings with the commander in chief than had often been the case at GHQ. Shortly afterward Kiggell went too, and Lawrence stepped up to become chief of staff.

Haig's own position was far from secure. Lloyd George later admitted that the problem in replacing him was to find somebody who would do better. "It is a sad reflection," he wrote after the war, "that not one among the visible military leaders would have been any better. There were amongst them plenty of good soldiers who knew their profession and possessed intelligence up to a point. But Haig was all that and probably better within limits than any others within sight." In January 1918 he sent the South African premier J. C. Smuts and the War Cabinet's secretary Maurice Hankey to the front in an effort to see who might replace Haig. Lloyd George described their report as "very disappointing," for it endorsed Haig. Robertson, who had for so long sought to cover Haig's back in London, was more vulnerable: in February he was replaced by General Sir Henry Wilson. Wilson, a clever, voluble francophile, was widely mistrusted by his own army and had been shunted off to be liaison officer to the French in 1915. In 1917 Lloyd George had appointed him British representative on the Allied Supreme War Council, and his promotion to Chief of the Imperial General Staff was bad news for Haig.

GHQ had little doubt that the Germans would attack. In December 1917 its intelligence branch, then still under Charteris, had given them an assessment that tallied accurately with Ludendorff's own: in the early spring the Germans would "seek to deliver such a blow on the Western Front as would force a decisive battle which she could fight to a finish before the American forces could take an active part." News of German concentrations around Mézières persuaded Haig that this might presage an attack toward Amiens and "an advance in force south-west of St-Quentin." In January he warned the War Cabinet that the next four months would be "the critical period of the war." This frank statement failed to ensure that his army was brought up to strength, and as Charteris gloomily opined on January 26 it entered the year with a longer front to hold, a reduced establishment with which to hold it, no hope of reinforcements, and the prospect of a heavy German attack.

| **THE MARCH OFFENSIVE** | At 4:40 on the morning of March 21 the German artillery shook the front between the Sensée and the Oise with the wild, impersonal malice of some natural disaster. |

aster. German guns fired over three million rounds that day. Lieutenant Herbert Sulzbach, a German artillery officer, wrote that it was:

THE WESTERN FRONT 1918:
THE GERMAN OFFENSIVES

HOLLAND

N
W   E
S

North Sea

Zeebrugge
Ostend
Bruges
Ghent

BELGIUM

Calais

GEORGE II

4th Army

Boulogne
Hazebrouck
Ypres   Passchendaele

R. Lys

GEORGE I

Brussels

Etaples
Armentières   Messines
Montreuil
Lille

GEORGETTE

Mons

Liège

1st Army
La Bassée
Lens
Vimy
Douai

MARS/
VALKYRIE

Charleroi   Namur

R. Meuse

Doullens
Arras

Cambrai

R. Sambre

Maubeuge

3rd Army

MICHAEL III
Le Cateau

Landrecies

R. Somme

Amiens
Bapaume
Albert
Péronne

MICHAEL II
MICHAEL I

Villers-Bretonneux
Chaulnes   Ham
St-Quentin

R. Oise

FRANCE

Roye   5th Army

Montdidier
Noyon
La Fère   Laon

BLÜCHER
Mézières

Sedan

Compiègne

GNEISENAU

R. Oise

Soissons

R. Aisne

REIMS-
MARNESCHUTZ

Longwy

*Chemin des
Dames*

Rheims

Verdun

R. Vesle

Château-Thierry

R. Seine

Meaux

R. Marne

St-Mihiel

Paris

---

*Disposition of British Armies as on
the eve of the first (March 21)
German offensive (2nd Army in
Italy at this period)*

0   25 Miles

0   25 Kilometers

Approximate line of the front
before the first offensive   ——————

Approximate limit of the German
advance, March to July   – – – –

Frontiers   –·–·–·–

as if the world was coming to an end. . . . During the firing I often have to interrupt my fire direction duties because I can't take all the gas and the smoke. The gunners stand with their sleeves rolled up and the sweat pouring down. Round after round is rammed into the breech, salvo after salvo is fired. I don't have to give orders any more because the men are so enthusiastic; they fire at such a rapid rate that no commands are necessary.

A British machine gunner on the receiving end thought that it "seemed as though the bowels of the earth had erupted, while beyond the ridge there was one long and continuous yellow flash." Lance Corporal William Sharpe had four youngsters who had only just turned eighteen in his section: this was their first experience of battle. "They cried and one kept calling 'mother!' and who could blame him, such HELL makes weaklings of the strongest and no human's nerves were ever built to stand such torture, noise, horror and mental pain." Their trench was blown in, and although Sharpe searched for the lads he never saw them again.

An artillery officer, almost blown off his bunk "by concussion like an earthquake," tried to telephone his batteries, only to discover that all the telephone cables, buried six feet deep, had been cut. The German artillery specialists Bruchmüller and Pulkowski had done their work well.

The German infantry loped forward behind the barrage. It was a foggy morning, which gave them protection from the surviving machine guns in the Forward Zone, but presented command and control problems which bugle calls, specially taught for just such an eventuality, only partially solved. Across much of the British front the picture was the same. Groups of storm troopers slipped in between the redoubts like wraiths, and the first many British soldiers saw of their enemies was when attacks curled in from flanks and rear. Under these circumstances some men fought to the last extremity, but the majority, fighting what was all too evidently a losing battle, surrendered. Most Germans behaved surprisingly well. Private J. Parkinson was changing the belt on his machine gun when he felt a bump in his back. It was a German officer's pistol, and its owner said: "Come along, Tommy. You've done enough." "He must have been a real gentleman," admitted Parkinson.

The personality and determination of individual leaders made a real difference. Manchester Hill, just west of St-Quentin, was held by elements of 16th Battalion the Manchester Regiment under its commanding officer, Lieutenant Colonel Wilfrith Elstob. A burly former schoolmaster who had joined the battalion as a private in 1914, Elstob knew, like so many others, that the attack was coming. When his men marched up to the line a few days before, their band played them out of camp, and as it turned about to return Elstob remarked: "Those are the only fellows who will come out of this alive." He had pointed out the position of battalion headquarters on a map, emphasizing: "Here we fight, and here we die."

The battle began early for the Manchesters when a scream from the fog told them a sentry had been bayoneted. There was then some firing, but no serious attacks, and when the fog lifted late in the morning the Manchesters could see German troops moving westward on both sides of them. Attacks proper started at about 3:00, as follow-up troops arrived. Elstob, wounded three times, was the heart of the defense, darting about with revolver and grenades. His field telephone allowed him to maintain contact with brigade headquarters, and he eventually reported that he had few men left, but declared: "The Manchester Regiment will hold Manchester Hill to the last." He was killed as he went back with more grenades.

Elstob's gallant stand earned him a well-deserved Victoria Cross, but his battalion had far more men captured than killed: there were limits to what even stoutly led men could achieve. In other cases leadership was less vigorous, often because officers believed that there was simply no point in ordering their men to fight on. Lieutenant Colonel Lord Farnham surrendered Boadicea Redoubt: the Germans reported the capture of one lieutenant colonel, a small white dog, three captains, seven subalterns, 241 men, and 41 machine guns and mortars. This sort of thing was scarcely last-ditch defense, and one nameless sergeant was scathing. "I must confess that the German breakthrough on 21 March 1918 should never have occurred," he maintained. "There was no cohesion of command, no determination, no will to fight, and no unity of companies or of battalions."

By nightfall the Germans had inflicted over thirty-eight thousand casualties on the British, including some twenty-one thousand prisoners. They had lost slightly more men, with hardly any prisoners, and had taken part of 3rd Army's Battle Zone south of the Scarpe, though the Flesquières salient was still secure, while 5th Army had lost a huge tract of ground north of Ham. The advance was less impressive on the 22nd, though Hutier made such good progress along the Crozat Canal that he suspected he might have caught Gough in the process of withdrawing. He had not, but the pace of his advance showed that 5th Army was now in real difficulties. That morning Gough declared that "corps will fight rear-guard actions back to forward line of the Rear Zone, and if necessary to rear line of Rear Zone." Given the fact that the Rear Zone consisted at best of "an immaculately patterned mock trench," this was pure moonshine.

All that week 5th Army slid back in defeat. One junior staff officer reported that:

> The troops were walking down a main road. They were in no formation and units were mixed up in strange confusion. Officers and men were together and it was just a rabble, but there was no panic, no hurry, not much talking, no shouting—just a dogged steady slogging towards the rear.

The divisional artillery commander ordered him to stop the rabble and make a line, but it was no use: "You might as well have tried to stop the sea." Guy Chapman saw similar sights. "The privates were all children," he wrote, "tired, hardly able to drag their aching shoulders after their aching legs. Here and there an exhausted boy trudged along with tears coursing down his face." Experienced officers knew that things were desperate. Captain Douglas McMurtrie of the Somerset Light Infantry strove to keep his men in hand when his colonel ordered him to retreat on March 24. "I was determined not to let the men start running," he wrote, "for once they did so in such a situation it was impossible to hold them. I had my revolver out and anyone who tried to run I immediately threatened to shoot. This stopped all running but it was the worst hour I have ever had with the only exception perhaps of the Cambrai counterattack on Nov 30th [1917]." And there were even more worrying signs. Some soldiers now doubted whether there was any point in the war: "The Boche can have this country as far as I'm concerned."

These worrying remarks were paralleled in the Allied command. Pétain, the French commander in chief, had honored an earlier agreement and sent six divisions to shore up Gough's right flank. On the 23rd, the day that Péronne fell, Haig asked Pétain to concentrate another twenty divisions around Amiens, only to discover that Pétain, concerned that the Germans might attack him, could not spare them. He made it clear that, in extremis, the French army would fall back to cover Paris. His reserve army group would fall back from Montdidier to the southwest if seriously attacked, and was not to be cut off with the British if the Germans succeeded in reaching Amiens and cutting the major rail link between the Allied armies. Haig had already faced the possibility that "the British will be rounded up and driven back into the sea," and now he wrote that he was "confronting the weight of the German army single-handed."

THE DOULLENS CONFERENCE

On March 26, Haig met some of his army commanders at Doullens, not far behind the shifting front. Gough was too busy to be there, and though Byng attended, old Plumer muttered that he ought to have been with his army, and then, helpful as ever, offered to send fresh troops south. Haig was then summoned to the town hall, where Lord Milner, a member of the War Cabinet, and Henry Wilson, the new Chief of the Imperial General Staff, were meeting a senior French delegation. Haig said that he proposed to hold Amiens and hold north of the Somme: he had placed elements of 5th Army south of the Somme under French command. Pétain, deeply pessimistic, observed that there was now very little left of 5th Army. Foch, rising to the occasion, burst out: "We must fight in front of Amiens, we must fight where we are now. As we have not been able to stop the Germans on the Somme, we must not now retire a single inch." Haig then said that if Foch was prepared to give him advice he would happily follow it, and after some discussion a document was drafted giving Foch authority to coordinate all Allied armies on the Western Front. It was the genesis of a unified command, in circumstances of far greater danger than had prevailed at the Calais conference which had subordinated Haig to Nivelle a year before. Yet this time the arrangement suited Haig, for it was Pétain who was overruled. Amiens would be held at all costs. United, the Allies might just stand: divided, they would certainly fall.

THE KAISER-SCHLACHT ENDS

Although the Allied leaders were not to know it, the attack was already running out of steam. In part this was due to what the Prussian military thinker Clausewitz had long ago called "the diminishing power of the offensive": as the attackers moved further from their bases they became ever more tired, and it became more and more difficult to supply them. German soldiers gorged themselves on captured food and drink, and discipline wavered. On March 28 Rudolf Binding entered Albert, which had just fallen, and saw:

> men driving cows before them on a line; others who carried a hen under one arm and a box of notepaper under the other. Men carrying a bottle of wine under their arm and another one open in their hand.... Men dressed up in comic disguise. Men with top hats on their heads. Men staggering. Men who could hardly walk.

He ordered an officer to press on with the advance, but was told: "I cannot get my men out of this cellar without bloodshed." As the momentum of the offensive faltered, Ludendorff kept tinkering with the lines of advance given to army commanders, sacrificing the grand plan of rolling up the British to capitalize on short-term local advantage, and on March 28 he unleashed Mars: it made little progress. Nevertheless, during those critical days many British soldiers felt themselves staring defeat in the face. On April 11 Haig issued an order of the day which concluded:

> There is no other course open to us but to fight it out! Every position must be held to the last man: there must be no retirement. With our backs to the wall, and believing in the justice of our cause, each one of us must fight on to the end. The safety of our homes and the freedom of mankind alike depend on the conduct of each one of us at this critical moment.

"Michael" at last sputtered to a halt, but not before Villers-Bretonneux—from whose long ridge the spires of Amiens can be seen on the horizon—had fallen. The Germans took it on April 24, using thirteen of their own tanks, the monster A7V *Sturmpanzerwagen* , to help them do so. Southwest of the town that morning a section of three British tanks moved out to engage them, and Second Lieutenant Frank Mitchell's Mk IV "male" (armed with 6-pounder guns, whereas Mk IV "females" had only machine guns) took on a German A7V in the world's first ever tank-versus-tank battle: Mitchell won it. Later the same morning seven British "whippet" light tanks, alerted by a reconnaissance aircraft, caught two German battalions in the open and drove right through them, machine gunning as they went. That night three brigades, two Australian and one British, counterattacked, and by dawn on the 25th Villers-Bretonneux was back in Allied hands. "Michael" was over. It had taken over ninety thousand prisoners and a thousand guns, and had overrun more territory than all the Allied advances of the past three years. But it had not won the war.

LUDENDORFF KEEPS TRYING

Yet the strategic logic that had persuaded Ludendorff to attack in March had not changed. He tried again, mounting "Georgette"—an attenuated version of "George"—on April 9. The brunt of the attack fell on an overextended Portuguese division holding the line around Neuve Chapelle, and the Germans advanced six miles that day. They went on to make a deep dent in British lines, running from Givenchy on the La Bassée

General Foch (left) appointed Allied Commander in Chief in
1918, with the American C-in-C General Pershing.

Canal to Merville on the Lys, and then on up to Ypres, where all those
painfully earned gains of 1917 were snuffed out. The Germans even wrested
Kemmel Hill from the French. But if the British blamed the French for this,
many Frenchmen were no less critical of the English. "Everyone says the
same," wrote Captain Henri Desagneux. "The English are useless, it's the
Scots, the Australians, and Canadians who do all the work."

Foch sent three divisions north to replace five British divisions that had
been badly mauled in the fighting, and these were sent down to rest on the
Chemin des Dames, now such a quiet sector that it was nicknamed "the sana-
torium of the Western Front."

These divisions, constituting Lieutenant General Gordon's IX Corps,
held part of the ridge under the command of the French 6th Army. But far
from having time to rest and refit in a quiet sector, they found themselves di-
rectly in the patch of the next of Ludendorff's offensives, "Blücher," which
began early on the 27th. As we have seen from German experience at Vimy,
holding a ridge was rarely easy, for it was always tempting to pack the vital
but vulnerable ground with troops. This is just what General Duchêne of 6th
Army did, and Bruchmüller's bombardment was so effective that in some
cases the principal opposition to the Germans came from the ripped-up

ground. By nightfall the Germans were across the Aisne, and by June 1 they had taken both Soissons and Château-Thierry. Tim Travers suggests that there was a "noticeable drop" in British morale, but highlights the fact that there were still examples of inspired and inspiring leadership. Lieutenant Colonel Dean of 6th South Wales Borderers was carried into an artillery headquarters, hard hit. Although "grievously wounded, obviously dying, and unable to speak, he made signs for writing materials—he managed to scrawl 'To my battalion—Stick it, Boys,' and died within a few minutes."

ENTER THE AMERICANS

Yet the story was the same as before—substantial tactical gains but no strategic success—with an added twist. General John J. Pershing, the commander of American forces in France, was insistent that his troops should fight as a unified American army and not be parceled out among the Allies. Nevertheless he was prepared to listen to reason and support Allied endeavors where the situation genuinely demanded it. American ground troops had their baptism of fire on June 3, when machine gunners of the U.S. 3rd Division shot up Germans trying to cross the Marne at Château-Thierry. Three days later 4th Marine Brigade assaulted Belleau Wood, west-northwest of the town. The Marines attacked in long, straight lines, with the sort of tactical innocence that European armies had long since lost. It took them until June 25 to secure the wood, and they lost five thousand men, including half their officers.

Yet their victory was a portent for the future. The Americans were inexperienced. Their logistics were clumsy. Their commander was not blown along by Foch's enthusiasm. Still, they had won one battle, and would win more. Henri de Pierrefeu coined a simile which many felt to be absolutely appropriate: the Americans were like a transfusion of blood arriving to reanimate the pallid body of France. The French Captain Desagneux's heart lifted when he saw his first Americans, "twenty strapping great fellows, sappers, admirably turned out with brand new equipment."

And as Allied spirits rose, so German resolve wavered. Ludendorff, like a driver pumping desperately at the accelerator as he feels the engine falter, launched two more attacks. On June 9–14, Operation "Gneisenau" pushed past Montdidier. Then on July 15 came the last attack, officially the "Reims–Marneschutz" but tellingly known as "Friedensturm" the Peace Offensive. The now-familiar tactical ploys, storm troops coming in behind a lightning bombardment, gained ground on either side of Rheims. But that was all: the Germans had shot their bolt.

THE ALLIED RIPOSTE: MANGIN, ST-MIHIEL, AND MEUSE-ARGONNE

Successive German attacks, which led to Foch and Haig demanding reserves to solve their own particular problems, made it hard for Foch to coordinate a cohesive Allied counterattack. Haig wanted reserves to reinforce the Lys sector in Flanders. And Pétain had prepared an attack by Mangin's 10th Army, but then canceled it to send reserves across to help contain the "Friedensturm" west of Rheims. Foch recognized that Mangin's proposed attack would focus Ludendorff's attention on the huge salient now in his possession, preventing him from attacking elsewhere. So he ordered Pétain to let Mangin's attack proceed. It thrust up from the forests of Compiègne and Retz on July 18. Although it had little chance of cutting off German forces in the salient, it took twenty-five thousand prisoners and forced Ludendorff to give up captured ground between Soissons and Rheims.

In late July and August Allied strategy coalesced. There would be a convergent offensive, with the Americans operating in Lorraine on the Allied right flank while the British took the lead in an attack eastward through Cambrai. *"Tout le monde à la bataille"*—"Everybody to battle"—declared Foch. The Americans began by pinching out the St-Mihiel salient south of Verdun on September 12–15. They then shifted their grip, attacking into the Argonne, parallel with the Meuse, on September 12 in a battle the Americans call Meuse–Argonne. Pershing had been offered the choice of attacking either there or into the more open country between Rheims and the Argonne. He chose the Argonne because, he thought, no troops but his own would have the fighting spirit for such a task.

It was certainly a battle that demanded fighting spirit aplenty. Although some Americans divisions had gained combat experience fighting under Allied command, Pershing's was still a largely untried army, and it was engaging an experienced opponent on ground ideal for defense. The Americans took Montfaucon Ridge on September 27, but two days later were sharply rebuffed at Exemont. They were now up against the main positions of the Kriemhilde line, and the Americans paused before launching an attack which saw them reach the Grandpré gap, where the valley of the River Aire divides the Argonne. On October 12–13, Pershing reorganized his command—getting bigger all the time—to form an Army Group, with two armies, 1st under Hunter Liggett and 2nd under Robert Bullard. It took more heavy fighting, with the Germans falling back yard by yard, before Liggett's men reached the Meuse just opposite the little town of Sedan, scene of a stunning German victory in 1870.

HAMEL AND AMIENS

Well before Pétain's scheme for a convergent Allied offensive was even sketched out, the British took important steps toward making it possible. The poor showing of 5th Army, which the condition of its defenses only partly justified, finished Gough. On March 28, Rawlinson replaced him, and the 5th Army disappeared from the British order of battle, to be replaced by a reconstituted 4th Army under Rawlinson. Haig's own position remained insecure, with Henry Wilson, the Chief of the Imperial General Staff, telling Lloyd George that he would fight a good defensive battle, "and that the time to get rid of him was when the German attack was over."

Rawlinson was pessimistic when he arrived, believing that a determined German attack would take Amiens. However, as we have seen, Ludendorff turned his attention elsewhere, and as he did so Rawlinson worked hard to improve his defenses, instituting a properly-thought-through system of deep defense based on a serious study of German methods of attack. It soon became evident that these defenses would not be put to the test. A variety of evidence—notably a large raid carried out by the Australians near Morlancourt on June 10—suggested that German troops in the sector were of poor quality and their defenses ill prepared.

As he considered the feasibility of launching an attack of his own, Rawlinson noted that the British army's diminishing manpower (for which, it must be said, his own efforts on the Somme were in part responsible) suggested that "all possible mechanical devices" should be used to increase the offensive power of divisions. The only two areas where such developments might be expected were in the increase of machine guns, and in extended "numbers and functions of tanks." He did not mention artillery, perhaps because he considered that the most significant developments—which we have previously traced—had already occurred.

An early demonstration of the Rawlinson method came on July 4 when the Australian Corps attacked the village of Hamel, northeast of Villers-Bretonneux. Because the Australians were badly below strength, Lieutenant General Sir John Monash, their newly appointed corps commander, proposed to attack with his infantry thinly spread: artillery, machine guns, and tanks would give the blow its real punch. The tanks were the new Mk V, slightly faster and more easily driven than the Mk IV, carrying its fuel under armor and, perhaps most important, more reliable than earlier models.

The original plan, which did without a creeping barrage, did not commend itself to some of those involved, whose experience of tanks had been marked

THE WESTERN FRONT 1918:
THE ALLIED ADVANCE

HOLLAND

N
W——E
S

North Sea

Zeebrugge
Ostend
Nieuport
Bruges

Ghent

Calais

2nd

Passchendaele

R. Lys

Boulogne   Hazebrouck   Ypres

Army Group
Rupprecht

Brussels

BELGIUM

Etaples

Messines

Armentières

5th

Mons

Liège

Montreuil   Laventie   Lille

La Bassée

Namur

R. Meuse

Lens   Douai

Charleroi

Vimy

1st

R. Sambre

Arras

Forest of Mormal

Maubeuge

Army Group
Boehn

R. Somme

Cambrai

Landrecies

Bapaume

Albert   Péronne

3rd   Le Cateau

Amiens

Villers-
Bretonneux   St-Quentin

4th

R. Oise

Army Group
Crown Prince

FRANCE

3rd till Sept 14   La   1st
Fère   Laon

Army Group
Gallwitz

Montdidier   Noyon

10th till Nov 27, then 3rd
Chemin des Dames

Mézières   Sedan

Compiègne

R. Oise

Soissons   *R. Vesle*

R. Aisne

5th

US 1st

4th

Rheims

Argonne   Verdun

R. Seine

Château-Thierry

R. Marne

US 2nd

Meaux

St-Mihiel

Paris

0	25 Miles	German forces in Army Groups under name of commander
0	25 Kilometers	

Albrecht

10th from Nov 27,
then 8th

Army Group
Albrecht

Approximate line of the Western Front, August

British and American armies   1st

French and Belgian armies   1st

Approximate line of the Western Front, November 11

by the Bullecourt fiasco in 1917. Monash and Rawlinson were flexible enough to permit "bottom up" influence on their plans. The final scheme embodied a lightning bombardment, which paid careful attention to German batteries, and then a creeping barrage moving ahead of the infantry and tanks. There was one holdup where tanks failed to reach an objective which the infantry had to storm in the old style, but elsewhere the day was a triumphant success.

In the weeks that followed, further raids suggested that German troops and the defenses they held remained poor, encouraging Rawlinson to plan for a much larger attack. The scheme, sent to GHQ on July 17, embodied an attack by eleven divisions on a nineteen-thousand-yard front from just north of the Somme to Demuin, south of the Amiens–Villers-Bretonneux road. There was to be a three-phase advance, its first objective the German front line and its third the outer Amiens defense line, built by the French in 1916. Troops taking the first objective would secure it while those attacking the second passed through, and after another brief pause these same troops would go on to the third. To ensure smooth command (and minimize national frictions) the three corps involved—the British III Corps north of the Somme, the ANZAC to their right, and the Canadians to the extreme south—would have their own sectors, with Canadians leapfrogging Canadians, and so on.

Both Foch and Haig tinkered with the plan. Foch decreed that the French 1st Army, on Rawlinson's right, would attack as well. Haig, in a dull echo of the Somme, visited Rawlinson just before the attack and told him to aim at going far deeper. The line Chaulnes–Roye, seven miles beyond Rawlinson's final objective, was to be taken, and Ham, another fifteen miles further on, was the general direction of the advance.

The odds were stacked in Rawlinson's favor. His Canadian and Australian divisions were first rate, and he had 342 Mk V tanks and an assortment of other supply- and infantry-carrying tanks. In addition to the eight hundred aircraft of his own, some dedicated to attacking German antitank guns and others to dropping ammunition to advancing troops, there were enough French aircraft on his right to give the Allies almost two thousand aircraft against fewer than four hundred German. Lastly, there were two thousand guns, which were to eschew preliminary bombardment but maintain a heavy creeping barrage in front of the advance. Robin Prior and Trevor Wilson observe that the ratio of artillery required per yard of attack front—for field guns, one gun per twenty-five yards firing four rounds per minute for the creeping barrage—was actually exceeded: "As a formula for victory, this could hardly have been bettered."

Rawlinson was meticulous about maintaining security: in particular, it was important that the presence of the Canadians should not be revealed, as the Germans, with good reason, regarded them as "shock troops" whose presence indicated a major offensive. It is likely that the Germans had some inkling of what was afoot, but news did not filter down the chain of command until it was too late.

The attack began at 4:20 on the morning of August 8. Sir John Monash recalled how:

> A great illumination lights up the Eastern horizon: and instantly the whole complex organization, extending far back to areas almost beyond earshot of the guns, begins to move forward: every man, every unit, every vehicle and every tank on the appointed tasks and to their designated goals, sweeping on relentlessly and irresistibly.

There were a few temporary setbacks, but determined men took them in their stride. A Canadian artillery sergeant was riding forward when he saw that a gun team in front had been hit:

> The first thing I saw was one of the drivers lying face down in the dust, dead. Some horses were lying in a heap, where the shell had landed. On the left I saw someone pulling one of the other drivers, also dead, out of the way into a shell hole. A man's feelings get blunted at these sights, and his mind being fully occupied by the work in hand he has no time to consider such things in the sad and awful light of what they really are. All I remember is that I turned round and shouted to the lead driver of my gun to swing out, so as to avoid the man in the road and the dead horses.

Captain Henry Smeddle's tank company went forward through batches of wounded and German prisoners, and it was clear that "very little infantry opposition was being met with." The scale of the surprise struck him when he reached Harbonnières station to see an ammunition train pull in as if nothing was happening. "It was immediately shelled by all the 6-pder guns of the approaching tanks," he wrote. "One shell must have struck a powder van for suddenly the whole train burst into one great sheet of flame."

Well might Rawlinson report that "we have given the Boche a pretty good bump this time," for his men advanced eight miles and inflicted twenty-seven thousand casualties. Only in the north, where III Corps was attacking over difficult ground with tired troops, were there serious disappointments. The German Official History called this "the greatest defeat which the German army had suffered since the beginning of the war.... The position divisions between the Avre and the Somme which had been struck by the enemy attack were nearly completely annihilated." Ludendorff himself was horrified. "August 8th was the black day of the German army in the war," he wrote. "This was the worst experience I had to go through." One black day, however, was followed by a hundred more, many scarcely less gloomy.

THE HUNDRED DAYS

The Amiens battle slowed down in the days that followed, though not before the U.S. 131st Infantry Regiment, fighting under III Corps, had taken the important Chipilly spur overlooking the Somme. Foch pressed Haig to hustle on both 3rd and 4th Armies, but Haig was concerned about stiffening resistance. Rawlinson, far more mature as an army commander than he had been two years before, was disinclined to be pushed into premature action. The official historian maintains that he asked Haig: "Who commands the British Army, you or Foch?" Haig himself was inclined to be less rigid, and not without reason, for while so many of the men under his command were eighteen-year-olds, his senior commanders knew their business as never before. On August 22 Haig told the army commanders:

> It is no longer necessary to advance in regular lines step by step. On the contrary, each division should be given a distant objective which must be reached independently of one's neighbor, and even if one's flank is thereby exposed for the time being.
>
> Reinforcements must be directed on the points where our troops are gaining ground, not where they are checked.

It was not until August 21 that Byng was ready to attack north of Albert, and found that the Germans had already begun to give ground. Rawlinson kept pace, taking Albert, and soon both armies were hustling the Germans back across the wilderness of the old Somme battlefield. On the 26th, 1st Army joined in, attacking east of Arras. The New Zealanders took Bapaume on the 29th, and the next day the Australians began their attack on Péronne, a strong position lying behind the Somme with its blown bridges. They took the dominating Mont St-Quentin on September 1, and Péronne itself fell the next day. Ludendorff's gloom deepened: he had hoped to winter in an intermediate line west of the main Hindenburg Line, but now there was no alternative but to fall back on to the line itself. However, it remained formidable. The British army had lost eighty thousand men in August, and even the Mk V tanks found it hard to keep up with the pace of battle. There seemed every chance that the front would freeze hard again, as it had so often in the past.

Things were different that summer. Haig's armies managed to maintain the tempo of their advance, and although the Germans never broke—day after day machine gun rear guards sacrificed themselves to buy time—the old spirit had gone. We must not detract from the achievement of the last Hundred Days—during which the British armies suffered over three hundred thousand casualties, a growing number of them a consequence of the influenza epidemic sweeping Europe—but German performance from August to November was undermined by the loss of the million men in the Ludendorff offensives, as well as by the long strain of the wearing-out fight.

In late September, 4th Army broke the Hindenburg Line north of St-Quentin in a battle where 46th North Midland Division, a Territorial formation, many of whose soldiers came from mining and pottery towns, distinguished itself by taking the bridge at Riqueval intact. As the sun broke through the mist, Major H. J. C. Marshall, one of the division's officers, described how:

> Over the brow of the rise opposite to us came a great grey column.
> Half an hour later a similar column appeared, and then another and
> another. We had broken the Hindenburg Line, and forty-two hundred
> prisoners, seventy cannon and more than one thousand machine guns
> were the trophies of the fight gathered by our single division!

Further north the U.S. 27th and 30th Divisions, fighting under Australian command, suffered heavy casualties: the 107th Infantry Regiment lost 377 killed and 658 wounded, the heaviest U.S. regimental loss in the entire war. Captain O. H. Woodward, an Australian tunneling officer, thought that "as individuals the Americans were not to be blamed, but their behavior under fire showed clearly that in modern warfare it was of little avail to launch an attack with men untrained in war, even though the bravery of the individual may not be questioned. . . . No wonder the German machine gunners had a field day." By nightfall on the 29th the German defensive system was in ruins, and Ludendorff warned that only an immediate armistice could avert a catastrophe.

OPPOSITE Moment of victory. Brigadier General J. C. Campbell addresses his brigade of 46th Division from the captured bridge at Riqueval. Some men are still wearing life jackets, and others have obtained German helmets.

Lieutenant General Sir John Monash, ANZAC Corps commander, decorates an Australian soldier in 1918.

In October the Germans were elbowed back, still struggling hard, across the downland of the Cambrésis, up to Le Cateau, and past the Forest of Mormal. There was vicious fighting on the Sambre Canal, where the poet Wilfred Owen was killed, and November saw the British armies back at Mons, where they had fired the first shots of the war in August 1914.

Despite all the efforts of the combatants on both sides over the previous four years, the Western Front was never truly broken. Even at this late stage in the war the Germans were pushed back in increasing disarray, but with their front intact. There was a very real probability that the Allied armies would shortly outrun their supplies, bringing their advance to a halt on the very borders of Germany. But it was not to be, for the Germans, undermined by military defeat and naval blockade, had reached the end of their tether.

THE ARMISTICE

In Germany, to starvation at home—largely a consequence of the blockade—was added unremitting bad news from the front. The government fell, and on October 1 a new one, headed by the moderate Prince Max of Baden, came to power. On October 23–24 the Italians beat the Austrians at Vittorio Veneto.

The Ypres salient had already been expunged, and on September 28 Plumer began to clear the Flanders coast: King Albert of the Belgians entered Bruges on the 25th. Ludendorff resigned on October 27; on November 1, Turkey capitulated. Three days later the High Seas Fleet began to mutiny, and Austria signed an armistice.

On November 7 a German armistice delegation arrived at a railway junction in the Forest of Compiègne. Foch received its members for a wintry interview in his carriage, and on the 10th the German government authorized acceptance of Allied terms. The armistice was signed at 5:15 on the morning of the 11th: it came into effect at 11:00 that day. Lieutenant R. G. Dixon of the Royal Garrison Artillery put that moment into words of which many would have approved:

> No more slaughter, no more maiming, no more mud and blood, and no more killing and disemboweling of horses and mules—which was what I found most difficult to bear. . . .
>
> There was silence along the miles and miles of thundering battle-fronts from the North Sea to the borders of Switzerland. . . . The whole vast business of the war was finished. It was over.

A Canadian soldier, Private Price, had the melancholy distinction of being the last man in the British armies killed in the war. He died at 10:58 on the morning of November 11, 1918, just two minutes before the armistice came into effect. Price lies in the little cemetery at St-Symphorien, just east of Mons. Nearby are the first and last British soldiers killed in the war: Private Parr of the Middlesex, killed on cycle patrol on August 21, 1914, and Private Ellison of the 5th Lancers, who died on November 11, 1918. I know of no more poignant comment on the Western Front.

RETROSPECT I was completing this book, and the television series it accompanies, over the eightieth anniversary of the armistice. At 11:00 on the morning of November 11, 1998, we were filming on Manchester Hill, near the spot where Wilfrith Elstob died. It was a beautiful autumn day, with the light slanting past the trees that circle the quarry where he had his command post. I have never known two minutes' silence seem more natural.

Much of the discussion surrounding the anniversary focused on whether the war was necessary or not. My old colleague John Keegan was among those who saw it as: "Unnecessary, because the train of events that led to its outbreak might have been broken at any point during the five weeks of crisis that preceded the first clash of arms." Alan Massie argued that Britain should not have fought in the war, and that the Russian Revolution, Fascist Italy, Nazi Germany, and the war of 1939, were among its baneful consequences.

It seems unquestionably true that, in common with so many other wars, the First World War could have been averted by astute diplomacy or more common goodwill. But we must neither credit our ancestors with knowledge of the future, nor seek to judge them by our standards. The threat to Britain seemed real enough to them in 1914, and a sense of national honor tugged their conscience harder than it does ours today.

This debate cannot obscure the central truth of the Western Front. For the only time in her history, Britain took the field in a major war against a first-rate adversary and confronted that enemy's main strength in the war's principal theater. She not only bore the enormous strain of the war, but also played a leading part in winning it. Well might Foch say of the Hundred Days: "Never in any time in history has the British army achieved greater results in attack than in this unbroken offensive."

Nearly three-quarters of a million Commonwealth soldiers, sailors, and airmen died on the Western Front. They rest in more than a thousand military and two thousand civil cemeteries. More than three hundred thousand of them have no known graves, and are commemorated on memorials to the missing: there are seven in Belgium and twenty-two in France. Some of these, like the Menin Gate and Tyne Cot at Ypres, and the Thiepval Memorial on the Somme, are well known and visited regularly. Others, like the Indian memorial at Neuve Chappelle, its "Indo-Saracenic" architecture incongruous among the lush fields and pollarded willows, are more lonely. Those they commemorate were Regulars, Territorials, volunteers, and conscripts, aged from fourteen to sixty-eight and ranging in rank from private soldier to lieutenant general.

Some had done their duty without flinching:

Not uncontent to die
That Lancaster on Lune might stand secure.

Others found military service itself a long agony, and would have sympathized with an unknown soldier whose letter, opened by the censor in June 1918, admitted: "Everybody is fed up with the war and don't care who wins so long as we can get it over." Death came in his capricious ways. Men were sniped, machine gunned, shelled, bombed, bayoneted, and mortared. They were kicked by horses, electrocuted by generators, and suffocated by charcoal braziers in winter dugouts. One NCO died of a heart attack behind the lines just as the Battle of Loos started. A military policeman was shot dead by a deserting officer, who was himself executed for the crime.

Some men were snatched away in an instant. Charles Carrington saw Corporal Matthews die on the Somme:

> I was looking straight at him as the bullet struck him and was pro-
> foundly affected by the remembrance of his face, though at the time
> I hardly thought of it. He was alive, and then he was dead, and there
> was nothing human left in him. He fell with a neat round hole in his
> forehead and the back of his head blown off.

Others died in pain and terror that we can only guess at. An Australian at Pozières saw "a shapeless black thing, flapping.... I ran over, ducking and weaving, till I got close. And it was a man, blackened, not a bit of flesh not burnt, rolling around, waving an arm stump with nothing on it." An unhappy few died by the hands of their comrades, and even here there was no consistency. Some stood square-shouldered, filling their lungs to face the volley, while others were tied to a chair, drunk and sobbing.

The sheer quantity of loss numbs our comprehension. Over seventy-three thousand missing are commemorated at Thiepval, and almost fifty-five thousand on the Menin Gate. Whatever the motive for their service or the manner of their death, they are united by the common humanity which we too share. As Lieutenant Colonel John MacRae, who himself died in the war, wrote, they:

> ... lived, felt dawn, saw sunset glow
> loved and were loved...

As we now are, so once were they; as they now are, so must we be. Let us remember them all, not with bravado or bombast, but with the respect that their sacrifice demands.

THE WAR IN OUTLINE

This brief summary aims to put the Western Front in the context of the war as a whole. While the battles there would have seemed all-consuming to those taking part, there were many other campaigns around the world, many other bloody battles, many other casualties on both land and sea.

On the Eastern Front, Germany and Austria-Hungary fought the Russians. Early in the war, in August–September 1914, the Russians suffered serious reverses at the hands of the Germans at Tannenberg and the Masurian Lakes, but did much better further south against the Austrians in Galicia. 1915 began badly for the Austrians, with the expensive failure of an attempt to relieve the beleaguered fortress of Przemysl. In the north, however, the Germans captured Warsaw and pushed on to Brest-Litovsk and Vilna. The Russian army was terribly mauled, and it is a tribute to its sheer dogged resilience that it remained in the field at all.

Following the early failure of the German army commander on the Eastern Front, Field Marshal Paul von Hindenburg was sent to command German forces there, ably seconded by Lieutenant General Erich von Ludendorff and Major General Max Hoffman. From November 1914 Hindenburg exercised overall authority over Austrian forces too, although the Austrian chief of the general staff, General Franz Conrad von Hötzendorf, took a close personal interest in the campaign. The association was not altogether happy, and soon the Germans were to complain that their alliance with the Austrians was like being "fettered to a corpse."

In 1916 the Russians responded to French appeals to distract the Germans from their offensive at Verdun by attacking them at Lake Narotch. Although this was a bloody failure, a bigger attack—known, from the name of the commander of the Russian southwestern army group, as the Brusilov offensive—was spectacularly successful. The Austro-Hungarian Fourth Army was almost destroyed, and German reinforcements had to be rushed in from the west to stabilize the situation. Brusilov's triumph encouraged Romania to join the war on the Allied side, but the ensuing counteroffensive saw Romanians and Russians alike badly beaten. Most of Romania was overrun, and even long-suffering Russia had reached the end of its tether. Hindenburg and Ludendorff departed for the Western Front, but German authority in the east was strengthened, leaving the Italian Front as the main concern of Conrad von Hötzendorf, who was himself relieved of his post as chief of staff in March 1917 and sent off to command in the South Tyrol.

In March 1917 the Czar abdicated, and a Provisional Government took power. It strove to remain faithful to the Allied cause, and launched another offensive in Galicia in July. German counterstrokes administered what was in effect the coup de grâce to Russia's military effort. In November a Communist coup overturned the Provisional Government, and in December Russia concluded an armistice which was confirmed the following year. Civil war followed in Russia, and although the Germans left some troops to watch their eastern frontiers, they were able to shift most to the Western Front.

Turkey entered the war in late October 1914, and her armed forces received considerable support from Germany, who had sent a substantial training team there in

1913. A Turkish invasion of Russian territory in the Caucasus was sharply rebuffed at Sarikamish in December 1914–January 1915. The war ebbed and flowed in 1915–16, with the Russians having rather the better of it, capturing Erzerum and Trebizond. Even this otherwise unimportant front cast a long shadow, for the initial Turkish success in 1914 encouraged the Russians to ask for Allied help against the Turks. This request played its part in initiating a campaign that had an appreciable impact on the Western Front: Gallipoli.

The Gallipoli peninsula, with its characteristic dogleg outline, forms the northern coastline of the narrow Dardanelles, which connect the Aegean Sea with the Sea of Marmara. Allied attention was drawn to the area by Turkey's plea for help, and the "easterners," who sought a more profitable theater than the Western Front, advocated forcing the passage of the Dardanelles to enable an Allied fleet to reach the Turkish capital Constantinople (now Istanbul) and drive Turkey out of the war. There were initial naval attacks in February and March, and landings in April and August. Although there were moments when the Allies might have taken Gallipoli, a combination of hesitance and misjudgment among their commanders coupled with dogged resistance and some inspired leadership on the part of the Turks produced stalemate. The Allies withdrew in December 1915 and January 1916.

Italy joined the Allies in May 1915 in the hope of making gains at Austria's expense. Her strategy was to hold the Trentino, Austrian territory jutting down into Italy north of Verona, while attacking into the Isonzo salient, Italy's northeast frontier. In a long and bitter series of battles on the Isonzo, too often ignored by Anglo-American historians, the Italian army made painful progress at great cost, but by the summer of 1917 the Austrians, worn to a thread, asked for German help. General Krafft von Dellmensingen's German contingent played a leading part in winning the Battle of Caporetto in October 1917. The Italians lost more than half a million men, and were bundled back to a defensive line just north of Venice. Six French and five British divisions were sent from the Western Front to support the Italians.

The rapid deterioration of Austria's economy and growing exhaustion of her army in 1918 did not prevent further attacks, but the Italians were now able to parry them. In October the Italians launched their own final offensive, beating the Austrians at Vittorio Veneto and pushing on, against diminishing resistance, in an advance ending in an armistice, which took effect on November 4.

The war originated in events in the Balkans, and fighting began early there. An Austrian invasion of Serbia initially made good progress, taking Belgrade, the Serbian capital, but soon stalled in the face of fierce Serbian resistance. In late September the Serbs counterattacked, retaking Belgrade and driving the Austrians from Serbian territory with considerable loss. However, Allied failure at Gallipoli encouraged Bulgaria, with her own territorial ambitions in the Balkans, to join the Central Powers, and in the autumn of 1915 a combined German, Austrian, and Bulgarian offensive crushed Serbian resistance, driving remnants of the Serbian army through Montenegro and down into Albania. The survivors were rescued by Allied ships in early 1916.

Bulgaria's entry into the war had alarmed the Greeks, who feared for their province of Macedonia, and called for Allied assistance. An Allied force was duly sent to Salonika, in northeast Greece, only to discover that Greece's pro-German king,

Constantine, dismissed his pro-Allied premier, Venizelos, and declared Greece neutral. The Allies, however, retained a substantial force at Salonika, which at least provided a command for the French General Maurice Sarrail, an ardent republican for whom a substantial post had to be found. There was some inconclusive fighting against the Bulgarians in 1916–17. In June 1917 King Constantine abdicated, and his successor, Alexander, reappointed Venizelos who brought Greece back into the war.

Sarrail's successor, General Guillaumat, reorganized Allied forces and successfully integrated the Greeks into his command. With the Allies on the Western Front showing signs of buckling under the strain of the German offensive, he was recalled to serve as military governor of Paris. However, his replacement, the resourceful General Franchet d'Esperey, began the Battle of the Vardar in mid-September. The Bulgarians, now denuded of German support, were swiftly beaten, and surrendered on September 30.

There were two theaters of war in the Middle East. Egypt was a British protectorate, and in February 1916 the Turks launched a halfhearted attack on the Suez Canal. The British followed up its repulse by advancing into Sinai, and prepared positions there for a possible advance into Palestine, part of the Turkish Empire. Turkish attention was distracted by an Arab revolt against their rule, which gained momentum in the second half of 1916 and included guerrilla attacks (in which the British Colonel T. E. Lawrence—"Lawrence of Arabia"—played a distinguished part) on the long and vulnerable Turkish lines of communication.

In March 1917 the British, under General Sir Archibald Murray, launched the first Battle of Gaza in an attempt to get into Palestine, failed, tried again the following month, and failed once more. Murray's successor was General Sir Edmund Allenby, who had commanded an army on the Western Front. In October–November 1917 he outflanked the Gaza positions by swinging through Beersheba on the desert flank and going on to take Jerusalem. Allenby's preparations for a renewal of the offensive were impeded by the steady leeching away of his troops to the Western Front, but in September 1918 he sprang a brilliantly successful attack on the Turks at Megiddo, and took Damascus on October 1: an armistice was concluded at the end of the month.

The second front in the Middle East was in Mesopotamia, now Iraq. General Sir John Nixon's expeditionary force from India landed at Basra, and began to advance, with inadequate supplies and no real campaign plan, along the Tigris toward Baghdad. Its leading elements took Kut-al-Amara in September 1916, only to be besieged there in December. Attempts at relief failed, and Kut surrendered in April 1916, a serious blow to British prestige, coming as it did so soon after failure at Gallipoli.

Nixon's successor, General Sir Frederick Maude, resumed the advance, winning the second Battle of Kut in February 1917 and taking Baghdad in March. He pushed on up the Euphrates and beat the Turks at Ramadi in September, only to die of cholera. His successor, Sir William Marshall, consolidated the gains, and although expeditions were sent out to the oil fields at Baku and Mosul, there was little more serious fighting.

There was sporadic fighting in Africa, the Allies overrunning German colonies in Togoland and South-West Africa. The Cameroons held out till early 1916, but in South-West Africa the talented German commander, Colonel Paul von Lettow-

Vorbeck, remained in the field for the whole war. In a brilliant guerrilla campaign, he held down one hundred and thirty thousand Allied troops.

Although the war at sea contained fewer of the main fleet actions than prewar theorists had expected, it was nonetheless important. In 1914 German maritime colonies worldwide—like Tsingtao on the Chinese coast—were snapped up quickly. Admiral Maximillian von Spee's German China Squadron, on its way home by way of South America, destroyed a British squadron off Coronel on the Chilean coast on November 1, 1914, but was caught off the Falklands eight days later and almost entirely destroyed. German commerce raiders caused some losses, and on September 22 a German submarine pointed the way ahead by sinking three old cruisers in the Channel.

In January 1915 a German squadron raided into the North Sea, but the British, alerted by radio intercepts, met it at the Dogger Bank. The action was inconclusive, but the Germans profited by the experience to improve precautions against internal explosions in their ships. The following month the Germans began an unrestricted submarine campaign against all merchant shipping, including neutral vessels, in the waters surrounding Britain. In May the Cunard liner *Lusitania* was sunk, with the loss of over a thousand lives, arousing a storm of international protest, and the campaign was suspended.

Allied vessels were still attacked, and during 1916 there were raids on the British coast. The year's main clash at sea was the Battle of Jutland, fought between the British Grand Fleet and the German High Seas Fleet on May 31. The Germans inflicted greater losses than they suffered, but were aware that they had courted great risk, and never again ventured out of port.

In February 1917 the Germans again adopted unrestricted submarine warfare, hoping that its effect on Britain would outweigh the risk of bringing the United States into the war. Although Germany had neither sufficient U-boats nor adequate tactics for their use, the campaign did terrible damage: in April 1917, its worst month, the Allies lost half a million tons of shipping. Adoption of the convoy system and increased Anglo-American naval cooperation—for the Americans did indeed enter the war in April 1917—helped reduce losses. However, the U-boat threat had its effect on the Western Front. One of the objectives of the Third Battle of Ypres, the British offensive launched in the summer of 1917, was taking the German submarine bases at Ostend and Zeebrugge, and the latter was the scene of a gallant raid on April 23, 1918, when the light cruiser *Vindictive* and smaller craft assaulted the port and inflicted some damage.

The war at sea was inconclusive, and certainly did little to justify the expenditure lavished on surface fleets. However, if the German submarine campaign managed neither to starve Britain out of the war nor to prevent the passage of American troops to Europe, the Allied blockade of Germany was a different matter. The Central Powers ran short of food and military raw materials, and although the blockade no more broke German morale than did Allied bombing a generation later, it led to growing problems on the home front and contributed to demands for an end to the war.

The First World War was indeed a conflict that spanned the globe, and its growing appetite for resources spread ripples of war even where armies and navies themselves did not reach. Yet from the British point of view, then as now, the war had one primary focus, the Western Front.

THE BRITISH CHAIN OF COMMAND

This simplified outline deals primarily with the infantry. Supporting arms (artillery and engineers) and ancillary services were to be found at divisional level and above. Establishments changed as the war went on. Terminology varied between arms: a company-sized body of cavalry was called a squadron, and a similar body of artillery (usually with six guns), a battery. The word regiment had no tactical significance in the infantry, though different battalions of a given regiment might find themselves in the same brigade. Confusingly, artillery batteries were grouped into brigades, although these artillery brigades (really the equivalent of infantry battalions) were designated by roman numerals in an effort to minimize confusion.

The BEF was effectively one army in 1914, becoming five by 1918. Commander in Chief was Field Marshal Sir John French till December 1915, then General (later Field Marshal) Sir Douglas Haig.

ARMY	(Commanded by a **General**) comprised about four corps, but precise numbers depended on the army's role.
CORPS	(Commanded by a **Lieutenant General**) usually comprised three or four divisions.
DIVISION	(Commanded by a **Major General**) usually had three brigades.
BRIGADE	(Commanded by a **Brigadier General**) had four battalions to winter 1917 and three thereafter.
BATTALION	(Commanded by a **Lieutenant Colonel**) had four companies.
COMPANY	(Commanded by a **Major** or **Captain**) had four platoons.
PLATOON	(Commanded by a **Subaltern** – **a Lieutenant** or **Second Lieutenant**) had four sections.
SECTION	(Commanded by a **Corporal**) with 8–10 men.

FURTHER READING

This is in no sense a comprehensive bibliography, simply a short guide for those wishing to read further. I have restricted myself to suggesting a handful of favorite books per chapter.

INTRODUCTION

Of the books marking the 80th anniversary of the armistice, both John Keegan *The First World War* (London 1998) and Niall Ferguson *The Pity of War* (London 1998) are likely to stand the test of time—though I disagree with their judgment on the war's origins. The former, beautifully written and illuminated by wisdom and humanity, is the best general account of the war. Although we must question some of its interpretations, for tactical narrative it remains hard to beat the British official history, Sir James Edmonds *Military Operations: France and Belgium*...There are several distinctive red-jacketed volumes for each year of the war, together with volumes of excellent maps. John Ellis *Eye-Deep in Hell* (London 1976) remains the most accessible review of life at the front. Of the many anthologies of war experience, Guy Chapman *Vain Glory* (London 1937, 1968) still repays the reader. The serious visitor to the Western Front will profit from taking Peter Chasseaud

Topography of Armageddon (London 1991), a selection of trench maps. Hugh Cecil and Peter H. Liddle (eds.) *Facing Armageddon* (London 1996) is a mine of valuable essays by many of the foremost contemporary scholars, and Brian Bond (ed.) *The First World War and British Military History* (Oxford 1991) is especially useful in charting the reputations of generals. Ian Malcolm Brown *British Logistics on the Western Front* (London 1998) is a long-overdue study of an important subject. Readers who wish to trace relatives can do no better than consult Simon Fowler, William Spencer, and Stuart Tamblin, *Army Service Records of the First World War* (London 1996).

MAKING THE FRONT

Paul Kennedy (ed.) *The War Plans of the Great Powers* (London 1979) is a useful introduction. My *Riding the Retreat: Mons to the Marne 1914 Revisited* (London 1995) tells the story of a ride from Mons in the footsteps of the BEF. For an evocative account of the opening campaign see the Moltke chapter in Correlli Barnett *The Swordbearers* (London 1963). Among the many memoirs, Edward Spears *Liaison 1914* (London 1930) and Walter Bloem *The Advance from Mons*

(London 1938) deserve mention. Lyn Macdonald *1914* (London 1987) is a marvelous anthology, and the well-illustrated Keith Simpson *The Old Contemptibles* (London 1981) remains the best overview of the British army of 1914. Michael Howard illuminates expectations and doctrine in "Men Against Fire: The Doctrine of the Offensive in 1914" in Peter Paret (ed.) *Makers of Modern Strategy* (Oxford 1986).

FEEDING THE FRONT

Tim Travers *The Killing Ground* (London 1987) is good for the war as a whole, and its chapter on the cult of the offensive is especially useful. Shelford Bidwell and Dominick Graham *Fire-Power: British Army Weapons and Theories of War 1904–1945* (London 1982), Ian F. W. Beckett and Keith Simpson *A Nation in Arms: A Social Study of the British Army in the First World War* (Manchester 1985), and John Turner (ed.) *Britain and the First World War* (London 1988) are useful for various aspects of the British background. For the New Armies see Peter Simkins *Kitchener's Army: Raising the New Armies 1914–1916* (Manchester 1988). Of David French's many contributions to our understanding of the war, see particularly *British Strategy and War Aims 1914–1916* (London 1986). Robin Prior and Trevor Wilson *Command on the Western Front: The Military Career of Sir Henry Rawlinson* (Oxford 1992) is invaluable for the spring offensives of 1915, Loos, the Somme, and 1918.

HOLDING THE FRONT

Despite its age, and the doubts that modern scholarship has thrown onto its views on Falkenhayn, Alistair Horne *The Price of Glory: Verdun 1916* (London 1962) remains a superb study. For the French military background see Douglas Porch *The March to the Marne: The French Army 1871–1914* (Cambridge 1981), and for France and the war see J. J. Becker *The Great War and the French People* (Leamington Spa 1985). *Les Combattants des Tranchées* (Paris 1986), Stéphane Audoin-Rouzeau's wonderful work on French trench journalism, is now available in English. For an important study of a French infantry division see Leonard Smith *Between Discipline and Obedience...* (Princeton 1994). The way the army was seen—and, no less important, saw itself—before the war is beautifully depicted in François Robichon *L'armée française vue par les peintres* (Paris 1998).

COMMANDING THE FRONT

Gerald Gliddon *The Legacy of the Somme* (London 1996) is a carefully annotated bibliography of fact and fiction on the Somme. Martin Middlebrook *The First Day on the Somme* (London 1971) is not simply a good book, but is one that changed the way many people felt about military history. Lyn Macdonald *Somme* (London 1983) is the best general anthology, while Malcolm Brown *The Imperial War Museum Book of the Somme* (London 1996) skilfully uses letters and diaries in the museum to reflect the two faces of the Somme, "the mud and the stars." Paddy Griffith *Battle Tactics of the Western Front: The British Army's Art of Attack 1916–18* (London 1994) sees the Somme as a key stage in the British army's learning process. The best general study of the battlefield is Martin and Mary Middlebrook *The Somme Battlefields* (London 1991), and several good slim volumes are published by Leo Cooper as an imprint of Pen and Sword Books in the Battleground Europe series.

ENDURING THE FRONT

Peter H. Liddle (ed.) *Passchendaele in Perspective* (London 1997) is the essential starting point for any serious study of 1917. For a penetrating view of the French army see Edward Spears *Prelude to Victory* (London 1939). John Terraine *The Road to Passchendaele: The Flanders Offensive of 1918: A Study in Inevitability* (London 1977) is one of the most important of its author's many studies of the war. Lyn Macdonald *They Called It Passchendaele* (London 1978) gives the view from the mud. Ian Passingham *Pillars of Fire* (Stroud 1998) is a good account of Messines Ridge. For the Australians see C. E. W. Bean *Anzac to Amiens* (Canberra 1983).

BREAKING THE FRONT

Tim Travers *How the War Was Won: Command and Technology in the British Army on the Western Front* (London 1992) is the most useful starting-point for the British army, and for the year in general see John Terraine *To Win a War: 1918, the Year of Victory* (London 1982). For the Germans see Bruce I. Gudmundsson *Stormtroop Tactics: Innovation in the German Army 1914–1918* and David T. Zabecki *Steel Wind: Colonel Georg Bruchmüller and the Birth of Modern Artillery* (London 1994). Shane B. Schreiber does justice to the Canadians in *Shock Army of the British Empire: The Canadian Corps in the Last 100 Days of the Great War* (Westport, Conn. 1997). Martin Middlebrook's *The Kaiser's Battle* (London 1978) and Lyn Macdonald's anthologies, *To The Last Man* (London 1998), both focus on individual experience. The best single volume on the U.S. war effort is probably still Edward M. Coffman's *The War to End All Wars: The American Experience in World War I* (Oxford 1968), while Frank Freidel's *Over There* (New York 1964) is good on the experience of the individual fighting man.

INDEX

7/02 ⑥ 2/01
12/05 16 3/05
3/07 ⑲ 4/06
2/10 ㉓